FOREST CAPITAL

A History of
Taylor County Florida

Joshua Goodman

Manufactured in the United States

Published by Sentry Press
424 East Call Street
Tallahassee, Florida 32301

ISBN 978-1-889574-49-3 Paperback
ISBN 978-1-889574-48-6 Hardcover

Library of Congress Control Number: 2020921194

Cover photo enhanced by William Wright
Cover design and formatting by Joney P. Perry

Notice: The information in this book is true and complete to the best of the author's knowledge and offered without guarantee on the part of the author or Sentry Press. The author and Sentry Press disclaim all liability in connection with the use of this book.

Table of Contents

Preface

Sometime in the spring when it's not too hot, take a kayak out to Clearwater Creek, located between Dekle and Jabo beaches on the Taylor County coastline. A motorboat works fine, but you'll miss out on hearing the birds and the relaxing sound of the breeze blowing through the palmettos. About halfway between the tree line and the Gulf of Mexico, you'll find a line of tiny sandy islands poking up out of the marsh. Getting to them can be a challenge, but the view is worth it.

Looking away from the coast, the Gulf stretches as far as you can see, usually dotted with a couple of crab trap balls and a few boats. Scallop season is the exception, of course—in those months it's so packed you could just about walk from boat to boat all the way from Spring Warrior to Steinhatchee. Not too many years ago, Greek spongers operated in this same area, pulling valuable Rock Island sponges from the water to sell in faraway markets. When it comes to beaches, Taylor County is nothing like Destin or Fort Lauderdale, but you won't get many locals to complain. After all, it's a lot more peaceful on the Taylor County coast, and it's one of the few places on Earth where mullet actually have a good flavor. Don't take my word for it, though—even in the mid-1800s people came from as far away as northern Georgia to catch and preserve them.

Looking north or south over the marsh, all those nameless little islands with their handfuls of cedars and cabbage palms may look insignificant, but many of them once served as shelter for saltmakers during the Civil War. Evidence of the salt works' existence is scarce—mostly unrecognizable balls of rusted metal and scattered rocks. In their time, however, they were a vital part of the Confederate war effort and a frequent target for Union blockaders.

Finally, looking inland, you're greeted by a solid wall of pines, the currency of the realm in this part of the world for more than a hundred years. A century ago, turpentine and virgin yellow pine lumber helped propel Taylor County into the modern industrial era. These days, the original stands of timber are long gone, but thousands of acres of replanted pine trees still keep the local economy going.

Truly, this one spot on the coast could be the starting point for dozens of stories, but even that would only cover a fraction of this county's remarkable past. I sometimes like to say that Taylor County is the center of the universe. There's no astronomical reasoning behind that assessment; it's just that so many accidents of history—good and bad—have brought either fame or notoriety to this precise area over the years. Two men who went on to become President of the United States made their headquarters here while serving as military commanders. The largest cypress sawmill in the world once operated here, around the same time that one of the co-founders of Sears & Roebuck had his own mills in the county. For decades, signs have given the distance to Perry from hundreds of miles away because so many U.S. highways converge there. And just recently, archaeologists found evidence in a sinkhole on the western edge of the county that is completely rewriting the book on when humans arrived in this part of North America. Clearly this is a special place with a lot of interesting stories. My goal in writing this book has been to string all of those stories together in a meaningful and accessible way.

Acknowledgements

I couldn't have done this alone. Taylor County has had no shortage of dedicated historians over the years, whose work has been essential to completing this project. W.T. Cash, Mary Lou Whitfield, Louise Childers, Henry and June McLeod, and many others have done an invaluable service by writing down their knowledge and encouraging others to pick up their pens and do the same. If this history of Taylor County is successful, it's only because I stand on their shoulders.

I have accumulated many other debts in writing this book. My family, who have always been my greatest source of support, have encouraged me at every stage. The Taylor County Historical Society has been tremendously helpful throughout the entire project, especially J.T. Davis, Angela Castelucci, Bettie Page, and the late Wanda Cash. They put up with me opening every drawer and flipping through every binder to find the details I needed. Others helped by answering questions by email and phone. Auley Rowell, Ann Taylor, Lydia Andrews, and Polly Waller are among them, but I know there were many more. I'm also grateful to the people who were kind enough to read the manuscript and offer their comments—Susan Moody, Donna O'Steen Mixon, William Wright, Dr. Jonathan Sheppard, Janis Owens, Toni Collins, Michael Morris, Dr. Joe Knetsch, Johnathan Grandage, David Goodman, and Katrina Harkness especially. Their advice and observations have helped me avoid more than a few mistakes. Any errors that remain are my own responsibility.

Archaeologist Neil Puckett prepares to hand Dr. Jessi Halligan a mastodon bone found in the depths of Half-Mile Rise in the Aucilla River. The bone, which bore signs of manipulation by humans, dates back more than 14,000 years.

(Photo courtesy of Dr. Jessi Halligan)

CHAPTER 1

Before 1856

In May 2016, a team of archaeologists led by Jessi Halligan of Florida State University reported a discovery in western Taylor County that is now rewriting the entire history of how humans originally made it to North America. For years, scientists agreed the first people to set foot in North Florida came about 12,000 years ago, making their way across the continent from a land bridge connecting it with Asia. All that changed when Halligan's team found artifacts buried in the muck at the bottom of a sinkhole in Half Mile Rise, a section of the Aucilla River. They brought up stone tools, including a double-edged knife, as well as mastodon bones that bore signs of scraping by humans. The scientists used carbon-dating to determine the age of mastodon dung they found near the artifacts, which turned out to be about 14,550 years old. For those tools to have been used to kill that mastodon, people would have to have been hunting along the Aucilla River more than 2,000 years earlier than virtually every previous estimate. For archaeologists, this meant a trip back to the drawing board to explain how and when humans made it to North America. For Taylor County, it just goes to show that people have found the area an appealing place to live for a very, very long time.[1]

Native Americans

The earliest inhabitants of North Florida, the Paleoindians, encountered a very different landscape from what we see today. The coast was about 60 to 100 miles farther out to sea, for starters. All that extra land, now covered by the Gulf of Mexico, was made possible by the enormous amount of seawater trapped in the glaciers left over from the last Ice Age. The land was also much drier. Groundwater levels were lower, which meant many of Florida's present-day lakes, rivers, and springs either didn't exist or were much smaller.

In Taylor County, the Aucilla River's many sinkholes would have been some of the only water sources around, which helps explain why they harbor such ancient Native American artifacts. Without as much surface water to support animal and plant life, these sinkholes would have been like little oases where man and beast alike would have come to find both water and vegetation for food. This also would have been a good place for ancient natives to ambush animals and kill them for their meat and hides. Archaeologists have found bones belonging to mastodon, mammoth, and bison just in Half Mile Rise alone. Other animals available to these earliest inhabitants included horses, camels, raccoons, deer, rabbits, and giant land tortoises. A number of these animals became extinct sometime after the end of the Pleistocene epoch, partly because of environmental changes, but also likely due to overhunting.[2]

Very few Paleoindian artifacts have survived aside from arrowheads and a few other stone tools. The Indians used chert (also called flint), a hard stone that forms naturally in limestone deposits, to make these objects. When struck at the correct angle, chert breaks off in thin flakes rather than chunks—the flakes can then be formed into the familiar shape of an arrowhead. Florida's Native Americans changed the standard design of their arrowheads over time. The earliest versions had a fairly simple oblong or teardrop shape, while later arrowheads were smaller with beveling, sharper points, and notches at the base to improve stability and accuracy. Arrowheads can be found all over the state, but Taylor County is a uniquely good place to find them, since so much of the land is frequently plowed to plant pine trees.

As Native Americans improved their hunting weapons and changed the way they organized their communities, the kinds of artifacts they left behind changed as well. One big transition happened around 500 BCE, for example, as the so-called Deptford culture began to emerge. The natives began crafting pottery tempered by sand rather than plant fibers. They also began creating burial mounds for interring their dead. Deptford sites are usually close to the coast, accompanied by large piles of shells (middens) left over from food gathering. The mouths of the Aucilla, the Fenholloway, Dallus Creek, and Spring Warrior Creek are especially rich with signs of the Deptford culture, although a few Deptford artifacts have been found as far inland as Tennille and Lake Bird.[3]

Between 1 and 250 CE, a new way of living—the Santa Rosa-Swift Creek culture, began to replace the older Deptford model. New ideas coming into northern Florida from the north and west probably provoked the change. Sites from this new era are larger, with circular shell middens and pottery with more complicated designs. There aren't many Santa Rosa-Swift Creek sites in the Taylor County area; most of the remains from this culture are located in the Panhandle. In fact, the so-called Stanaland site, located just inland from

Hagan's Cove, is one of the southernmost Santa Rosa—Swift Creek sites ever found.[4]

Most of Taylor County's prehistoric sites belong to the Weeden Island culture, which began to appear around 250 CE. These sites, usually built on top of the remains of preexisting villages, occur both along the coast and as far inland as Salem, Athena, and Eridu. This was the last group of Native Americans not to practice agriculture. Between 600-750 CE, Indians moving in from present-day Georgia and Alabama brought farming techniques into the area, which revolutionized the way Floridians acquired their food. Some of the earliest evidence of farming in Taylor County has been found in Tide Swamp along the coast, where the natives appear to have borrowed ideas from the Alachua culture farther inland.[5]

By the time the Spanish arrived in Florida in the 16th century, most of the local natives had settled into stationary villages organized into chiefdoms, with Timucuan as a shared language. The Timucuans dominated the area for the next two centuries, although diseases brought by the Spanish reduced their numbers greatly over time. By the early 1700s, northern Florida was inhabited very sparsely, and new tribes began filtering in from Georgia and Alabama. Many of these newcomers were Creek Indians fleeing from intertribal warfare back home. These natives would eventually be called the Seminoles by their white neighbors.[6]

Taylor County's Native American heritage is most obvious in its place names. The names of each of the rivers in Taylor County all come from either the Creek or Timucuan languages. The name "Steinhatchee," for example, is formed from the Creek words *isti*, meaning "man," *in*, meaning "his," and *hachi*, meaning "river." Part of the name, an "ack" sound at the beginning, has been dropped over time. This syllable is derived from the Creek *ak*, meaning "down." Altogether the name translates to "Dead Man's River," which also explains the name of the bay into which it drains.[7] The name "Fenholloway" is derived from the Creek *fina*, meaning "bridge" or "foot-log," and *halwi*, meaning "high." The end result translates to "high bridge."[8] The Fenholloway may also have been known to some people as the "Chattahatchee," which translates in the Creek language to "red river," possibly so-called because of the dark tannic acid that leaches into the river where it spills over into the surrounding woods. The only prominent reference to the Chattahatchee comes from John Lee Williams's history of Florida, but it must be considered since it does correctly place the stream by identifying San Pedro Bay as its origin and giving an accurate distance from its mouth to the mouth of the Aucilla.[9] The Econfina

River is named similarly to the Fenholloway. It is formed from the Creek words *ikana,* meaning "earth," and *fina,* meaning "bridge" as in the Fenholloway, so essentially the name means "earthen bridge."[10] This almost certainly refers to the natural bridge over the Econfina River on the north side of U.S. 98 near Oakland Baptist Church.

The names of the remaining streams are somewhat trickier to define. Spring Warrior Creek has been referred to at least as long ago as the Civil War era as either the Spring Warrior (Creek) or the Warrior River. However, before that Spring Warrior was referred to by names from the Creek language. An 1837 map of Florida drawn by John Lee Williams labels the river as the Chattaposche River.[11] A map dated two years later calls it the Ocitlota Funka. This second map was commissioned by General Zachary Taylor during the Second Seminole War.[12] Clearly the true name of Spring Warrior Creek depended on who you asked.

Excerpt from an 1837 map by J. Lee Williams showing two of the earlier names for some of Taylor County's waterways. Spring Warrior Creek appears here as the Chattaposche River, while the Steinhatchee River is spelled "Achenahatchee."

(Map courtesy of the State Library of Florida)

The name "Aucilla" seems to originate from the Timucuan, not the later Creek language. One of Hernando de Soto's chroniclers, who identifies himself in his work only as a "Knight of Elvas," recounts a stop at a town he calls "Aguile," located on the boundary of Apalachee territory, which was historically the Aucilla River.[13] During the Spanish occupation, a Franciscan mission was established at San Miguel de Asyle, the last town in the Timucuan province in a sequence from east to west, which puts it in the same spot.[14] Based on this evidence, it seems the Aucilla got its name from that single village.

Spanish Colonial Era

Florida's Spanish colonial era began in 1513 when explorer Juan Ponce de Leon stumbled upon it while searching for the fabled isle of Bimini. His crew spotted the land on March 27, but it was April before the ships could find a good place to land. Once ashore, Ponce de Leon claimed the territory for the Spanish Crown and named it "La Florida," after Pascua Florida, the "feast of flowers" associated with Easter. Unequipped to start a colony right away, Ponce headed back to Puerto Rico after a bit more reconnaissance, and would not attempt to settle the new territory until 1521. When he did return, he brought 200 colonists, fifty horses, livestock, and everything necessary to sustain a new community, most likely to a location near present-day Charlotte Harbor. The experiment was short-lived. Native Calusa Indians attacked the Spanish colonists soon after they landed, killing several of them and wounding Ponce, who later died of his injuries in Cuba.[15]

The next few Spanish visitors sought to explore Florida rather than settle it. That was Pánfilo Narvaez's plan when he landed at Tampa Bay in April 1528. Once ashore, he sent his supply ships up the coast toward present-day Apalachee Bay, intending to meet back up with them after the land expedition had scouted the Florida peninsula. Narvaez then led his force of 300 men and forty horses into the interior. The natives around Tampa Bay had spoken of a chiefdom called Apalachee to the north, a land with gold mines and other enticing riches. Narvaez pointed the expedition in that direction, eventually reaching Apalachee but not finding the treasure he was hoping for. Along the way, the Spaniard may very well have crossed through present-day Taylor County, although contemporary descriptions are too vague to say for sure. The treasurer of the expedition, Alvar Núñez Cabeza de Vaca, described the lands they passed through as sandy, flat, pitted with lakes, and covered in stands of oak, pine, cypress, and cedar trees. If they were not in Taylor County, they couldn't have been too far away.[16]

At any rate, the Narvaez expedition came to an unfortunate end. After spending a month in Apalachee trying in vain to make contact with the supply ships, the explorer led his followers to the Gulf coast—possibly around the mouth of the St. Marks River—and began constructing a series of barges to transport the party to safety in Spanish Mexico. By the time the expedition sailed into the Gulf on these crude boats in September 1528, only 242 of the original 300-man landing party remained. The barges made it as far as the Texas coastline, but a violent spring storm pulverized them in early 1529, forcing the survivors to take shelter on an island. Between the wreck and the harsh conditions they encountered on land, the expedition quickly dwindled to fifteen members, and then to only four. The survivors eventually made it to Mexico City in 1536, carrying with them the history of the ill-fated journey.[17]

Hernando de Soto is probably the best known Spaniard to have reputedly traveled through Taylor County while exploring Florida. The true "De Soto Trail," like that of Narvaez, is not entirely certain. Scholars generally agree that De Soto landed in the vicinity of Tampa Bay in May 1539 and embarked on an expedition into the interior. From there, however, finding the route requires interpreting contemporary records written by people who did not use our modern place names for rivers, lakes, or other features. Archaeologists and historians estimate that De Soto's trek took him through the area around Zephyrhills, across the Alafia and Withlacoochee rivers, and into the Timucuan province of Ocale, near present-day Marion County. From there, the explorer went as far north as Live Oak before turning almost due west to head for Apalachee, crossing the Aucilla River in October 1539. That month the expedition encamped at the Apalachee town of Anhaica, the only undisputed site along the De Soto Trail thanks to a series of dated artifacts. Whether any part of the expedition actually visited present-day Taylor County is difficult to say, but again – they couldn't have been very far away if they didn't.[18]

The next known Spanish presence in the vicinity of present-day Taylor County involved friars rather than conquistadors. Eager to crush a small French outpost near present-day Jacksonville and protect the Spanish claim to Florida, explorer Pedro Menéndez de Avilés founded St. Augustine in 1565. Soon after, Catholic missionaries arrived to establish a church and begin Christianizing the natives. These friars belonged to the Order of Friars Minor of the Regular Observance of St. Francis of Assisi—Franciscans for short. Starting in 1587, they began making contact with the Timucuans north and west of St. Augustine, building missions and developing relationships with the various chiefs.[19]

The area between the Aucilla and Suwannee rivers belonged at this time to the Timucuan province of Yustaga. Located far away from St. Augustine, this area did not receive much attention from the missionaries until 1608, when Fray Martín Prieto crossed through Yustaga seeking to end a long-standing feud between the Apalachees and the tribes east of the Aucilla. Along the way, Prieto visited the village of Cotocochuni, located on Lake Sampala in present-day Madison County. The local chief had no interest in converting to Christianity at the time, but by 1623 he had relented, and by 1635 the Franciscans estimated they had converted 13,000 natives in Yustaga province. Cotocochuni itself became the site of a Franciscan mission—San Pedro de Potohiriba—from which San Pedro Bay gets its name. Numerous maps from the 18th and 19th centuries also show a San Pedro River running through the Taylor County area, although the mapmakers vary wildly in their placement of the stream.[20]

There has long been some suspicion that one of the Franciscan missions was located closer to the Gulf coast along the Fenholloway. Historian W.T. Cash thought this might have been San Lorenzo de Ivitachuco, established in 1633 according to Spanish records. Multiple contemporary sources identify Ivitachuco as being in Apalachee territory, however, which means it would have to have been on the west side of the Aucilla River. Most likely, the Fenholloway and other Taylor County waterways did support a number of Timucuan villages ministered by the Franciscan missions, but they were *visitas*, meeting places without a resident friar. Any Franciscans serving the Taylor County region would almost certainly have been headquartered at San Pedro de Potohiriba along the *camino real* or "royal road" connecting St. Augustine with Apalachee province. This route is still marked in a few places today as the Old Spanish Trail. Another trail, called the "Suwanney Path" by Andrew Jackson's topographical engineer in 1818, split from the Old Spanish Trail near present-day Lamont and crossed Taylor County en route to the Suwannee River. Another contemporary officer called this the "lower trail," an alternative route to the Suwannee from the Miccosukee territory near Tallahassee. This path was probably used more by the Indians than the Spanish, but no doubt it served as a useful means of communication for mission friars and other travelers during the Spanish colonial era.[21]

Florida's Transfer to the U.S. and the Seminole Wars

Florida changed hands twice during the 18th century, with both transactions being decided across the Atlantic by diplomats in Paris. The first transfer came at the end of the French and Indian War, the North American portion of the broader Seven Years' War fought by numerous European nations and their colonists between 1756 and 1763. Britain and France did most of the fighting in that war, but Spain allied itself with the French, fearing the consequences of a British-dominated North American continent. That turned out to be a poor choice. The British defeated the French and also captured Havana, one of Spain's most valuable possessions in the New World. To get Havana back from the British, Spain agreed to hand over Florida, which at that time extended as far west as the Mississippi River.[22]

Florida did not stay British for long. Less than two decades after the French and Indian War ended, Britain found itself fighting yet again in North America, this time against its own subjects, who declared their independence in 1776. Spain, still feeling the sting from its losses to the British in the French and Indian War, gave indirect aid to the Americans, but stopped short of making a formal alliance. With their own colonies in the Western Hemisphere, the Spanish were hesitant to give full-throated support to an upstart nation of revolutionaries aiming to overthrow their colonial overlords. The help they did give, however, earned them some credit at the negotiating table once the war was over. Britain transferred Florida back to Spain as a condition of the Treaty of Paris in 1783.[23]

Neither the British nor the second colonial Spanish administration was able to get much going in Florida, particularly not on the Gulf side—Pensacola being a slight exception. Both European powers hoped to make the province profitable through large-scale agriculture, but this activity was concentrated along the Atlantic coast for the most part. Maps from the second half of the 18th century demonstrate that little exploration was done to ascertain the location of major rivers and landmarks along the upper Gulf coast. Available land records also suggest very little activity. When the U.S. officially acquired Florida in 1821, it agreed to honor existing land grants made to private individuals, provided they brought their claims before a commission so they could be confirmed. Of all the cases brought before this commission, no one claimed any land in the vicinity of present-day Taylor County.

Native Americans made up the bulk of the local population during this time. The Timucuans were decimated by disease and conflict during the first Spanish colonial period, which left large swaths of land in North Florida virtually uninhabited by the turn of the 18th century. Creek Indians from present-day Georgia and Alabama moved southward into these open lands, driven from their home territory by conflicts with other tribes and the expanding presence of British colonists. Villages developed on the lower Suwannee (around present-day Old Town), at Alachua on the northern edge of Payne's Prairie, and near Lake Miccosukee around Tallahassee. The British trading firm Panton, Leslie and Company also operated a store at St. Marks, where they traded weapons, gunpowder, and other commodities for animal furs and skins. Contemporary accounts from traders and government officials traveling between these centers mention the Aucilla and Econfina rivers, as well as San Pedro Bay. No doubt the Indians trading at St. Marks hunted for game in the swamps and hammocks of Taylor County.[24]

As more white settlers began moving into the territory north of the Florida border, tensions between the U.S., Spain, and the Indians became more serious. Runaway slaves from Georgia and Alabama often escaped into Spanish Florida and attached themselves to the Seminole tribes they encountered. This sometimes led American citizens and non-Florida Indians to conduct raids south of the border, occasionally prompting retaliation from the Florida Seminoles. Spanish authority over the Seminoles was almost non-existent; the government at St. Augustine did very little to control these border issues. U.S. officials protested strongly at the Spanish government's weakness, but it confirmed something many Americans had already been thinking for some time—that Florida would inevitably have to become part of the United States.[25]

The dominoes began falling in 1816 when the U.S. government established Fort Scott only a few miles from the Florida border and determined to supply it by bringing a boat up the Apalachicola River through Spanish territory. The black garrison of a fort along the river attempted to block the U.S. supply boat's advance, which prompted the Americans to fire on the fort, exploding its powder magazine. Soon afterward, Miccosukee Indians led by Chief Neamathla fired on another U.S. boat coming up the Apalachicola, prompting Secretary of War John C. Calhoun in 1818 to order Major General Andrew Jackson to the Florida border to rectify the situation. Jackson took a broad view of his authority and decided to invade Spanish Florida in pursuit of the Seminoles, an episode now called the First Seminole War.[26]

Accomplishing this mission took General Jackson right through present-day Taylor County. After destroying the Indian town on Lake Miccosukee in late March, Jackson and his force of nearly 5,000 militia, volunteers, and friendly Creek Indians headed for the Spanish military outpost at St. Marks. The garrison of the fort capitulated on April 6, and soon Jackson set out for the Seminole village located along the lower Suwannee River near present-day Old Town. Captain Hugh Young, Jackson's topographical engineer, kept a remarkably detailed account of the terrain the army passed through. Based on Captain Young's description, Jackson's forces retraced their steps in the direction of Lake Miccosukee until they reached the "lower trail" or "Suwanney path," which crossed the Aucilla near present-day Lamont. An 1848 plat of Township 3 South, Range 5 East shows "Jackson's Trail" heading south through Gibson's Pasture before making a sharp turn to the east to cross the Econfina River just northeast of the present location of Oakland Baptist Church. According to one of Jackson's letters to the Secretary of War, the army encountered a band of Indians near the Econfina on April 12. Jackson sent about fifty Tennessee volunteers and friendly Creeks under the command of General William McIntosh to pursue them. In the skirmish that ensued, they killed 37 warriors and captured more than a hundred prisoners and five hundred head of cattle.[27]

From the Econfina, Jackson's army proceeded to the Fenholloway River ("Slippery Log Creek"), likely crossing below Hampton Springs near where Fort Andrews would later be built during the Second Seminole War in the 1830s. Captain Young's memoir mentions four more streams between the Fenholloway and Steinhatchee rivers, one of which would almost certainly have been Spring Warrior Creek. He mentions another one on the edge of what he called "Live Oak Swamp" (probably Tide Swamp), which may have been either Fish Creek or Dallus Creek. The army then crossed the Steinhatchee River at the falls before arriving at their final destination near Old Town on April 16.[28]

Excerpt from a map drawn by Mark F. Boyd showing the approximate route taken by Andrew Jackson through Taylor County during the First Seminole War in 1818.

(Map courtesy of the State Library of Florida)

While passing through this region, Captain Young wrote down what is likely one of the earliest American descriptions of a Taylor County delicacy—swamp cabbage. He commented on the abundance of cabbage palmettos, which he said had tops like "large pineapples." He went on to describe the structure of the plant, offering these remarks: "The vegetable substance from which the stems and leaves are supported has in its center a white brittle mucilaginous mass composed of the centre folds of the leaves forming it, which may be eaten raw and when boiled has a taste somewhat like parsnips. In times of scarcity the Indians live on it, and it is said to be wholesome and nutritious." As time would tell, Indians weren't the only ones who found this unusual dish appealing. Taylor Countians are still eating swamp cabbage with gusto two hundred years later. Plenty more Americans enjoy the raw variety under the name "hearts of palm."[29]

Andrew Jackson's foray into Florida provoked strong protests from Spain, but was immensely popular in the United States. Jackson and his defenders maintained that the Spanish colonial authorities had been unable to restrain Indians or people of other nationalities from using Florida as a base from which to harass American citizens in Georgia and Alabama. Jackson, they argued, had merely done what the Spanish would not do—ensure the integrity of the border. Calls to annex Florida increased in intensity. President James Monroe ultimately turned the forts Jackson had seized back over to the Spanish, but at the same time American and Spanish officials began hammering out the details of a treaty ceding Florida to the U.S., which was eventually ratified in 1821.[30]

American migration into Florida picked up once U.S. ownership of the territory was established, but present-day Taylor County remained relatively devoid of white settlement for the first two decades. Government surveyors came through the area in 1825 and 1826 to stake out township lines to facilitate land sales, but in many cases the terrain was so desolate and swampy they delayed surveying the interior section lines for years afterward. Special agents of the U.S. Navy arrived in 1831 hunting for stands of timber that might be useful for shipbuilding. One of the agents, Eli B. Whitaker, recommended the Navy reserve a few sections of land along the Steinhatchee River on account of the red cedar and live oak he found there. Some of the cedars he encountered were reportedly as much as three feet in diameter. As for the area around the Fenholloway and Econfina rivers, however, Whitaker wasn't impressed. "It is indeed a poor, pine, barren, dreary country," he wrote. "No live oak there—and if there was, no water sufficient to transport it."[31]

White settlers may have bypassed Taylor County in those early days, but Indians continued to make their home there even as Americans began pouring into the new Florida Territory. Unlike the Spanish and British, American settlers were highly interested in the land between the Apalachicola and Suwannee rivers—what was then called "Middle Florida." This area had formerly belonged almost exclusively to the Indians; now white settlers insisted on establishing their plantations there. The proximity between the Seminoles and their new neighbors only exacerbated the problems that had existed before the First Seminole War, and white settlers quickly called for action to remove the Indians from the region once and for all.[32]

Federal Indian agents convened a treaty conference at Moultrie Creek in 1823, where they convinced a delegation of Seminoles to move their tribes to a reservation in Central Florida and stop harboring runaway slaves. The agreement was flimsy and unsatisfactory to all involved, and Seminole warriors frequently left the reservation in search of food and supplies for their families. White settlers entered the reservation, even though they were forbidden to do so, and complained of seeing runaway slaves among the Seminoles. The only solution many Americans saw was for the Indians to be removed from Florida entirely. Federal authorities convinced a few Seminoles to emigrate west of the

Mississippi River, but many others declined to leave. Tensions broke out into open conflict in 1835, touching off what would become the Second Seminole War.[33]

The territory where Taylor County sits today was still mostly unpopulated by white Americans when the war began. Plenty of land had been purchased, but it went to speculators and investors rather than settlers. Jefferson County planters like William Nuttall and John G. Gamble bought up huge tracts of land around the Aucilla and Steinhatchee rivers, believing these waterways would eventually prove key to the growing cotton industry. Other big buyers included Seaton Grantland, a Congressman from Griffin, Georgia; Simeon A. Smith, probably from Georgia; and Richard Hayward, a planter from Leon County with a history of dueling and gambling. All of this territory still belonged to Madison County, as did that of present-day Lafayette and Dixie counties. In the 1830s, this was ownership only by name—the reach of law enforcement didn't extend very far south from the county seat at San Pedro, located close to where county roads 14 and 360 now intersect on the way to Madison.[34]

Early on in the war, most of the action took place east and south of the Suwannee River, and it was confined to skirmishes between the Seminoles and the regular U.S. Army. By December 1835, however, Indian sightings just across the river from Madison County led local citizens to take action on their own. A group of Madison Countians had gone to St. Marks to purchase a large load of merchandise, and they were planning to bring it up the Suwannee by way of a pole barge. Fearing trouble, about forty additional citizens gathered at Charles's Ferry on the Suwannee and formed a militia company to ensure safe passage for the cargo. Thomas Livingston was elected captain. At least two future Taylor Countians were among Livingston's militia group—Moses Barker and Edward Henderson, who became the company's second sergeant. The pole barge crew finished their voyage without incident, but Livingston's company remained on guard.[35]

Indians attacked at least one plantation in Madison County in early 1837, prompting nearby settlers to abandon their homes and seek refuge in San Pedro and Hickstown. Robert D. Bradley, who had been a member of Livingston's company, formed a new militia unit at San Pedro with 52 men, including future Taylor Countians William Biven (or Bevan) and Stephen Godwin. Captain Bradley's company scouted the countryside that summer, chasing the Indians and killing several. Bradley wrote in his report to Governor Richard Keith Call that there were "considerable signs of Indians on the Suwannee, and trails where they have been driving cattle recently toward the upper part of the Suwannee Hammock and Deadman's Bay." Further attacks confirmed Bradley's observation; in July 1838 a party of Indians attacked the home of a Mr. Baker in Madison County, killing most of the family inside and setting fire to the house. Other attacks targeted plantations and settlements within only a few miles of Tallahassee.[36]

The United States Army struggled to control the situation using conventional means, but they were dealing with an unconventional enemy. The Seminoles lacked some of the heavy weaponry held by the U.S. troops, but they used guerilla tactics that made those weapons and the normal rules of warfare less effective. Floridians criticized the regular army's reliance on orthodox methods, and urged the government to accept more local volunteers into service. A number of commanders in the regular army doubted the local volunteers could do much better, but over the next couple of years many new companies were established by Floridians. At least thirty men who would later become heads of households in Taylor County appear on the muster rolls for these units.[37]

Zachary Taylor, the general for whom Taylor County is named, took command of the Army's forces in Florida on May 15, 1838. He proposed a plan to rid Middle Florida of Indians by setting off the area into 18-mile squares, building roads around the perimeter of each square, and putting a fort in the center with a garrison of twenty soldiers. The officer commanding each garrison would make a map of his square and organize daily patrols. Taylor received authorization from the Secretary of War to put his plan into effect on February 15, 1839.[38]

Portrait of Zachary Taylor, commander of United States troops in Florida during a portion of the Second Seminole War, as well as 12th president of the United States.

(Photo courtesy of the Library of Congress)

The Army constructed at least six forts in what is now Taylor County as a result of this plan. The term "fort" is a bit generous; soldiers built them hastily out of whatever materials happened to be nearby. One staff officer named Woodburne Potter described the general appearance of the forts like this: "The pickets are made by splitting pine logs about eighteen feet in length into two parts, and driving them upright and firmly into the ground close together, with the flat side inwards. These are braced together by a strip of board nailed on the inside. The tops are sharpened, and holes are cut seven or eight feet from the ground for the fire arms. A range of benches extends around the work about three feet high, from which the fire is delivered. All our forts in that country are so formed."[39]

Fort Pleasant and Fort Frank Brooke were the first posts to be established in present-day Taylor County. Fort Pleasant was founded on November 12, 1838, by Company E of the 6th Infantry Regiment, which had marched up from Micanopy to begin putting General Taylor's plans into action. The soldiers built the fort near the bank of the Econfina River just downstream from present-day Shady Grove. Fort Pleasant was one of the largest and longest serving Taylor County forts. It was the headquarters for the First Infantry Regiment in 1840, and post returns show that a number of units were stationed there throughout the war.[40]

Fort Frank Brooke was founded about the same time as Fort Pleasant on the other end of the county on the west side of the Steinhatchee River, not far from the mouth. Government surveyor Alfred H. Jones showed the site of the fort in the southwest quarter of Section 19 of Township 9 South, Range 10 East on his 1851 plat of the area, which would put it close to the present-day Steinhatchee Landing resort. The post was named for Francis Brooke, a lieutenant who was killed during the Battle of Lake Okeechobee on Christmas Day in 1837. Companies from the Sixth Infantry Regiment occupied Fort Frank Brooke from its founding until it was abandoned in June 1840, and for a while in late 1838 it served as Zachary Taylor's headquarters. Fort Frank Brooke was never directly attacked by the Indians, but evidently there were many camped in the area. Taylor wrote in January 1839 that more Indians appeared to have spent the previous summer around the head of the Steinhatchee than anywhere else north of the Kissimmee River.[41]

Fort Andrews was established on March 2, 1839, on the south side of the Fenholloway River near Couey Island, downriver from Hampton Springs and the river's junction with Rocky Creek. The fort was likely named for George Andrews, a graduate of the United States Military Academy and a captain in the 6th Infantry who was severely wounded in 1837 at Lake Okeechobee. Forts Andrews and Frank Brooke were connected by a road that ran near the coast, similar to the present-day Beach Road but possibly a bit farther inland.[42]

This was dangerous territory, and soldiers traveling through it often faced attacks from Indians patrolling the area. On May 3, 1839, a detachment of soldiers commanded by Lieutenant William Hulbert set out from

Fort Andrews to check on an express rider who failed to arrive on time. Hulbert halted the detachment for the night about halfway between the two posts, but continued on with one of the privates, intending to spend the night at Fort Frank Brooke. Before the two soldiers could reach the fort, however, they were ambushed at "the 14 mile creek," possibly Dallus Creek or Bivens Creek, and killed. The bodies were discovered the next day by the remainder of the detachment, and they were buried near Fort Frank Brooke.[43]

Excerpt from an 1843 map of Florida drawn by Henry Schenk Tanner showing the locations of the three largest Second Seminole War forts in what would later become Taylor County.

(Map courtesy of the State Library of Florida)

More attacks occurred on this same road in the following months. On July 20, 1839, two wagons left Fort Frank Brooke for Fort Andrews, having an escort of four soldiers, plus the hospital steward from Frank Brooke. About halfway between the two posts, Indians fired on the party, killing the hospital steward and one private instantly. The remaining privates retreated to Fort Frank Brooke for reinforcements, but by the time they returned the Indians were gone. The body of the private had been badly mutilated; the body of the hospital steward was missing entirely. In another skirmish on July 29, a party of about forty Indians attacked a detachment of seventeen soldiers from Fort Andrews as they were building a bridge along the road to Fort Frank Brooke. Two soldiers died and were buried at Fort Andrews; five additional soldiers were wounded.[44]

These depredations began to wear on the soldiers stationed at Fort Andrews, as correspondence from its commander, Second Lieutenant Samuel Woods, reveals. "Indians are constantly hovering about the Fort Frank Brooks Road," he wrote in one letter. "We are more like a besieged garrison than anything else. We cannot even supply ourselves with subsistence without a great risk of an ambuscade." In another letter, he expressed his frustration that so few soldiers were assigned to this dangerous area when so many more were available. He noted that while twelve companies guarded the settlements farther north where Indians were only seen once a month, the area between Fort Frank Brooke and Fort Andrews was assigned to only two companies separated by 38 miles. "The post has been most sadly neglected," he wrote, and what few soldiers there were could not safely perform their duties.[45]

General Taylor beefed up patrols of Middle Florida in late 1839, sending large scouting parties under colonels John Garland and William Davenport to comb the area between the Georgia border, the Suwannee, and the Gulf of Mexico. Colonel Davenport was reportedly moving in the direction of Andrew Jackson's old trail, which means he would have swept present-day Taylor County from northwest to southeast. Colonel William Bailey led another scout of the region later in the spring of 1840, and found significant Indian settlements between the Econfina and Fenholloway rivers. Bailey reported finding three separate Indian villages in Thomas Mill Hammock, one of them having seventeen lodges. All were destroyed by the soldiers as they passed through, and the Indians fled toward the Suwannee.[46]

The Army also established at least three more forts in the Taylor County region to quarter the troops patrolling this active part of the countryside. Forts Mitchell and Hulbert were established on February 2, 1840. Fort Mitchell was located near present-day Foley where the south (main) branch of the Fenholloway River crossed the trail leading from Fort Pleasant to Fort Barker in Cook's Hammock. Fort Hulbert, named for the young lieutenant who had been killed by the Indians the previous year, was established not far from the scene of the murder along the road connecting Fort Andrews with Fort Frank Brooke. An 1840 map of the area places Fort Hulbert on the next major creek down the coast from Spring Warrior Creek, possibly Blue Creek near Keaton Beach. This fits with written descriptions of the fort's location, which put it anywhere between 17 to 22 miles northwest of Fort Frank Brooke at the mouth of the Steinhatchee. A third post, Fort Econfinee (Econfina), was established by Captain Jacob Brown in March 1840 about five miles up the Econfina River.[47]

All three of these forts were fairly short-lived. Fort Econfina was reportedly abandoned only two months after it was established. By the end of 1841, the buildings at forts Hulbert and Mitchell had been destroyed by fire, as had the buildings at Fort Andrews and Fort Frank Brooke. Fort Pleasant, on the other hand, remained in service until at least October 1842, very near the war's end.[48]

The Second Seminole War did not end suddenly or with any great fanfare. It was a war of attrition, one that required the Army to slowly chase the

Indians back and forth across the territory, burning and destroying their camps as they went. The last action of any consequence within the boundaries of present-day Taylor County happened in the spring of 1842, when Colonel William J. Worth coordinated a final sweep of the area between Fort Pleasant and Fort Fanning on the Suwannee, creating a pincer movement designed to squeeze the last remaining Seminoles out of their hiding places in the swamps and hammocks around the headwaters of the Steinhatchee River. By 1843, Worth estimated that only about 300 total Seminoles remained in Florida, and that they were not a threat. The rest had been killed or shipped west of the Mississippi for resettlement.[49]

While the Seminole Wars were devastating to many established settlements in Florida, that did not stop new people from moving into the territory. On the contrary, the population continued to increase, and new towns began to form, especially in the Middle Florida region. Even in the midst of the war, Floridians sent delegates to draw up a state constitution in 1838, and in 1845 Congress admitted Florida into statehood. New counties emerged as settlers began arriving in previously uninhabited corners of the state. Reaching the county seat to do business could be a serious hardship, especially for a county like Madison, which for much of its early years stretched from the Georgia border to the mouth of the Suwannee River. It wasn't long before settlers along the Steinhatchee River, the Fenholloway, the Econfina, and Rocky Creek began wondering if maybe the county ought to be divided.

Portrait of an early Taylor County family.
(Photo courtesy of the Taylor County Historical Society)

CHAPTER 2:

Early Settlers

Most of Taylor County's first families came from Georgia and the Carolinas. Of the 221 households listed in the 1860 census, more than 130 were headed by individuals born in Georgia. Another 59 heads of household hailed from the Carolinas, and 12 were born in Florida. The four household heads from northern states included John E. Jenkins, Sr., and his son Reuben, a carpenter and farmer, respectively; John O. Woods, a millwright; and Charles Francis O'Hara, a shoemaker. One Taylor Countian, Thomas Green, reported being born in England.[1]

Florida was an alluring destination for both wealthy elite Southerners and not so wealthy yeomen farmers. For rich planters, the relatively uninhabited territory of Florida seemed to be a blank canvas, ready to be molded into a productive landscape even more bountiful than the Carolinas and Georgia had become. Cotton was only one crop they dreamed of; they also hoped to establish large sugar plantations and revel in some of the same successes their European counterparts were enjoying in the Caribbean. Yeoman farmers, often called "countrymen" by their elite neighbors, had simpler desires. Cash crop agriculture had made good land in Georgia and the Carolinas too expensive for them to buy. Wealthier families already owned the best land, and even if a countryman cleared off a new plot for a homestead, when he went to purchase it he often found it had been bought by a speculator. Florida was a new American territory, and it offered an opportunity for countrymen to purchase a homestead of their own, plus the freedoms that came with it.[2]

A family's move to Florida typically took place in stages, and sometimes over multiple generations. The southward migration of families from the Carolinas and Georgia toward Florida began when the Second Seminole War was still in progress and much of the new territory had yet to be surveyed. As a result, migrating families often paused in southern Georgia before moving into Florida. Many of Taylor County's earliest residents followed this pattern. Allen

O'Quinn, for example, was born in South Carolina in 1802, but lived, married, and even owned land in two different counties in Georgia before finally ending up in Taylor County around 1856. Samuel Blue similarly was born in North Carolina around 1820, but shows up in Dooly County, Georgia, married to his first wife Margaret Spradley in 1850 before appearing in the census records for Taylor County a decade later. Many more of Taylor County's founding settlers were born in Georgia, but their parents or grandparents had previously migrated from the Carolinas. This was the case with the Englishes that moved to Taylor County prior to 1860, as well as the prolific Robert McFail Hendry family.[3]

Portrait of Robert McFail Hendry, an early settler of Shady Grove.

(Photo courtesy of the State Archives of Florida)

Once settlers arrived in Taylor County (or Madison County prior to December 1856), they had to find a place to live. Many of the county's earliest families started out as squatters, meaning they had no legal title to the land where they built their homes. In the 1850s, title to most land in present-day Taylor County still rested with the federal government. A few speculators had picked up plots of land around the Aucilla and Steinhatchee rivers, but the broad territory in between was almost entirely unspoken for. In those days, squatting was not uncommon, nor was the government very concerned about it. Officials did not patrol unsold public lands, and if the land was owned by a speculator that person probably lived many miles away and would never know the squatters were even there.[4]

Families could either purchase land from the federal government with cash when it came up for public auction, or "pre-empt" the land, essentially reserving it to purchase later by establishing a homestead and improving it. The State of Florida also held title to a large amount of swampland and certain sections reserved to raise money for education. These were available for sale as well. Some settlers received land as a bounty for military service—either their own service or that of a friend or relative. Robert McFail Hendry and his brother Neal Hendry both received parcels of land in Shady Grove in this way.

Neal received land from the federal government in 1853 as compensation for the service of James House during the Seminole Wars. Robert received his the following year as compensation for the military service of Green B. Harrell. All of these transactions took place at the General Land Office in Tallahassee, and many of the sale records are available online through state and federal databases.[5]

Federal land records offer clues as to where and when Taylor County's first settlements began to take shape. The northernmost stretch of land between the Aucilla River and present-day Shady Grove was the first area where actual settlers bought large amounts of land. Between 1848 and 1860, the Sever, English, Sheffield, Blanton, Wallace, Wheeler, Rowell, Sapp, and O'Quinn families— among others—purchased land in this zone. During that same period, the Rountree and White families purchased land near present-day Athena. The Towles family, connected with the Rountrees by marriage, would also eventually own a considerable amount of land there. Several Carltons and Hendrys purchased land near where Puckett Road crosses the Fenholloway River— hence the Carlton Bridge, Carlton Cemetery, and Carlton Spring in that area. A very large number of families purchased land in the vicinity of present-day Foley and the abandoned town of Fenholloway southeast of Perry. Records show that the Sutton, Ezell, Henderson, Harrell, Hendry, Parker, Townsend, Albritton, and Kelly families all bought land in that area prior to the Civil War. A final concentration of land purchases appears just to the east of present-day Perry, stretching northward toward the Pisgah community. John and Reuben Jenkins, John O. Woods, William Wallace, William McMullen, Boyd D. Poppell, Henry Smart, John O'Steen, and John J. and Britton Edwards are among those who purchased land there prior to 1860.[6]

Several families got their start living farther away from these early settlements, usually because they had a specific occupation in mind. William J. Biven, for example, bought land near Steinhatchee in 1860 and started a fishery. Hampton Springs was also a center of activity, although not just by the Hampton family. William McMullen was the first private citizen to obtain legal title to the springs when he bought the surrounding forty acres of land in 1852. Less than a decade later, records show Henry Parker tried to set up a hotel at the springs. Parker mortgaged his place on Rocky Creek in 1860 to pay off Daniel Ladd, a merchant at Newport who had been selling him "provisions &c … to enable me to carry on Hotel Keeping at the Hampton springs in Taylor County."[7]

Creating the County

Taylor County was officially established along with Lafayette County by an act of the Legislature signed by Governor James Broome on December 23, 1856. Barton C. Pope, Madison County's representative in the Florida House of Representatives, had tried the year before to get Taylor created, but he ended up withdrawing his bill before it could be voted on. Growth was likely the impetus for wanting to divide Madison County into smaller parts. The state census of 1855 showed the county had gained 2,546 white citizens since 1850 for a total of 5,348. To put that into perspective, Leon County only had 3,506 whites in 1855; Jefferson County only 3,086. Moreover, Madison's population was spread out over 2,300 square miles of territory from the Aucilla to the Suwannee. Politics no doubt had a role to play as well. More Middle Florida counties meant more representatives in the state legislature, and therefore a stronger voice for Middle Florida leaders in making decisions about the state's future.[8]

The act creating Taylor County called for a March 1857 election to choose the first slate of county officials. The Madison County judge of probate was to conduct the election. Stephen R. White was elected sheriff; Alexander Ezell became the first tax assessor and collector; John O'Steen became the first county judge; Daniel C. Barker became the first county clerk; and J.R. Mott, James Martin Towles, Edward Jordan, and John M. Wilder became the first county commissioners. The law ordered the new officers to conduct their business at the home of Daniel Bryant until the voters selected a permanent place for a courthouse. Taylor County citizens chose the current site of Perry, and on October 2, 1857, the state deeded over the forty-acre parcel of land where the courthouse and much of downtown now exists.[9]

The first courthouse was a log cabin built on the site of the current courthouse, probably in late 1857 or 1858. Documentation of its construction is lacking, but in 1940 a team of researchers working for the Works Progress Administration interviewed Abner Parker, who remembered seeing the building as a young boy. Parker described it as being about 20 feet by 18 feet, having only one room with a judge's stand and a couple of windows. The county ordered a few renovations for the building in 1869, but then ended up constructing a new two-story courthouse to replace it in 1873.[10]

The rest of the county's forty-acre courthouse site became the original town of Perry, named for Florida's governor at the time, Madison Starke Perry. For generations, the traditional wisdom has always been that Perry started out in 1869 as a post office called Rosehead, and the name was changed to Perry in

Portrait of Florida's fourth state governor, Madison Starke Perry, for whom the town of Perry was named.

(Photo courtesy of the State Archives of Florida)

1875. Archival evidence tells a different story, however. Several deeds in the county's official records refer to lots in the "Town of Perry" being sold as early as 1859, ten years before the Rosehead post office even existed. More deeds were recorded for lots in the "Town of Perry" while the Rosehead post office was active from 1869 to 1875. In other words, not only did Rosehead and Perry exist at the same time, but Perry was actually the older of the two.[11]

So what was Rosehead supposed to be, and what was its relationship to Perry? The best available evidence suggests that Rosehead may have started out as a separate settlement intended to replace Perry as the county seat. When Allen O'Quinn applied to establish Rosehead as a post office in 1869, he described it as being located in the northwest quarter of Section 5, Township 4 South, Range 7 East. That puts it miles away from the courthouse near the Pisgah neighborhood and the old road connecting Perry with Newport. This district was already well established, and several of the county's earliest pioneer families had lived there for years. Two months after O'Quinn applied for the post office, the county commission called for a special election to decide whether the county seat would remain at Perry. The commissioners gave no explanation for potentially wanting to abandon the town, but it is possible they were looking at the Rosehead-Pisgah neighborhood as a replacement.[12]

If that was the case, however, they did not look for long. Either the special election never happened or the voters rejected the idea of abandoning Perry as the county seat. Two months after the vote was supposed to take place, the county commissioners announced they would let a contract to repair the original courthouse, a sure sign they meant to keep it where it was. They also ordered in March 1870 that "the town of Perry" be re-surveyed into quarter-acre lots. They did this despite the fact that citizens had already owned lots in Perry for more than a decade, which suggests that very little if any development had occurred around the courthouse during that time. Perhaps that was why the idea of moving the county seat had been proposed in the first place.[13]

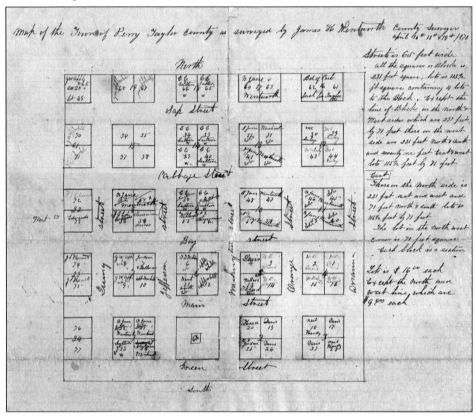

Map of the original town of Perry, drawn by James H. Wentworth in 1870.
(Image courtesy of the Taylor County Historical Society)

Adding to the confusion is the fact that at some point the Rosehead post office was relocated to Perry without changing its name. An 1873 map of Florida even gives both names over the same point. In 1874, the Postmaster General in Washington wrote to Rosehead postmaster Henry Tillman, asking him to explain the relationship between Rosehead and Perry. Tillman replied that Perry and Rosehead were "one and the same place," and that the name should always have been Perry. The Postmaster General responded by changing the name of Rosehead post office to Perry, effective May 28, 1875. No explanation was ever given for why Rosehead had been moved from where Allen O'Quinn originally established it.[14]

Life on the Taylor County Frontier

Most Taylor County families lived away from town on small farms, growing corn and food crops and tending cattle and hogs. Fencing was very limited; livestock ranged freely throughout the woods. Each farmer branded his stock or used a special pattern to mark their ears in order to keep them separate from the cows and hogs belonging to his neighbors. These marks and brands were registered with the county government, and they frequently appear in legal documents showing transfer of ownership from one person to another. For example, in 1860 John Grantham deeded all of his livestock to his five children. He indicated he didn't actually know how many cows he had, but they all had the same mark and brand, "swallow fork and under bit in one ear, crop and under bit in the other and some markes [sic] changed but branded 7S."[15]

Almost all of the earliest homes in the county were built from split logs, as were other buildings like churches and storehouses. Most of these log cabins had a single room, with either one or two porches. Some of the cabins used a "double-penned" pattern, with two rooms and a breezeway down the middle. Windows had wooden shutters rather than glass, at least in the vast majority of early homes, and wooden pegs generally held things together rather than nails. The roof was usually made from cypress shingles. Kitchens were usually in a separate building far away from the house. This kept the heat of the cooking fire away from the living quarters, and reduced the risk of burning the main house down by accident. A good example of this Florida Cracker architecture is the Whiddon house, located next to the Florida Forestry Museum at Forest Capital Hall. That cabin was built by

The Wiley W. Whiddon House at the Cracker Homestead at Forest Capital Museum State Park south of Perry. The cabin has the typical double-penned layout with a breezeway down the center.

(Photo by the author)

Wiley Whiddon around 1863 in western Taylor County, where it remained until it was transported to its current location in 1972.[16]

Building these houses was a community affair. A settler looking to start a new home would call on his nearby relatives and friends to come for a "log-rolling." This involved cutting down the trees for building materials, moving them to the home site, and assembling the log "pens" that made up the rooms. This was difficult work, but it was also a chance to socialize. Families got together for other chores as well, including splitting rails for fences, killing and dressing hogs, and "pulling fodder," which meant pulling the leaves off corn stalks and drying them for feeding livestock in the winter.[17]

The inside of the typical early Taylor County cabin was fairly simple, with bare floors and handmade furniture. Kerosene lamps and the glowing blaze from stick-and-mud fireplaces provided light. Store-bought goods were rare and valuable, although every home had at least a few such items, as county records show. In one 1863 inventory, for example, Julia Willis listed among her property 30 hogs; a bedstead, mattress, two sheets, and two quilts; a water bucket; a spinning wheel; a butter churn; three chairs; 14 geese; a jar; a loom for weaving cloth; two pots; a tea kettle; a milk bucket; a cow and yearling; and a table. Those were her most valuable possessions, the ones worth reporting for legal purposes. Wealthier families usually had a few more household goods on hand. The 1871 household inventory of Mamie Delilah Wilcox, for example, listed many of the same items as Julia Willis, but also included books, a store-bought wardrobe, glass tumblers, silverware, and a double-cased silver watch.[18]

Consumer goods were rare, not just because of the high costs and difficulty of getting them all the way out to Taylor County, but also because the mid-19th century South was a very cash-poor society for most citizens. Even if a farmer made a good cotton or corn crop, that crop was only sold once annually, and by then the farmer had so many debts from the preceding year that very little of his profits could be converted to cash. Florida farmers, both large-scale planters and yeoman farmers alike, dealt mainly through credit and barter. The official records of Taylor County are full of examples of citizens mortgaging everything they had—land, draft animals, slaves, the next cotton or corn crop—just to get a few dollars to pay off debts or buy essentials. Often these mortgages were made out between the farmer and whichever merchant he went to for his farming supplies and other needs. W.L. Blanton & Company and A.J. Williams appear frequently in the records as mortgage holders.

Aside from a few specialties only available from a grocer or the general store, settlers got their food from their surroundings. Since most Taylor Countians were in the livestock business to some extent, they generally had a steady supply of pork and beef. Wild game was widely available as well, just as it is now. Many residents also traveled to the coast from time to time to catch mullet in seine nets, which they would either smoke or brine to preserve it. Gardens provided a variety of vegetables for the family table, especially corn and sweet potatoes. Corn could also be ground to make corn meal. A number of early Taylor County residents had water-powered mills for this purpose. Zachary O. Lovett had a mill on a creek just east of Shady Grove. John E. Jenkins had one on Rocky Creek near Pisgah, and Mills W. Parker had one on Spring Creek west of present-day Perry. Many more mills existed over the years; these are just some of the earlier ones. Residents would bring corn to a nearby mill to be ground, giving the miller a portion of the processed meal as payment.[19]

The plantation owners' dreams of turning Middle Florida into a lucrative source of sugar cane never quite came to fruition, but Taylor Countians did grow enough for home use and sometimes a little extra to sell in trade. The growing season was shorter than in the Caribbean islands, but residents reported being able to get twelve or more barrels of syrup to the acre if the land was good. Processing the cane required a labor-intensive series of tasks—cutting the cane, pressing the juice from the stalks with an animal-driven machine, and then boiling the juice down. Locals often used this as an excuse to get the neighbors together for a party, and "cane grind-ings" became one of the hallmarks of autumn.[20]

Managing live-stock and keeping food on the table was a family affair that required every-one's participation. Families tended to be larger in those days; more hands meant more help. Slavery existed in antebellum Taylor County, but

Cane grinding equipment at the Cracker Homestead at Forest Capital Museum State Park. Cane was fed between the two rotating cylinders, where it was crushed, releasing the cane juice.

(Photo by the author)

only about 25 families owned slaves during the brief period between the coun-ty's founding and the outbreak of the Civil War, which ended that institution. Even among those families in the county that did have slaves, only five had more than five slaves in 1860—those of William H. Sever, Francis and Rebecca Rountree, Matthew Fane, Thomas Brannen, and Bryant Sheffield. The rest of Taylor County's slaveholders only owned enough slaves to supplement, but not replace, the family's own labor.[21]

Frontier life was not entirely about work, however. Early settlers regularly got together with their neighbors to socialize and have fun. These gatherings were called "frolics," and they often followed a big community project like a log rolling, a fodder pulling, or a cane grinding. Many of the county's early Protestant churches forbade dancing, yet that was one of the most popular activities. Fiddlers sawed out tunes like "Cindy," "Arkansas Traveler," "Drunkard in the Sawgrass," and "Hell After the Yearling" while the settlers danced well into the night. The cotillion was the favorite dance at these events. An equal number of men and women would line up in the middle of the dance floor and follow the lead of someone who called out instructions. The caller would yell out commands like "Honor your partner, lady on the left," "All promenade," and "balance your partners." These dances could last for hours, sometimes even until after daybreak the following morning.[22]

Religion was another critical part of early Taylor County social life. The 1860 census reported four churches in the county—two Baptist churches with a combined capacity of 350 and two Methodist churches with a combined capacity of 300 seats. The first church founded in the territory of present-day Taylor County was almost certainly Rocky Ford Primitive Baptist Church, which was established on September 12, 1846, with elders James Connell and Seaborn Jones at the helm. Shiloh Primitive Baptist Church was established a few years later in 1853.[23]

Congregation at Rocky Ford Primitive Baptist Church near present-day Eridu, 1898.

(Photo courtesy of the State Archives of Florida)

Springhill Missionary Baptist Church was another early church, said to be founded by free blacks living in the area as early as 1853. The church was originally located near the corner of Buckeye Nursery Road and East Green Street, where its cemetery can still be found today. The Colson family, at least five of whom were among the first African Americans to vote in Taylor County after the Civil War, were key leaders in Springhill's earliest days. Tony Colson was among Springhill's first pastors.[24]

The Baptist and Methodist faiths were well-suited to the Taylor County frontier. The music and traditions were simple, and the Methodists even had circuit-riding ministers who traveled to multiple worship sites in the region rather than preaching at a single building. This expanded the reach of the church into even the most remote neighborhoods far outside of town. Many early worshippers in Taylor County took their spiritual learning at brush arbors or in private homes rather than traditional churches.[25]

The Hendry family was virtually synonymous with the Methodist faith in early Taylor County. Robert McFail Hendry, who settled in Shady Grove in the early 1850s, was a circuit rider and preached at locations in both Taylor and Lafayette counties. Three of his sons—Thomas Bowden Hendry, James Madison Hendry, and John Wright Hendry—also became Methodist ministers. James A. Blanton is listed in the 1860 census as a Primitive Baptist minister active in the county. Isaac Munden and Z.G. Wheeler are also listed, although their denominations are not specified.[26]

Services at the early Taylor County churches—whether Methodist or Baptist—involved a combination of hymns, testimony, and fundamentalist preaching. Many of the most popular songs from the mid-19th century are still in the hymn books of today, such as "Rock of Ages," "There Is a Fountain Filled with Blood," "The Lord Will Provide," and "On Jordan's Stormy Banks I Stand." Church was also an important social space, and more than a few young people discovered their future spouses at religious functions.

The early settlers valued education, even if their access to it was limited. The first known school for Taylor County children was established in 1850, when the area still belonged to Madison County. A group of settlers near the Pisgah community contracted with John W. Mixson to teach "such branches as reading, writing, and arithmetic," for which services the subscribers agreed to pay Mixson a dollar a month per student, payable in corn, pork, or bacon "at cash price." The agreement was signed by Mixson, Nathan Smart, Mary Rogers, Maria A. Jenkins, and Harriet E. Parker.[27]

State and county governments became more active in the education of

Florida's youth after the Civil War. Following the state's establishment of a statewide school system in 1869, Taylor County organized its first board of public instruction. W.C. Carlton was the first chairman of the board, and James H. Wentworth was the first county superintendent. In his initial report to state authorities, Wentworth stated there were eight schools in operation with a total of 230 students. Each school had a single teacher earning an average of $25.37 per month plus contributions from local citizens. Seven more schools were in the works.[28]

Fifteen schools for a much smaller Taylor County population might seem odd, but remember this was an age before school buses. Children had to be able to get to school on their own, which meant there had to be a school near every major cluster of homes. Also, these schools were not the top-notch facilities we have today. Wentworth's report to the state reveals that each schoolhouse had been provided by local citizens and was given rent-free. Each building, a log cabin of course, had a broom, a drinking cup, and a well for drawing water. None of them had blackboards or even outhouses. Only three had tables and chairs for the teachers. The students likely sat on benches.[29]

Educational opportunities for Taylor County's African American children were available but very limited in the 1800s. The first volume of the local school board's minutes has been lost, but the oldest surviving volume shows that by 1887, there were 21 schools operating for some portion of the year. Only one of those schools, Springhill, was open to African American students. Henry Nesbitt was appointed to teach the school that year. Records indicate that some years the board did not operate a school for African Americans at all, but in these years the community itself may have stepped up to fulfill the need. According to local tradition, Cordelia Colson, who was born into slavery between 1850 and 1860, learned to read and write as a child while working for a white family, probably in Georgia. She and her daughter Alberta were instrumental in teaching members of Taylor County's African American community to read and write when resources from the county were short.[30]

Teaching school in those days—much like today—was not a career for building great wealth. By 1870 Taylor County's teachers were doing a little better than John W. Mixson's dollar per pupil worth of pork and corn, but it was still a tough profession. No school in the county had more than one teacher, which meant an instructor often faced a class with as many as a dozen or more students from five or six years old up through the teenage years. He or she would be paid in cash when the county had it to give, but often it was not enough to make a complete living. Moreover, in especially cash-poor times teachers were often paid in scrip, which merchants might or might not honor. Teachers were frequently re-assigned to different schools to fill in vacancies, which led many of them to board with nearby families rather than move or make the difficult trek each day from wherever they lived. Some of the county's leading lights got their start as teachers, however. W.T. Cash, who went on to become Florida's first State Librarian, taught at Bethpage, Pleasant Hill, Blue Creek, Seven Mile, and Rockville schools. Cary Hardee, who taught at Pisgah and in Perry, later became Florida's 23rd governor.[31]

James H. Wentworth once called Taylor County "the industrious poor man's paradise," and indeed the county's earliest residents must have felt that way about it. Unlike Georgia and the Carolinas, from which they and their families had moved, they could actually afford to purchase land and establish farms here. They could build their own society, virtually free from the stifling presence of large plantation owners like the ones who controlled the politics and public institutions of neighboring counties. Indeed, Taylor Countians might not have enjoyed great wealth, but most did enjoy a tremendous measure of personal liberty, as well as the comfort of living in a tight-knit community of like-minded families. The strength of this community was about to be tested, however. Only four years into Taylor County's existence, its citizens were plunged into the most divisive conflict in United States history, as well as one of the most complex. The Civil War meant far more to Taylor Countians than just North versus South. It pitted neighbors against neighbors, friends against friends, and even family members against their kin, bringing destruction and disruption that would take decades to fully heal.[32]

Florida's Ordinance of Secession, adopted January 10, 1861 by delegates to a "Convention of the People." Taylor County's William Henry Sever was one of the men who voted in favor of the Ordinance, and his signature is included on this document.

(Image courtesy of the State Archives of Florida)

CHAPTER 3:

The Civil War

O n the morning of January 11, 1861, a convention of delegates in Tallahassee signed an ordinance of secession declaring Florida independent from the United States of America. The measure had almost unanimous support; 62 of the 69 convention members approved it. After the signing ceremony on the east portico of the Capitol, several of the delegates went down the street to visit former territorial governor Richard Keith Call and tell him the news. "Well, Governor—we have done it!" they shouted. Call was a fiercely conservative slaveowner, but in his mind Florida's decision to secede was a fateful mistake. "And what have you done?" he shot back. "You have opened the gates of Hell, from which shall flow the curses of the damned which shall sink you to perdition!"[1]

Call was at least partly right; within a few months Florida was at war along with the rest of the Confederate states in the most destructive conflict in American history. Florida may not have been the scene of the Civil War's most storied battles, but the trials and hardships Floridians faced were as serious as those anyplace else in the Confederacy. Basic goods they could normally take for granted became scarce, and then disappeared altogether. As more men went off to fight, farms languished. Families did the best they could, and government authorities made a few feeble attempts to help, but by the end of the war most Floridians were desperate for relief.[2]

Taylor County played a complex role in the war, its people torn in many cases between a sense of duty to the Confederacy and a desire to save their families from ruin and starvation. By 1864, longtime residents of the county were fighting on both sides, sometimes directly against one another. Understanding how this happened requires understanding that Taylor Countians of that era— like most Floridians—did not have the luxury of thinking about the war solely as a contest between the Union and the Confederacy and the ideals they each stood for. Lofty principles like the right of secession or the value of remaining in the Union meant little to families pushed to the brink of devastation by the war. As the suffering became increasingly acute, Taylor County settlers did what they felt would best ensure their families' survival and help return them to the peaceful life they had known before the war.

A Call to Arms

The Civil War was the culmination of a long series of grievances between the northern and southern states, mostly relating to slavery and the right of a state to practice it unmolested. Florida's elected officials adopted a clear stance on the issue well before secession. In 1849 the Legislature passed a resolution condemning any law prohibiting the extension of slavery into new U.S. territories. In the 1850s, Florida voters consistently backed pro-slavery Democrats over the Whigs and the short-lived "Know-Nothing" Party, both of which were willing to compromise on the slavery question. By the election of 1860, the state legislature and the governorship were occupied by staunch Democrats who increasingly saw secession as the only way to preserve Southern interests. Sixteen of the state's newspapers, including all of the major ones, supported them.[3]

Very little evidence exists to reveal exactly how Taylor Countians felt about these issues, but their voting habits offer a few clues. Local voters chose secessionist Democratic candidate John Milton for governor by a small majority in 1860. The secessionist Democratic candidate for Congress, R.B. Hilton, won Taylor County by two votes over his opponent, Richard C. Allen, who ran on the Constitutional Unionist ticket. The Constitutional Unionists favored a solution to Southern grievances that did not involve secession. In the presidential race, Southern Democrat John C. Breckinridge won the county decisively with 86 votes, his Constitutional Unionist opponent John Bell only receiving 64 votes. The Republican candidate, Abraham Lincoln, did not appear on the ballot.[4]

With the Democratic vote divided across the South, Lincoln ultimately won the presidential election of 1860, which raised the cry for secession in Florida to a fever pitch. Governor Madison Starke Perry used his authority to summon a special session of the Legislature, which in turn called for a special convention in January 1861 to decide whether Florida would secede from the Union. Taylor County voters chose William H. Sever, a slaveowner and resident of Shady Grove since at least 1850, to represent them at this assembly. The delegates met on January 3, 1861, at Tallahassee, and in a week's time had decided in favor of secession. Throughout the proceedings, Sever voted against every measure that might have delayed Florida's departure from the Union, and on January 11 he added his signature to the list of names certifying the convention's decision.[5]

Secession did not mean immediate war. Lincoln did not take office until March 1861, and lame duck President James Buchanan claimed the federal government had no authority to force the seceding states to return to the Union. The newly formed Confederate states were not taking any chances, however. Florida lawmakers passed an act in February 1861 reorganizing the state's militia and establishing new infantry regiments. Taylor Countians were among the many who enthusiastically volunteered to serve in these units. Joseph H. Sappington was one of the first, joining the First Florida Infantry in April. More local men joined the Third Infantry later that year, includ-

William Henry Sever, who represented Taylor County in Florida's 1861 secession convention, and later served in the Taylor Eagles.

(Photo courtesy of the State Archives of Florida)

ing Thomas, Leonard, and Ezekiel B. O'Steen; William W. and Francis M. Whitfield; and James G. Green. All these men served in Company G of the regiment, which formed in nearby Madison. The First and Third Florida regiments served in the western theater of the war, seeing action at Chattanooga, Chickamauga, Kennesaw Mountain, and Atlanta.[6]

In October 1861, Governor John Milton called the Taylor Eagles into service, captained by John M. Hendry. More than 45 men volunteered to serve with the Eagles, mostly from Taylor County. Assisting Captain Hendry as lieutenants were William H. Sever, Taylor County's representative at the state secession convention, J.H. Baker, and William J. Smart. The unit trained at St. Marks before being sent to Fernandina to defend Amelia Island from a Union invasion. The Confederate troops were forced to abandon Fernandina, however, and the Taylor Eagles disbanded shortly thereafter. Dr. Wilson T. Hendry, a descendant of John W. Hendry, who enlisted in the Taylor Eagles, reported having been told that the unit was sent home because it did not have enough men to be absorbed into the Confederate army as a complete company.

Many of the Eagles ended up joining other Confederate units in 1862, however. At least six of them enlisted in Company I of the Second Florida Cavalry, including two sets of brothers—Robert W. and John W. Hendry, and David J., Thomas J., and Edward H. McMullen. This regiment stayed in Florida during the rest of the war and saw action at the battles of Olustee and Natural Bridge, where they successfully blocked the Union from capturing Tallahassee. At least another dozen of the Taylor Eagles joined the Fifth Florida Infantry, which became attached to General Robert E. Lee's Army of Northern Virginia and fought at Gettysburg and Antietam.[7]

The six sons of Robert McFail Hendry and Nancy Ann Carlton Hendry. Standing left to right are David A., Alderman C., and Eli M. Hendry. Seated left to right are Thomas B., James M., and Robert W. Hendry.

(Photo courtesy of the State Archives of Florida)

Several Taylor Countians were captured in battle. A few, like James G. Green, who was captured near Atlanta while serving in the Third Florida Infantry, were released or exchanged fairly quickly. Others remained in Union prisons for the remainder of the war. This was the case for James B. Watts, who was captured at Resaca, Georgia in 1864 and sent to Rock Island Prison in Illinois until the end. James Hamilton Wentworth, who would later become Taylor County's first school superintendent, was captured at Gettysburg in 1863 and imprisoned at Fort Delaware and Johnson's Island, Ohio. He kept a diary while in prison, which provides some interesting details about life for Confederate prisoners of war. Wentworth reported being given rations of bread, beef, pickled pork, coffee or chicory, sugar, beans, peas, rice, and hominy, which he described as "tolerable." Being an officer, Wentworth's rations at Johnson's Island would have been far better than what the Confederate rank and file received at other Northern prisons. Indeed, at Fort Delaware, before the captured officers were sorted out from the enlisted men and sent to other locations, Wentworth reported only receiving two meals a day, each consisting of a slice of "dingy light bread" and a slice of "beef boiled in dirty water." Even with better food, Wentworth and other Florida officers at Johnson's Island still faced serious hardships. The Floridians were poorly prepared for the cold Ohio winter, which brought subzero temperatures and numerous cases of frostbite. Diseases like smallpox, dysentery, and typhoid fever were prevalent, although not as much as at other Northern prisons.[8]

On the Home Front

Back in Taylor County, things were busy as local families tended their farms and did what they could to support the Confederate war effort. Saltmaking was one of the county's most critical contributions. Floridians normally imported most of their salt, but once the Union blockaded the Gulf and Atlantic coasts, shipping slowed to a trickle. This was a serious blow to the Southern states because it severely restricted their ability to export cotton to make money, and it prevented critical shipments of weapons and supplies from reaching Southern ports. Salt was an especially important commodity at this time, because without refrigeration it was urgently needed to preserve and flavor the meat used by the Confederate army. Florida's Big Bend region was the perfect place for boiling seawater to make salt. The area's meandering tidal creeks were filled with especially salty, slow-moving seawater, with lots of marshy land and small clumps of trees to shelter the saltmakers from the guns of the Union block-

ade ships. It also helped that the Gulf was so shallow along this part of the coast; the ships could rarely get close enough to attack the saltmakers by sea with any accuracy.[9]

The salt shortage in Florida became serious only a few months after the war began, and only got worse as the weeks went by. The *Florida Sentinel* noted in an editorial that salt was just as necessary for the war effort as corn and gunpowder and urged any Floridian who

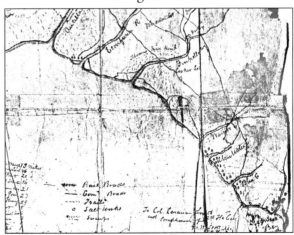

Excerpt from a map drawn by George Washington Scott showing the locations of salt works (represented by teardrop shapes) along the Taylor County coast.

(Map courtesy of the State Archives of Florida)

could make salt to do so. A number of the saltmakers who operated along the Taylor County coast were from other places, but historian W.T. Cash recalled that many were locals, such as Gabriel Harden, Jackson Sapp, John Taylor, Randall B. Williams, William H. Sever, James W. Faulkner, John Towles, Wyche Fulford, William and Rufus Stanaland, Thomas Young, Wiley W. Whiddon, John R. Morse, and John G. Pettus. Most of these men purchased land close to the coast so they could expand their businesses.[10]

The saltmakers used pumps to draw the water up from tide holes or creeks to large kettles with furnaces underneath. They usually took the water at high tide when its salinity was highest. The kettles ranged in size from less than a hundred gallons to almost a thousand gallons, and were often made from sugar kettles or parts of boilers and smokestacks from steamboats. Workers boiled the water in several stages, removing impurities and getting the concentration of salt as high as possible. After adding a bit of lime to the solution and letting everything settle, salt crystals would form, and they could then be extracted, packed into baskets, and dried.[11]

Evidence of the saltmaking industry still survives along the Taylor County coastline. Many of the small islands of trees and high ground in the marsh contain evidence of "salt works," such as piles of limerock that were used as foundations for the furnaces. The salt kettles, which were generally made of iron, have long since been taken, destroyed, or have rusted away, but orange patches of mud indicate where pieces of the metal once were. At least one wooden cistern has been located near Adams Beach, and one of the larger salt works is located within a stone's throw of the Jug Island Road.

Cattle raising was another key Taylor County contribution to the war effort. Beef and pork were staples in the Confederate diet, and Florida's supply of both meats became critical as the herds in other parts of the rebel nation were depleted or cut off by the fighting. The beef situation became especially dire after the Union Army captured Vicksburg, Mississippi in 1863. With the Union in control of the entire Mississippi River, beef from west of the river could not be transported to the Confederate armies fighting farther east. Florida beef became essential to sustaining the Confederate war effort.[12]

Getting the beef to the front lines was a serious challenge. Florida had very few rail lines at this time, and none extended far enough south to help transport beeves raised in Central and South Florida. Shipping the cows or their meat by sea was difficult due to the blockade. The best option was to drive the cattle northward to the rail connections at Baldwin, or into Georgia after those rail lines were destroyed. This system obviously had its natural draw-backs—cattle frequently got lost or were attacked by predators, and they lost a significant amount of weight over the long trek north. Some of the danger was man-made. By 1864 when Florida beef became most critical, a number of deserters and other men collaborating with the Union military were operating in the state, and they often attacked the cattle drives as they worked their way northward.[13]

To deal with these challenges, Confederate authorities established the First Florida Special Cavalry, better known as the "Cow Cavalry," led by Colonel Charles I. Munnerlyn. Munnerlyn's men were a combination of Confederate commissary agents, cattle ranchers, and other locals. Their job was to round up cattle and hogs in Florida and prepare them for transporting up north. They also guarded the herds from the roving bands of deserters and Union sympathizers. Captain James W. Faulkner of Taylor County commanded Company A of this battalion, which operated mainly in Taylor and Lafayette counties. The company was headquartered at Camp Carlton on the Fenholloway River and had at least twenty men. A number of these cavalrymen reported spending much of their time serving the unit while living at home. Thomas L. Gunter, for example, wrote in his pension application that Captain Faulkner tasked him with gathering, jerking, and shipping beef. William H. Ezell wrote that his job was to make barrels for the company. Edward Benjamin Sanders, a member of the company from Madison County, reported having a pack of dogs trained to hunt down deserters, which he used everywhere from the Taylor County coast to Jasper. Faulkner's unit was not always successful in chasing away their foes; Sanders reported in his pension application that on at least one occasion a group of the deserters kicked Faulkner's company out of Pumpkin Swamp. Sanders and a squad of cavalrymen turned the tables and chased them toward the Gulf, but their pursuit came to an end when they reached Deadman's Bay and were greeted by a Union gunboat.[14]

Indeed, those Union gunboats made many visits to the Taylor County coastline, in part because the creeks and rivers emptying into the Gulf in this area were frequently used as bases for blockade runners. The Union blockade was tight but not perfect, and small, fast-moving ships could sometimes sail quickly enough to escape the blockaders and deliver a few bales of cotton or a few head of cattle to traders in Cuba and other Caribbean islands. They typically brought back much-needed supplies and cash on the return trip.

Deadman's Bay was an especially busy port for blockade runners, as both official and personal records reveal. Sylvanus M. Hankins, a Lafayette County

Illustration from Harper's Weekly showing a U.S. vessel chasing a Confederate blockade runner.

(Image courtesy of the State Archives of Florida)

native in the 11th Florida Infantry, wrote extensively about his experiences picketing the coastline near the mouth of the Steinhatchee River. In the winter of 1864, Hankins's company was ordered to guard a blockade runner that was scheduled to come into the bay with supplies and then leave with a load of cotton bound for Nassau. The ship made it into port safely, but it ran aground on the sand bar when it tried to exit the bay. A detachment of sailors from a nearby Union blockade ship headed for the grounded vessel, but the captain and crew set fire to it and escaped to the shore. According to Hankins, the Union blockaders reached the burning boat just in time for it to explode. There were several similar episodes up and down the Taylor County coastline throughout the war. On June 5, 1862, Union blockaders surprised the Confederate steamer *Havana* while it was in port at Deadman's Bay offloading a large cargo of supplies. The crew set fire to the ship and escaped, leaving ten tons of lead aboard that eventually melted and sank with the vessel.[15]

Some blockade runners were unable or unwilling to scuttle their ships to avoid capture. In April 1863, the commander of the U.S.S. *Huntsville* reported capturing the Confederate sloop *Minnie,* which had been headed from the Aucilla River to Cuba with 13 bales of cotton aboard. In January 1865, the U.S. schooner *Fox* captured a British vessel called the *Fannie McRae* near the mouth of Spring Warrior Creek. The captain admitted he had been heading for the mouth of the Aucilla with a cargo from Cuba. In cases like this, the Union blockade ship would usually put a small crew aboard the captured Confederate vessel and sail it to Key West for disposal by a "prize court."[16]

Union blockaders received most of their supplies by sea, but occasionally they sent small detachments ashore to get fresh water, firewood for their boilers, and other necessities. This could be dangerous, as one such mission by the U.S. bark *Kingfisher* proved. On June 2, 1862, two cutters from the *Kingfisher* went up the Aucilla River to collect fresh water, guided as far as the mouth by a local pilot named Charles Welles. When the boats did not return, Welles went upriver to the landing point, where he saw casks floating in the water and one of the cutters capsized. He hurried back to the *Kingfisher* to report this discovery, whereupon the commander, Joseph Couthouy, sent the ship's mate back up the Aucilla to secure as much of the lost equipment as possible and find out what happened to the watering party. The mate confirmed that a skirmish had taken place, which prompted Couthouy to send him under a flag of truce with a message for the Confederate officer at the St. Marks lighthouse, Lieutenant D.W. Gwynn. Couthouy asked for permission to send a party under a flag of truce up the Aucilla to bury the remains of the Union soldiers killed in the skir-mish, and to give money and clothing to the sailors who were captured. Gwynn granted both of Couthouy's requests. A party went out from the *Kingfisher* the next day and located the remains of two sailors, Antoine Faulkner and Antonio Euphrates, which they buried. According to the sailor in charge of the burial party, the graves were located about two and a half miles up the Aucilla on the west bank, fifty yards back from the water's edge, and marked with a painted head-board. So far as anyone knows, the bones of these Union sailors are still buried there today.[17]

Portrait of Joseph Couthouy, commander of the U.S. bark Kingfisher.

(Photo courtesy of the University of Illinois)

A War Within a War

Taylor County citizens contributed to the Confederate war effort in a variety of ways, but pro-Confederate sentiment was not uniform among local families, nor was it constant throughout the war. In fact, by 1864 the region had become a serious trouble spot for Confederate military officials, who received numerous reports of deserters hiding out in the coastal swamps. They were joined by individuals who had never deserted, but rather had either been discharged on account of disability or were trying to avoid military service altogether. They were also not entirely made up of locals; many people came to Taylor County from other parts of the Confederacy to avoid military service, sometimes bringing their families along. They often made contact with the Union blockaders just offshore, swapping information and cooperation in return for supplies and ammunition. Despite the presence of Faulkner's cow cavalry and other home guard units, these refugees occasionally left their hideouts to ambush Confederate cattle drives and capture supplies and equipment from local farms and storehouses. By the end of 1864, at least 70 men from Taylor County had joined the Second Florida Union Cavalry, headquartered at Key West, the sworn enemies of many of their friends, neighbors, and even family members.[18]

The Taylor Countians who threw their lot in with the Union were not necessarily Unionists, at least not in an ideological sense. Judging by election returns, most of them probably voted for secessionist Democrats in 1860, believing the Southern states would be better off as a separate nation. Many of them also served in Confederate units at the beginning of the war. As the conflict dragged on, however, conditions became dismal at home for many Taylor County families, and the Confederate government in Richmond persisted in adopting policies that only made the situation worse. As a result, a number of Taylor County men felt as though they had to choose between loyalty to the Confederacy and the livelihood of their own kin.

Conscription was one of the major causes of disaffection. In April 1862, the Confederate government established a draft, requiring all able-bodied men aged 18 to 35 to register for military service. In September, the age range increased to include men aged 18 to 45. Many Taylor Countians had already volunteered for military service, believing as most of the South did that the war would be short and a single tour of duty would be enough to get the job done. The North ended up being a more formidable foe than expected, however, and many Floridians were held in service longer than they or their families had prepared for. For families on large plantations with money, large fields, and slave labor, this was not quite as serious a problem. In Taylor County, however, families tended to be younger, smaller, and poorer, and slave labor was almost nonexistent. This placed an enormous burden on those left on the home front—old men, young children, and women—and prompted many men to avoid being conscripted at all costs. Some moved their families closer to the coast, away from the main roads used by military officials. Others tried to escape entirely. In July 1863, the U.S.S. *Fort Henry* captured a small boat near Cedar Key piloted by Joseph H. and William English, who said they were trying to get to a Union blockading vessel to escape conscription. The following month, eight elected Taylor County officials wrote to Governor John Milton, asking that the families in their juris-diction be exempted from conscription. They argued that there were only about 15 to 20 men left who were subject to Confederate service anyway, and that nearly 100 soldiers' families were already nearly destitute for want of food and basic necessities. "If this petition is not granted," they warned, "in our humble opinion the women and children of our county are bound to come to suffering if not starvation."[19]

On top of the conscription issue, Taylor Countians who were already in the Confederate service sometimes received very callous responses to their requests to take short leaves of absence to help their families, even when they were stationed very close to home. Tul-

Portrait of John Milton, governor of Florida for most of the Civil War.

(Image courtesy of the State Archives of Florida)

lius Kinsey, for example, received a letter sometime in 1864 informing him that his mother was very near death at her home in Jefferson County. Kinsey's company was camping only a few miles away in Madison County, but the captain would not grant him a pass. Kinsey chose to leave on his own account to see his dying mother, but returned to his unit in time to see action at the Battle of Natural Bridge. Similarly, William Wilson Strickland learned just before Christmas 1862 that his wife—Mary Ann Johnson Strickland—was danger-ously ill, possibly from complications associated with the birth of a son. Strick-land's company was located only about twenty miles from his home, but his captain refused to grant him permission to see her. Strickland visited his wife anyway without leave, and upon his return was court-martialed and sentenced to grub a stump while wearing a placard with the word "coward" printed on it. Strickland deserted once again rather than subject himself to this degrading punishment, and he went on to become the leader of one of the largest bands of deserters in the region.[20]

The Confederate government in Richmond continued to enact policies that ultimately worked against poorer families in North Florida. In 1863, the Confederate Congress passed a series of acts permitting government agents to collect a 10% tax in kind of all agricultural products, including the corn and livestock that many families depended on for survival. Some called it the "Confederate tithe." To make matters worse, government agents sometimes confiscated property from Florida families without compensation when they objected to the low government price they were offered. Some people who went about collecting property were not even government agents, and the scrip they offered their victims was worthless. Another sore spot was the Richmond government's decision to cancel an exemption from conscription for saltmakers. A number of Taylor County salt manufacturers had found their industry to be an elegant solution to the question of military service, because they could support the Confederate war effort while remaining close to home. When their exemptions were lifted, however, some of them turned to the Union rather than submit to the Confederate military officers. William S. Stanaland and Wyche W. Fulford were among the Taylor County saltmakers who made this choice.[21]

By the fall of 1863, declining morale and desertion were two of the Richmond government's most pressing domestic concerns. Florida's political and military leaders were feeling much the same way. Judge John C. McGehee of Madison County sent a letter to General Joseph Finegan in October on behalf of a group of local citizens, noting the growing number of refugees in Taylor County and asking that a force be sent to bring them to heel. Finegan already had a plan in mind to do just that, hopefully without force. Having heard from his superiors that the Richmond government would offer a general amnesty to all deserters and draft dodgers with a few conditions, the general sent Confederate Marshal E.E. Blackburn and Captain P.B. Bird to Taylor County to speak with the leaders of the refugees and convince them to return to the Confederate military. Blackburn and Bird met the following day with James Moody, brother-in-law to the Coker family, which ran one of the largest bands of refugees along the coast. Moody agreed to arrange a meeting between the Confederate representatives and the refugees at Hampton Springs on October 1, 1863, but when the appointed time came the refugees did not show. Blackburn reported that he believed the refugees had no intention of coming back to the Confederate military and ought to be rounded up instead. As for the families, Blackburn recommended they be removed from Florida altogether in order to compel the refugees to obey.[22]

When Finegan reported these findings to Thomas Jordan, chief of staff for General P.G.T. Beauregard, Jordan responded that Beauregard had authorized Finegan to employ as much force as was necessary to "capture, or slay and destroy, the deserters … banded together in Taylor County." Finegan had his hands full at the moment, however, as Union forces had occupied Jacksonville and were preparing to march westward toward Tallahassee. When the military finally got around to addressing the Taylor County refugee issue in March 1864, General Finegan had been replaced, and Brigadier General William M. Gardner had decided to try his hand at offering amnesty. On March 18, 1864, he circulated a proclamation inviting all refugees in Taylor and Lafayette counties to return to the Confederate military with a full pardon. Those who did not, Gardner warned, would be "shot without mercy," their livestock driven away or shot, and their families sent to the interior of the country.[23]

General Gardner included in his proclamation that military operations against the refugees would continue while the amnesty offer was in effect, and he kept his word in a most destructive way. Confederate scouting expeditions along the Econfina River and Rocky Creek had revealed several refugee camps, which prompted Gardner to order Lt. Colonel Henry D. Capers and Major

Portrait of Henry D. Capers, from William Mickle's Well Known Confederate Veterans and Their War Records (1907).

Charles Camfield to march their Georgia troops into Taylor County to make a thorough search of the coastal swamps. Capers ordered Camfield's men to take the eastern bank of the Econfina River, while his own troops took the western side. Together, the Georgia troops moved downriver, reaching the camp of William W. Strickland's refugee band at Snyder's [Snipes'] Island on March 24. The camp was deserted, although Capers reported finding a muster roll belonging to Strickland's group, which called itself the "Independent Union Rangers" of Taylor County. Believing that, much like the Seminoles had done, the refugees would be difficult to defeat by traditional means, Capers ordered the destruction of every house along the Econfina and Fenholloway rivers belonging to the refugees.

Each family was given a few moments to gather their belongings before being sent to a camp outside Tallahassee, their homes reduced to ashes behind them.[24]

Before leaving the county, Capers left a letter for Strickland with his father-in-law, William Johnson, asking what it would take for Strickland to bring his men in and rejoin the Confederate military. Strickland sent back a response saying he could no longer control his men since they had seen their homes destroyed, and that he was no longer accountable for their actions. As for himself, Strickland offered to help his father-in-law pen and drive cattle for the Confederate military, and to convince the members of his band to do the same. If these conditions were not met, however, he would be like a flea. "When you put your thumb on me and then raise it up," Strickland warned, "I will be gone." Confederate military authorities seriously considered Strickland's terms, with Capers' endorsement, but they ultimately decided it would set a dangerous precedent to allow conscripts to negotiate their role within the military. The terms of General Gardner's proclamation would have to do. The deadline for returning to the Confederate fold came and went, however, and none of Strickland's men took the offer. They instead looked to the Union blockaders for their salvation.[25]

Meanwhile, Capers and Camfield's cruel and destructive raid had caused a humanitarian crisis for the Confederate military. Following their capture, the families living along the Econfina and Fenholloway rivers were taken to Camp Smith, located about six miles south of Tallahassee near the Bel Air community. Local planters built nine double-penned log cabins with stick-and-dirt chimneys and wooden shutters for the refugee families. Despite this bit of hospitality, Governor John Milton complained bitterly to Confederate military leaders about the Capers raid, noting that some of the burned homes had belonged to loyal Confederate citizens, and that now there were wives and children of Confederate servicemen being held at Camp Smith. The raid, he insisted, had only made the refugees angrier and more determined to get revenge, spring their families from prison, and collaborate with the Union. He recommended that the Confederate government immediately free the refugee families and rebuild their homes where the old ones had been burned. "I cannot approve of a warfare upon women and children," he wrote.[26]

As for the refugee women confined at Camp Smith, they merely wanted out. A dozen of the wives wrote to Milton in July 1864, asking for permission to return to their husbands, fathers, and brothers behind Union lines. "However much they may be to blame in having left the Confederate States," they explained, "we are their wives and daughters [and] are eternally united with them." Milton had initially opposed letting the refugee families rejoin their menfolk, but after reading this petition he relented, and arranged for the women and children to be transported to one of the Union blockade vessels off the coast near St. Marks.[27]

By this time many of the deserters and other refugees who had been hiding out in the Taylor County swamps were now full-fledged Union soldiers, inducted into the newly formed Second Florida Union Cavalry. Taylor County refugees had been trading information and supplies with the Union blockade ships since at least early 1863. In February 1864, they joined forces with sailors from nearby blockade ships to destroy over 400 kettles, 170 furnaces, 150 pumps, and nearly 300 buildings belonging to salt works between the mouth

of the Steinhatchee River and Adams Beach. David Harmony, commander of the U.S.S. *Tahoma,* gave the refugees about a thousand head of cattle for their trouble.[28]

Convinced that the coastal refugees could be very useful, David Harmony organized them into two unofficial companies. He doubted men like Strickland would join the regular U.S. Army since their disagreement with the Confederate

USS Tahoma, one of the blockade vessels that patrolled the Gulf of Mexico off the Taylor County coast during the war.

(Image courtesy of the United States Naval History and Heritage Command)

military revolved mainly around their objections to being taken from their homes and families. Brigadier Daniel P. Woodbury, commander of the Union army's district of Key West and the Tortugas, was eager to try, however. In March 1864, he headed for the Taylor County coast to meet with the three largest bands of refugees—Strickland's Independent Union Rangers, along with the groups led by James Coker and William White. The Union army officials' timing could not have been better. Shortly after they began their talks with the refugees, the Capers-Camfield expedition destroyed the Taylor Countians' homes and removed their families, taking away the only reasons they had avoided a deeper relationship with the Union. Woodbury recognized his advantage and declared he could not continue to support the refugees as irregulars; they needed to join the United States Army if they wanted the Army's help. And join they did. By early April, 77 men from Taylor County had enlisted in the Second Florida Union Cavalry, with more on the way from William White's band near the Steinhatchee River. The unit eventually boasted more than 700 soldiers, mostly refugees from the Florida coast.[29]

The Second Florida Union Cavalry set up its headquarters at Cedar Key, which the Union had occupied since early 1864. Many of the refugees' families camped on Seahorse Key, where the Union military provided a few supplies to help them since most had left their possessions behind. The white refugee soldiers camped on Depot Key, while a regiment of U.S. Colored Troops camped on Way Key. Conditions were crowded and tough, supplies were short, and mortality was high. One refugee recruit from the Peace River region, William McCullough, reported that a whole shipment of flour from Key West had to be kept outside because it was so full of worms and weevils. McCullough noted in August 1864 that people were dying at a rate of four of five a day from disease and starvation. Wyche Fulford, John O. Woods, Reuben Jenkins, Jacob Madison Bishop, Augustus and David Easters, Henry Poppell, and James Madison Strickland were among the Taylor County refugees who succumbed to illness and died while stationed at Cedar Key. The Union post at Cedar Key had several contract physicians, including Dr. Samuel A. Wilcox of Taylor County. Wilcox's commission was withdrawn, however, after the unit commander, Major Edmund Cottle Weeks, accused him of medical malpractice causing the death of a sentry. Weeks had shot the sentry one night while drunk, but he mounted a fierce defense at his court martial in Key West with the help of two private attorneys from Boston. They convinced the court that the sentry's wound had been minor, and that it was Wilcox's incompetence that ended the man's life.[30]

Despite these hardships, the Second Florida Union Cavalry carried out a number of successful raids against Confederate cattle operations in the region, and gathered more disaffected Floridians into their ranks. The unit's most dramatic military action came in March 1865, when almost all the men participated in the battle of Natural Bridge. This was also one of the most tragic actions of the war, as Taylor County natives ended up on both sides of this fight, and were literally shooting at each other.

The object of the Union attack at Natural Bridge was to close the port of St. Marks to blockade running and attempt to capture Tallahassee. Sixteen ships and a thousand troops assembled near the mouth of the St. Marks River, and three advance parties disembarked to destroy bridges that would be critical to the Confederate defense. One of those parties was sent to Sandy Ford on the Aucilla River to obstruct the railroad and stop Confederate reinforcements at Madison from reaching Tallahassee. Both sergeants in charge of the mission, William S. Stanaland and Charles Kidd Martin, were from Taylor County, as were at least four of the privates, including William W. Strickland, John William Poppell, John R. Brannan, and William P. Johnson. Two others, Thomas W. Crosby and Eli M. Bishop, were from neighboring Jefferson County. The men reached the trestle and set it on fire, but it did not burn quickly enough to stop the train carrying troops from Madison. According to Sylvanus M. Hankins of Lafayette County, who was on the train, the engineer saw the smoke coming from the trestle, but was unable to stop in time. Instead, he gunned his engine and shot across the burning bridge, only moments before parts of it fell into the Aucilla. The train continued to Tallahassee to deliver reinforcements to the defenders at Natural Bridge, and the Union men were forced to flee when a Confederate patrol chased them into the nearby woods.[31]

Once the troop train reached Tallahassee, a detachment including Green C. Denmark of Taylor County was sent to round up Stanaland, Martin, and their troops with dogs. Denmark wrote in his pension application that when he and his comrades caught up with the bridge burners, they shot Martin and Johnson and took Strickland and Brannan back to Tallahassee to face trial. Both men were court-martialed and executed on the morning of March 18, 1865. The remaining members of the Union party were captured and held as prisoners of war.[32]

The Legacy of the Civil War in Taylor County

The Battle of Natural Bridge was a decisive victory for the Florida Confederates, who managed to hold the line at Newport and defend Tallahassee despite the bulk of their force consisting of young military school cadets and old men. The win did nothing, however, to stop the tide that was turning against the Confederacy elsewhere in the South. On April 9, 1865, General Robert E. Lee surrendered his army at Appomattox Courthouse in Virginia, and by May 20 the United States flag was flying once again over Tallahassee.

For Taylor County citizens, whether allied to the Confederacy or the Union, the war could not end soon enough. The Capers-Camfield raid had destroyed dozens of homes. Refugee families languished in their hastily set up accommodations at Cedar Key. Hundreds of acres of normally active farmland in the county lay fallow for want of men to plant and tend crops. According to W.T. Cash, even the Strickland execution weighed heavily on the minds of Taylor Countians who had remained faithful to the Confederacy. He was a deserter, certainly, but many locals knew that he had left the military out of concern for his family. Moreover, his Johnson relations had provided cattle and other supplies to needy families in the area, something Strickland had been willing to help with if the Confederate military had only let him. Given these considerations, Cash wrote that he believed the execution—however lawful it might have been—lost Confederate authorities more support among Taylor Countians than it gained them.[33]

The end of the war brought significant changes, especially in terms of the population. Dozens of Taylor County men had perished on distant battlefields, while many refugee civilians and soldiers had died while enduring the hardships of life at Cedar Key. In his 1870 report to state education authorities, James Hamilton Wentworth wrote that out of 230 students in the county, 83 had no father, and ten were orphans. Indeed, the 1870 federal census reveals that a number of households combined to pool resources and manpower to make a living. Family ties and friendships became more critical than ever.[34]

The county gained many new residents as well. Many of the men and women who had come to Taylor County to make salt or escape conscription ended up staying. Several former members of Strickland's Independent Union Rangers, including John Henry Ayers and Jackson Sapp, plus former members of the Second Florida Union Cavalry like John Perry Taylor, chose to make Taylor County their home after the war. In at least one case, a decision to remain in the area grew out of newfound love. Elizabeth Grooms, for example, came to Taylor County with her husband Francis from Mitchell County, Georgia in 1863. Francis joined Strickland's Independent Union Rangers, and Elizabeth ended up being sent to Camp Smith with her children after the Capers-Camfield raid. After the refugee families' release, Elizabeth learned that Francis was serving at Cedar Key and began making her way there. While passing through Taylor County, she learned that Francis had died of dysentery. With seven children in tow, Elizabeth decided to camp out while deciding what to do next. She discovered the vacant farm of Samuel Blue, who was also serving at Cedar Key. His wife had recently died, and his children were all staying with relatives. At some point in 1865, Samuel Blue returned home to find Elizabeth Grooms and her children occupying his house. At first, Samuel and Elizabeth reached an arrangement whereby Elizabeth would help care for Samuel's children in exchange for room and board for her family. Within a year, however, the two had married, and they ended up having a child of their own, Melinda Blue.[35]

As Taylor County moved into the Reconstruction era, divisions between those citizens who had remained loyal to the Confederacy and those who had chosen to support the Union healed quickly in some cases, others not so much, especially once the Democrats regained political control over the state and local governments in the 1870s. Nancy Poppell, for example, whose father, Hendry D. Poppell, had fought for the Union, feared that some of her fellow Taylor Countians might have been responsible for her being dropped from the federal pension rolls. "If I have any secret enemies that is writing anything against me, please inform me," she wrote officials in Washington. "There are many people that are against the Union pensioners here and elsewhere." Colen Blue, who wrote to Washington several times on Nancy's behalf, also raised this issue. "There is so much prejudice here," he said. "The county has rejected [Nancy] on the pauper list here because her father fought for the Union."[36]

Gravestone for Colen Blue, a private in Company D of the Second Florida Union Cavalry. Colen Blue is buried in Pisgah Cemetery northwest of Perry.

(Photo by the author)

In the immediate aftermath of the war, however, most Taylor Countians seemed ready to put the fighting behind them and try to rebuild the peaceful life they had known in earlier years. As W.T. Cash noted years later, the permanent results of the war were "more hatred for [African Americans], a distaste for political control by the wealthy, a desire to be left severely alone, a greater detestation than ever of outside authority, and a permanent appetite for the corn bread and collards to which the Civil War had accustomed them."[37]

Taylor County's third courthouse, completed in 1892.

(Photo courtesy of the State Archives of Florida)

CHAPTER 4:

Frontier Cattle Country

In March 1945, a freelancing author named Jack Murray published a story called "Florida's Flaming Six Guns" in the pulp fiction magazine *Adventure*. The tale begins with a little frontier flirtation between partygoers from two rival cattle families, and ends a few pages later in an explosion of angry gunfire and lawless bloodshed. One commentator later remarked that the story made the showdown at the OK Corral in Tombstone look like a pillow fight.[1]

The setting for this scandalous legend was Taylor County, Florida. Murray's sensational account featured two prominent local clans—the Towles and the Brannen families—and leaned heavily on details he allegedly learned from a Taylor County citizen while both men were inmates at the Florida State Prison in Raiford. Not surprisingly, the story caused an uproar when it appeared in 1945. Local citizens destroyed issues of *Adventure* magazine and demanded it be removed from the public library. Even today, the story is still controversial, and people who hold onto copies of it do so quietly.[2]

"Florida's Flaming Six Guns" is rife with omissions, exaggerations, and outright falsehoods, but there is still a little truth to the story. Taylor County really was the scene of a considerable amount of violence in the late 19th century, and some of it really did stem from disagreements between major cattle ranching families and their allies. Racial tensions also contributed to the violence,

Cover of the March 1945 edition of Adventure, which contained Jack Murray's "Flaming Six Guns of Florida" tale based on events in Taylor County.

especially during Reconstruction as both black and white Floridians adjusted to new realities brought on by the results of the Civil War. Whatever the cause, by the 1890s the county had earned a reputation for being a rough neighborhood, mired in what state official David Lang called a "deplorable condition of society."[3]

But there was also progress. Between the Civil War and the turn of the twentieth century, the county's population nearly tripled. New roads and bridges criss-crossed the territory, clearing the way for new communities to take shape. More than two dozen post offices opened during this era. Stephensville, forerunner of the modern town of Steinhatchee, became a commercial outpost for the first time. A state-mandated system of public education emerged, with small log cabin schoolhouses appearing across the county. And, at the courthouse, land changed hands at an increasingly rapid rate as investors began dreaming of the money they could make by exploiting the area's virgin pine forests, if only they could get a railroad into operation.[4]

Reconstruction

When the Civil War ended, Taylor County was in a shambles. Although it was never the scene of a battle like Olustee or Natural Bridge, the area had seen plenty of action. Dozens of homes still lay in ashes after having been torched during the Capers-Camfield raid. The fledgling town of Perry lay unfinished and relatively uninhabited, and may have also been damaged during the war. The county commission even ordered a referendum in 1869 to determine whether Perry would remain the county seat. Saltmakers along the coast had seen their property destroyed and their cattle either confiscated by the Union or driven off. Many of the cows belonging to citizens of the interior had been taken by Confederate commissary agents for military use.[5]

The county government still existed at the end of the war, but the officers' authority was unclear at first. The state government in Tallahassee was in total limbo. Abraham K. Allison, who replaced John Milton as Florida's governor after the latter's death in April 1865, attempted to convene the state legislature and negotiate a settlement with President Andrew Johnson. Union military authorities halted Allison's plans, declared martial law, and refused to recognize the authority of any state officials. The occupiers encouraged local officers, however, such as judges, justices of the peace, and clerks of court to continue functioning as usual.[6]

How much actual functioning they did is hard to say. State records show that Robert Henderson, judge of probate since the establishment of the county government in 1857, stayed at his post after the war, as did the sheriff, Edward Jordan. Wiley W. Whiddon represented Taylor County at Florida's 1865 constitutional convention and signed the finished product. The county commission may have also met during this time, but evidence of their meetings does not appear in the records until 1868.[7]

Florida's new state constitution did not last long. The former Confederate states infuriated the Republicans in Congress by passing a series of "black codes" that essentially recreated the old slave codes in all but the name, and also by refusing to ratify the 14th amendment, which was designed to afford some degree of federal protection for the rights of the recently freed slaves. With President Andrew Johnson actively encouraging the Southern states to take this approach, Congress wrested control of the reconstruction process away from him by passing a sweeping series of new laws over his veto. The so-called Reconstruction Acts reinstated martial law in the South and declared most of the new state governments invalid. The act also directed Union military authorities to register all eligible citizens—including African Americans—to vote, and for

Portrait of Dr. Samuel A. Wilcox, one of the three men who registered Taylor County voters—including African Americans— in 1867.

(Image courtesy of the Taylor County Historical Society)

the states to hold a new round of constitutional conventions. Once a state had established a new constitution that properly acknowledged the end of slavery and the right of African American men to vote, Congress would approve the document and readmit the state to the Union.[8]

Union military authorities divided Florida into nineteen registration districts and selected three-person boards to travel around each district and register all eligible citizens to vote, including black men over 21 and even former Confederate soldiers. The only people specifically excluded from registering were former federal or state officials who, after taking an oath of allegiance to the United States, had participated directly in the war on the Confederate side.[9]

Taylor County's registration board consisted of Dr. Samuel A. Wilcox, John A.J. Cruce, and Jessee Colson, all three men being relatively disconnected from the late rebellion. Wilcox, as Chapter 3 explains, had contracted with the U.S. Army to serve as a surgeon for the Second Florida Union

Cavalry. Cruce, who was about 46 years old when the war began, does not appear to have served in the Union military, but two of his sons did. Colson was an African American man born in Georgia. It is unclear whether he was enslaved in Taylor County or the surrounding area before the war, but his family remained in Taylor County for several generations afterward.[10]

The three registrars registered a total of 270 men in the county between August 1867 and April 1868. Only 33 of these voters were listed as non-white. The white voters included both Union and Confederate veterans, plus others who served in neither army. A handful of citizens who had held public office before or during the war were questioned about their qualifications, but the records show that almost all were eventually allowed to register.[11]

The newly registered voters went to the polls in November 1867 to decide whether to hold a state constitutional convention, and to determine who their delegates would be. Taylor and Lafayette counties were allotted one delegate between them. The voters chose Dr. John Newton Krimminger, a North Carolina native who had been drafted into the Confederate army before deserting and joining the First Florida Union Cavalry. After the war, Krimminger and his wife Rebecca moved to New Troy in Lafayette County. Dr. Krimminger and his fellow delegates assembled at Tallahassee in January 1868, where they drew up a new state constitution, which Congress accepted, and the voters ratified in May.[12]

While the politicians were sorting out Florida's political institutions, federal agents sought to help the newly freed African American slaves adjust to their new situation. The War Department's Bureau of Refugees, Freedmen and Abandoned Lands—more commonly called the Freedmen's Bureau—took the lead. Union military officials and civilian employees set up headquarters in Florida's major towns to help negotiate contracts between former slaves and their former masters to get the freedmen back to work as quickly as possible. The bureau also issued rations, set up schools, transported freedmen to areas in need of labor, and helped them take advantage of new homestead provisions designed to help them get started as private citizens.[13]

Taylor County was mostly uninvolved in this phase of Reconstruction. As of 1870, there were only about 75 African Americans in the county, mostly in the northern part where the largest farms were located. Lieutenant J.E. Quentin, Freedmen's Bureau agent in charge of Madison, Taylor, and Lafayette counties, wrote in his May 1866 report that there were relatively few freedmen in Taylor County, and that resistance to the Union occupation was lessened by the presence of so many whites who had been refugees from the Confederacy during the war. With the situation fairly quiet, Quentin let local justices of the peace handle issues involving the freedmen.[14]

There was one interesting exception. The Freedmen's Bureau hired "locating agents" to find plots of public land all around the state that were unoccupied and available to give to the freedmen as homesteads. One of these agents, A.A. Knight, turned in a report in December 1867 describing land he had found in Taylor County for this purpose. All the plots were located in the western part of the county in the vicinity of Powell Hammock. Knight's report lists 21 individuals who had applied for a homestead, mostly African Americans from Jefferson and Madison counties. None of these people ever actually received title to the parcels Knight located. This was likely due in part to the agent's own dismal appraisal of the land. It had recently flooded, and Knight wrote that the whole area was "covered with palmetto and almost impenetrable." Most of the freedmen on Knight's list seem to have chosen to remain in Madison and Jefferson counties as sharecroppers rather than start over in such tough conditions.[15]

The social and political upheaval of Reconstruction did not go without a response. White Floridians grudgingly acknowledged the Union victory and cooperated with the occupying military authorities to an extent, but they resisted efforts to change the existing social structure of the state. They generally expected African Americans—even as free men and women—to be deferential in their relations with whites, and for them not to have any real control over the institutions of society or government. Samuel A. Wilcox of Taylor County, for example, was appointed to public office by Governor Harrison Reed, a pro-Reconstruction Republican. Dr. Wilcox later wrote that he was unable to honestly support Reed's government because he did not agree with Reed appointing black Floridians to serve in public office. Even though he had served the Union army during the war, he continued to vote like his neighbors who had served the Confederacy, as a Democrat.[16]

The legal system also reflected this attitude. Freedmen's Bureau agents often wrote to their superiors asking for permission to intervene on behalf of African Americans in the county courts. J.E. Quentin wrote in 1866 that "ninety-nine percent goes against the freedmen in the civil courts—there is positively not a particle of justice done them. They base all their verdicts on the statement of the whites, perfectly ignoring those of the freedmen." William Bryson, judge of the Third Judicial Circuit, which included Taylor County, later testified that in many cases perpetrators of crimes against African Americans or their white allies could not even be brought to court in the first place.

The sheriffs simply would not make the arrests. If they did stand for trial, no jury would convict them.[17]

In many cases, resistance to Reconstruction turned violent. Throughout the state, especially in counties where black Floridians made up the majority of voters, conservative Democrats and vigilante groups like the Ku Klux Klan used terror tactics to intimidate African Americans and whites who condoned their participation in the political arena. In Madison County, arsonists burned down the store of merchant Simon Katzenburg in 1868, ostensibly because of his willingness to sell goods to blacks. Two years later, David Montgomery, the county's much-disliked pro-Reconstruction Republican sheriff, was attacked and wounded just before Election Day.[18]

Taylor County, having a relatively small black population for most of Reconstruction, experienced only a small share of the interracial violence that marked this time period, but it was not entirely immune. Secretary of State Jonathan Gibbs testified in 1871 that based on letters received in his office, at

least seven African Americans and white Republican supporters had been murdered in Taylor County since the end of the war. The Ku Klux Klan had been in the area as well, although Gibbs' account is unclear as to whether the members were local or from elsewhere. He said several citizens had visited his office and reported that a band of men had come into Taylor County carrying a flag with three K's on it, alarming the locals and committing acts of violence. Further along in his testimony, Gibbs attributes some of the trouble in Taylor County to conflict between the conservative Democrats and what he called "Union men"—the former refugees from the Confederacy who had taken up with the Union army during the war. Conservative Democrats, Gibbs reported, often swore that no Union man or Republican would live among them. We know, of course, that many former refugees from the Confederacy did in fact continue to

Portrait of Jonathan Clarkson Gibbs, Florida's Secretary of State for much of Governor Harrison Reed's administration. He was the state's first African American member of the Cabinet.

(Image courtesy of the State Archives of Florida)

live in Taylor County and even serve as county and state legislative officials. Gibbs' testimony reveals, however, that not everyone was happy about it.[19]

Perhaps the most notorious local instance of political violence during Reconstruction came in 1871 when Dr. John Newton Krimminger was assassinated at his home in New Troy. Krimminger, a pro-Reconstruction Republican, had been elected state senator for Taylor and Lafayette counties after representing them at the 1868 constitutional convention. The assassin was John C.C. Ponchier, Lafayette County's clerk of court and a conservative Democrat. Ponchier escaped and went into hiding, but was eventually gunned down on July 5, 1873, at Deadman's Bay, where he owned property.[20]

Postwar Growth

The founding families of Taylor County had had very little time to establish basic community institutions before the Civil War broke out. Once the war ended, however, they went back to work carving a civilization out of the swamps and piney woods.

The county commission led the way with infrastructure projects that aided both public and private business. Getting the county seat into shape was a top priority. Interest in moving the courthouse away from Perry lasted only a brief moment in 1869; after that the county commissioners focused on improving the town they had already started building. One of their first priorities seems to have been improving the office space for county officials. In August 1869, the commissioners ordered Sheriff H.H. Wilder to raise the judge's stand two and a half feet higher and install a new window. The next year, the commission looked into the cost of building a separate office for the sheriff and county clerk. That project was initially shelved, but by 1873 the need for space was great enough to warrant building a whole new courthouse. The commissioners specified that it should be thirty feet by thirty feet with two floors. The courtroom was to be on the second floor; the first floor would house offices for the county officers.[21]

The commissioners also took steps to help bring new residents into the town of Perry. Lots had been sold as early as 1859 according to the county deed books, but there was some confusion about who the current owners of each lot were. The county commissioners instructed all town lot owners to confirm to the tax assessor which lots they owned, or else they would be resold. At the same time, the board ordered the town to be re-surveyed so sales could begin once again. They also announced that any citizen could cut down timber in the streets or on the public square. This demonstrates that even though town lots were up for sale, the streets had yet to be cleared. Still, local residents did buy lots. Between 1871 and 1874, the county sold parcels to Donald McAulay, John Timmons, Moses Simmons, Jane Wentworth, George W. Applewhite, Christian Sutton, J.S. Howell, and Thomas J. Edwards.[22]

Improving transportation was another key to building up the new town.

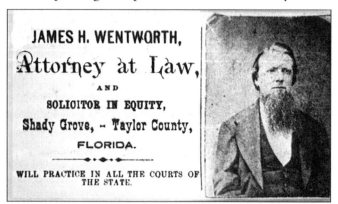

JAMES H. WENTWORTH,

Attorney at Law,

AND

SOLICITOR IN EQUITY,

Shady Grove, -- Taylor County,

FLORIDA.

WILL PRACTICE IN ALL THE COURTS OF THE STATE.

Business card advertising the services of James Hamilton Wentworth, who served as Taylor County's first superintendent of public schools and surveyed the town of Perry in 1870.

(Image courtesy of the State Archives of Florida)

In the late 1860s, local residents were still using the same trails the military had used during the Seminole Wars to get between Perry and the surrounding countryside. County commissioners appointed road markers to lay out new public roads, and road commissioners to monitor them. In January 1869, they tapped Moses Simmons, James H. Wentworth, John P. Carlton, David Gamble, J. Ellis Blanton, and Henry DeCausey as the county's first known road commissioners. Two months later, they appointed James H. Wentworth, William H. Sever, Robert M. Hendry, William Tedder, and J.A.J. Cruce to determine the best place for a new bridge across the Econfina River near Shady Grove. They also declared the old trail connecting Perry with Shady Grove via Z.O. Lovett's mill on Rocky Creek a public road, as well as the road leading from Perry to Rocky Ford on the Aucilla River, via the Fulford Bridge across the Econfina. Only short segments of these two roads are still widely used by the public; U.S. highways 19 and 221 are now the preferred connections between Perry and points to the north.

More roads followed the next year. In August 1869 the county commissioners tasked Joseph L. Hampton, Allen and James Coker, William C. Carlton, and Miles W. Parker with laying out a road connecting Perry with Deadman's Bay. A year later, they ordered Joseph L. Hampton, James Coker, Richard Sadler, and Greenberry Hill to mark out a road between the Carlton Bridge across the Fenholloway River and the mouth of Spring Warrior

Creek. The route between Perry and Deadman's Bay is somewhat uncertain, but the road between the Carlton Bridge and the mouth of Spring Warrior Creek almost certainly followed the general path of the present-day Puckett Road. The commissioners finished out their run of road projects in late 1870 with one final route from the Lafayette County line to the Fenholloway River, and from there up to the Wallace Ford on the Econfina River near present-day Shady Grove, likely skirting the western edge of San Pedro Bay. J.H. Ezell, Robert W. Hendry, John M. Towles, J.H. Sappington, Daniel N. Cox, and Moses Simmons were in charge of staking out the route.

Better roads meant better communication, including through the postal service. Although some were short-lived, more than two dozen post offices were established in Taylor County between the end of the Civil War and the turn of the twentieth century. Rosehead post office was established in 1869, but not as the forerunner to Perry as is often thought—the application puts it several miles away just west of the old Pisgah community. Shady Grove post office was established in 1870, with Thomas Bowden Hendry as postmaster. A

post office opened at Deadman's Bay in 1876, but the name changed to Stephensville shortly thereafter in 1879. Salem post office was first established in 1878, with Micajah A. Cockroft as postmaster. Cabbage Grove got a post office the following year, with Thompson P. Hamilton in charge. Halfway between Cabbage Grove and Perry was the Waylonzo post office, established in 1889 and named for its first postmaster, Waylonzo Johnson. James A. Blanton, who operated a store in the northern part of the county, had hoped to have a similar office named Blantonville that same year, but it appears he settled for the name Iddo instead.[23]

Portrait of Thomas Bowden Hendry and his wife Josephine Williams Hendry. Thomas was the first postmaster of the Shady Grove post office, which was established in 1870.

(Image courtesy of the Taylor County Historical Society)

Commerce picked up after the Civil War as well. As of 1870, the county had at least seven merchants: Thomas J. Edwards, John P. Carlton, Henry Stevens, Henry G. Jordan, George W. Applewhite, and two brothers, William "Barn" and Robert T. Davis. There were also at least three wheelwrights, Charles Ezell,

Moses Simmons, and Macon Lemons, plus two blacksmiths, Joshua Moody and Garrett Sanders. The county also had three physicians at that time—John Simmons, Thomas P. Bradley, and of course Samuel A. Wilcox. Bradley Spring near Steinhatchee was reportedly named for this Dr. Bradley. More businesses were on the way as the end of the 19th century approached. More merchants like John J. Gornto, Samuel Hiram Peacock, and Thomas J. Faulkner added stores in the 1870s and 1880s, and the county got its first newspaper, the *Taylor County Banner*. Jefferson L. Davis was the publisher, and the first issue went out on July 13, 1888. Two more newspapers, the *Perry Herald* and the *Taylor County Advocate*, succeeded the *Banner* in 1891 and continued on for a few years.[24]

The coastal region also began to see some development after the Civil War. The United States Commission on Fish and Fisheries reported that in 1878, fishermen caught and preserved about 202 barrels of mullet while oper-

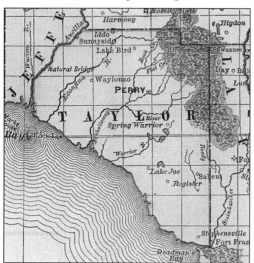

ating from camps near the mouths of the Aucilla, Econfina, and Fenholloway rivers, plus Blue Creek. The Steinhatchee, Spring Warrior, and other waterways were left out of this report, but these were also important known sites of mullet fisheries. According to the report, the fishermen were mostly visitors from the interior who stayed along the coast for just a few months each year—typically October, November, and a part of December. After catching and salting or smoking their mullet, the fishermen would store it in cypress barrels and return to their homes, saving back the majority of the haul for their own table and selling the remainder for cash. Cash might be too strong a word for it; the government's report states the going price of salted mullet was only three cents per fish.[25]

Excerpt from an 1892 map of Florida by Rand McNally & Company showing a number of newly established post offices in Taylor County. Shady Grove is missing because the map was drawn during the brief period between the closure of the original Shady Grove post office and the establishment of the Luther post office, which changed its name back to Shady Grove in 1909.

(Map courtesy of the State Library of Florida)

Spongers were also beginning to appear off the Taylor County coast. Until about the 1840s, most of the world's natural sponges came from the Mediterranean Sea. Around that time, a French merchant began shipping sponges to Europe from the Bahamas, and more sponge beds were quickly discovered off the Florida Keys and up both coasts. Tarpon Springs became a major hub for Gulf spongers in the 1870s, and Deadman's Bay resident John B. Carrin reported seeing their boats as early as 1886.[26]

Carrin headed up one of a handful of families that established Stephensville as a commercial center near the mouth of the Steinhatchee River after the Civil War. James Howard Stephens and his relatives were among the most prominent in this group. Stephens was a Confederate veteran, having left his farm in Hamilton County to serve in the 9th Florida Infantry during the Civil War. When he moved with his family near Deadman's Bay around 1872 he began cutting red cedar and cypress timber, forming it into rafts, and sending it down the coast to Cedar Key for processing, a lucrative business at a time when cash was in short supply.[27]

John Baptist Carrin arrived shortly after Stephens, but with a very different background. Carrin was born in Calais, France in 1834 and immigrated to the United States with his parents in 1850. He spent his later teenage years and early adulthood in Illinois, serving the Union Army in the 130th Illinois Volunteers during the Civil War. After the fighting ended, Carrin moved to Florida, stopping first in Suwannee County but moving to the Deadman's Bay area by 1876. That year, he applied to open a post office at Deadman's Bay, and he served as the postmaster for a number of years. Despite having fought on a different side of the war from his neighbor James H. Stephens, Carrin must have held him in some regard, because it was Carrin's name on the application to change the name of the post office to Stephensville in 1879.[28]

If James H. Stephens was the leading businessman of Stephensville, Carrin was its greatest spokesman. He wrote several letters to the editor of one of Florida's leading periodicals at that time, *The Florida Dispatch*, describing Stephensville as ideal for settlement. He painted a rosy picture of the region, praising the mild winters, the rich hammock lands, and the easy availability of game, fish, and oysters. "Starvation is impossible," he wrote, "for one able and willing to work." Carrin also wrote to larger newspapers up north like the *National Tribune* in Washington, urging Civil War veterans to relocate to Stephensville. Florida still had a reputation for political and racial violence at this time, which Carrin sought to tamp down. "The people are very peaceable and hospitable," he wrote in one editorial. "No danger whatever to any one on account of his political opinion. What is said to the contrary in political papers is all bosh."[29]

Outside of Perry and the few instances of industrial development along the coast, the majority of Taylor County was still farm country, with cotton, corn, hogs, and cows being the primary products. As of 1884, the county had an estimated 8,742 acres under cultivation. About 60% of that land was planted in corn, which could feed both humans and stock animals. About 23% was planted in cotton, mainly the long-staple, Sea Island variety that produced heartily even in sandy soil. The rest was divided up between oats, sweet potatoes, and sugar cane.[30]

As for cattle and hog production, Florida still operated almost exclusively on the open range system. Stock animals wandered the hammocks and piney woods at their leisure, with only their owners' unique marks and brands to set them apart. Courthouse records list hundreds of different patterns that stock owners stamped or cut into the animals' ears and flanks. Many owners registered multiple marks and brands, since they frequently traded or sold stock with other farmers, and the patterns often could not be modified to match the new owner's existing marks and brands. The differences between many of the patterns were minute, but they became critical in the event of a challenge in court or out on the range itself.[31]

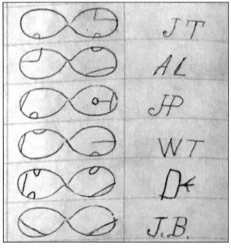

Excerpt from Taylor County's official record of marks and brands, showing the patterns used by local farmers to identify their cattle and hogs. From top to bottom, these marks and brands belonged to James Towles, registered in 1875; A.L. Towles (1885); J.P. Tuten (1893); Dr. William Woodruff Tyson (1895); Daniel Towles (1901); and J.B. Thomas (1904).

Most families owned at least a few head of cows and other animals, but some herds ran into the hundreds or even thousands. In 1873, William N. Johnson was taxed for 700 head of cattle, while John Martin Towles reported having 400, Wiley W. Whiddon 450, Boyd Dias Poppell 164, and Z.O. Lovett 150. By 1880 many of these herds had grown, and Neal Hendry had become one of the major cattlemen with a reported 800 head. Some of the largest herds were actually owned by Madison County citizens, but they appear on the Taylor County tax rolls because the cows ranged in that area. W.D. Griffin of Greenville, for example, had over a thousand cattle in Taylor County in 1873. John J. Norton had about 175 head, Chandler Smith about 600, and J.K. Williams & Company about 700 head.[32]

Farmers with smaller herds typically used their cows for meat, milk, and local barter, selling one or two as needed to get cash for the general store or to pay off debts. The best money, however, came from selling in larger markets, including Key West, Nassau, and especially Havana, Cuba. With no railroad to transport the cattle, Taylor County farmers had to either drive their cows to market or sell them to a bigger outfit that would do it on their behalf. Early on, cattle had to be driven all the way to Tampa, Manatee, or Punta Rassa to be loaded onto a schooner bound for market. In 1871 an enterprising cattleman named J.S. Turner began shipping cows from Cedar Key on barges. This was critical for maintaining the value of the herds that North Florida farmers sent southward. Long drives often resulted in leaner cows and losses due to disease, injury, or other mishaps. Both outcomes meant a lower payout when selling the cows, so the less time they spent hoofing it the better. William H. Towles illustrated this concern when negotiating a deal with Tampa cattleman John T. Lesley, who ran one of the largest outfits in the Cuba trade. "I would like

Portrait of William H. Towles, who was successful in business not only in Taylor County, but also in Bartow and Fort Myers.

(Photo courtesy of the Taylor County Historical Society)

… some insurance that you would take the cattle that I take to you," Towles wrote Lesley in 1879, "as you know it would be very disagreeable to have them turned loose on my hands there."[33]

Towles went on to play a much larger role in the story of the Florida cattle industry. He got his start managing his family's growing herd in Taylor County, buying up cows from his neighbors and consigning them to large buyers farther south. He also became one of the county's earliest store owners, going into business with S.H. Peacock in the late 1870s. By the early 1880s he was acting as an agent for Dr. Howell Tyson Lykes, a physician who turned to cattle after the Civil War when the market began to heat up. Towles sold his interest in the general store business to Peacock in 1883 and moved to Bartow in Polk

County. He ran another store there for a while before moving to Fort Myers in 1884, where he became one of the town's leading citizens. He helped lead the effort to establish Lee County, founded or co-founded several successful businesses, and continued raising cows, making a fortune by shipping them to Cuba during the Spanish-American War. His house, built in 1885, was added to the National Register of Historic Places in 2008.[34]

One more major development from this period deserves mentioning, although its effects would not be felt until after 1900 for the most part. By the early 1880s, Congress had granted millions of acres of land to the state government, hoping it could either improve the land or sell it to someone who could. Much of the unsold land left in Taylor County was part of this transfer. The state's Internal Improvement Fund was in charge of managing this massive amount of land, as well as doling it out at reduced rates to railroad companies and other developers. The Fund got into financial trouble in the 1870s, which led Governor William D. Bloxham to seek a buyer who might purchase a large enough portion of the Fund's holdings to wipe out the debt. He found such a buyer in Hamilton Disston, a young Philadelphia man who had recently inherited the largest saw and file company in the world, Henry Disston & Son. Disston agreed to purchase four million acres of "swamp and overflowed lands" in Florida at 25 cents an acre. That was enough money to retire the Internal Improvement Fund's debt, and it also made Disston the United States' largest private landowner.[35]

Disston immediately sold half of his Florida purchase to a syndicate of foreign investors headed by Sir Edward James Reed, a British naval engineer. This portion of the sale spread across 29 counties, including 172,228 acres in Taylor County, over 20 percent of the county's total area. Reed's syndicate formed a corporation, the Florida Land and Mortgage Company, to develop and sell off their property at a profit. Many of the timber and turpentine companies that operated in Taylor County in the 20th century obtained their land either from the Florida Land and Mortgage Company or its successors. Some of the largest parcels from the original Disston-Reed purchase are still intact, especially in the western and coastal regions of the county. Much as they did in the early 20th century, these lands continue to be an important part of the local economy.[36]

A Rough Neighborhood

While the county was making progress at the end of the 19th century, there were some troublesome developments as well. "It is an unpleasant duty to call your attention to the condition of affairs in Taylor County," Circuit Court Judge John F. White wrote to Governor William Bloxham in 1898. At one time, White said, Taylor County had been "one of the most quiet counties in the state." Now, he explained, it was "one of the most lawless, and if possible rapidly growing worse." State's Attorney L.E. Roberson wrote the governor that same day with a similar assessment. "The most deplorable state of affairs exists there," he wrote, "that it has ever been my misfortune to witness."[37]

Although White and Roberson had some specific cases in mind when they wrote to Governor Bloxham, the situation they were describing was only the culmination of a remarkably violent decade for Taylor County. The 1890s saw an unusually high number of murders, gun fights, and other serious crimes. State officials blamed the isolated location of the county for its lawlessness, noting that the maze of swamps and hammocks and piney woods made it an ideal place for illegally distilling liquor and harboring fugitives from the law. There is certainly some evidence backing this up; plenty of stills were broken up during this period and wanted men did occasionally make their way to Perry. Charley and Jack Kelly were an example of this, although they were not exactly hardened criminals. The two brothers were convicted of murder in Georgia around 1870 after getting caught up in a big fight that broke out at a circus. They escaped from prison and made their way to Florida, eventually settling in Taylor County. The public had never been fully convinced of their guilt, and in 1887 Georgia Governor John Brown Gordon pardoned the two Kelly brothers. By that time, Charley was superintendent of schools in Taylor County, and Jack was serving in the legislature.[38]

One of the most violent outbursts occurred in 1892, when two young men, Thomas Walters and William Parker, got into a fight in Perry that quickly turned deadly. Jack Murray's "Flaming Six-Guns of Florida" describes this episode in gory detail, claiming that when the dust and smoke finally cleared, nine people had died and several others were injured. Newspaper accounts from the time describe the fight in equally dramatic fashion, but report only two deaths. According to the

Photo of the Gornto family residence in Perry, circa 1890. Judge J.J. Gornto and A.S. Gornto are standing on the steps.

(Image courtesy of the State Archives of Florida)

Pensacola News, Robert Parker, William's brother, died, along with J.J. Gornto, a store owner and former county judge who ran out into the street to try to break up the violence.[39]

Another bout of bloodshed followed in late 1894 and 1895, after the alleged assault of a young white woman named Ella Jones. Locals identified three African American men as her attackers, and organized posses to hunt them down. Two men were captured in Lafayette County within a few days and lynched without their having been tried in court. According to newspaper reports, the two men confessed before meeting their death that they had been part of a larger group, and white citizens then began searching for the other members. In July 1895, newspapers reported that a dozen African American men had been lynched, and that groups of armed white men had invaded at least one local African American church and broken up the services.[40]

Perhaps the most dramatic quarrel of the decade was that between the Towles and Brannen families, the one that formed the basis of Jack Murray's "Flaming Six-Guns" story. Murray's account is best described as historical fiction, based on real events but significantly altered to make the story more theatrical and enjoyable for the reader. More reliable accounts of the feud are found in the papers of William D. Bloxham, governor of Florida in the late 1890s. Bloxham's files include letters from allies of both the Brannen and Towles families, plus county officials, the circuit court judge, and the local state's attorney. While some details of this unfortunate episode remain debatable, these documents do collectively offer a more dependable timeline of events.

Portrait of John Fletcher White,
the circuit judge who presided over
the court proceedings relating to the
Towles-Brannen feud in the 1890s.

(Image courtesy of the State Archives of Florida)

Judge John F. White, who presided over the trials associated with this feud, wrote Governor Bloxham that while trouble between these families had been brewing for years, it intensified because of two killings in 1895 and 1897. Brad Hampton, an African American man who worked for James X.

Towles, was shot dead while ploughing a field on May 10, 1895. Newspaper reports at the time connected Hampton's murder with the racial violence that had started with the assault of Ella Jones the year before, but Judge White said locals believed the Brannens or their allies had done the deed to settle an old score. At any rate, the identity of Hampton's killer was never ascertained; the shooter had reportedly fired from the bushes and disappeared undetected.[41]

Then, on October 27, 1897, Thomas Brannen was shot as he sat by a campfire in Tide Swamp, where he had been cutting red cedar to send to Cedar Key. He survived, but sustained significant damage to his arm. As with Brad Hampton's murder two years before, the shooter fired from a distance and was not immediately identified. According to Judge White, however, suspicion quickly fell on Bump (or Bunk) Padgett, another one of the Towles family's woods riders.[42]

Just over a month after Thomas Brannen was shot in Tide Swamp, Padgett was standing in a wagon in his yard raking out clay to build a chimney when he was fired on from the nearby bushes. According to a letter from his brother Ward, the first shot hit Bump's pistol, rendering it useless. Seeing that his weapon would not fire, Padgett headed for his house, but the shots kept coming, and before he could reach the door he fell dead. John C. Calhoun, clerk of the county court at that time, told the governor's private secretary that a coroner's jury investigated the scene, but could find no clues as to who was responsible.[43]

The violence did not stop there. On December 18, 1897, just days after Bump Padgett's death, Henry Horace, a Brannen ally, was shot from the bushes while walking along a public road. Like Thomas Brannen, he eventually recovered from his wounds, but not without serious damage to his arm. John C. Calhoun speculated that Winchester rifles had been the weapon used against both Brannen and Horace.[44]

By this time, Governor Bloxham's mailbox was filling up with letters about these incidents. Bump Padgett's brother D.B. in Suwannee County wrote in late December, describing what had happened to Bump and enclosing a letter written by a third Padgett brother, Ward, who had been responsible for closing up Bump's affairs when he died. William H. Towles, the Taylor County cattleman who had moved south to chase bigger prospects, heard about the feud and urged the governor to do something to stop the violence. "I have both relatives and property in that county," he wrote, "and I feel that something should be done."[45]

But in 1898, there were limits on what the governor could do. There was no state law enforcement agency at this time, and it hardly seemed appropriate to declare martial law or bring out the militia. The biggest problem, state officials felt, was that Sheriff A.J. "Jud" Head was not making any arrests, and even when he did, the juries were not finding anyone guilty. "If the people of Taylor County want the law enforced," Governor Bloxham's secretary told William H. Towles, "they must lend their aid to the executive authorities to that end... [until] the individual citizen assumes his own responsibility for the enforcement of the laws, a better condition of things in Taylor County cannot be hoped for."[46]

The one thing Bloxham felt he could constitutionally do that would help the situation was offer a reward for the capture and conviction of the people responsible for this bloodshed. On Valentine's Day 1898, Bloxham's secretary David Lang wrote to county clerk John C. Calhoun, asking him to state what facts he had about the case and advise whether a reward would be more effective if announced publicly or circulated quietly outside the county. Calhoun responded that the second option would work better, and Governor Bloxham quickly signed a proclamation offering $200 for the arrest and conviction of Bump Padgett's murderer. He also offered a $100 reward for the arrest and conviction of the parties responsible for shooting Thomas Brannen and Henry Horace.[47]

Portrait of William Dunnington Bloxham, Florida's 13th and 17th governor. Bloxham was in office when the Towles-Brannen feud came to a head in the late 1890s.

(Image courtesy of the State Archives of Florida)

The violence continued, however. Less than a month after Governor Bloxham offered the rewards, John Scroggins, who worked with James X. Towles, was shot from the bushes, the bullet breaking his leg. William H. Towles anxiously wrote the governor once again, likening the situation to the tense standoff that was then taking place between the Spanish and Americans over Cuba. "It seems the war has opened in Taylor County whether it opens in Spain or not," he remarked. John C. Calhoun wrote the governor, asking if he could either declare martial law in the county or send detectives to help bring the fighting to an end. David Lang shot back an angry response, saying the governor would do neither, and it was up to Taylor County's elected officials to do their sworn duty and apprehend the people responsible for this violence. "You must realize," he said, "that the citizens of Taylor County are more interested in the enforcement of the law in their own county than anyone else can possibly be, and unless they take active measures to do so, all efforts of the Governor to bring the guilty to punishment are worse than futile." The most the governor could do, Lang wrote, was to double the rewards.[48]

The people of Taylor County had an opportunity to take Lang's advice at the spring term of the circuit court, which opened on April 5, 1898 in Perry. Judge John F. White later reported that the mood was tense, and while people seemed to have knowledge about who was responsible for the various unsolved murders and attempted murders, no one was talking. The grand jury did return an indictment, however, against Henry Horace for the murder of Bump Padgett. James X. Towles was also indicted for distilling and selling spirituous liquors without a license. Judge White said there was "overwhelming" evidence that Henry Horace had not acted alone, yet the jury would issue no more indictments for Padgett's murder or for the assaults on Thomas Brannen, John Scroggins, or the now-suspect Henry Horace. Horace was arrested sometime after the circuit court session ended, but his trial would have to wait.[49]

By the time the circuit court reconvened in the fall, the grand jury had more to say. It returned an indictment once again against Henry Horace for the murder of Bump Padgett, but this time the jurors also indicted Thomas and George Brannen. James X. Towles also came under fire once again, the jury indicting him this time for breaking and entering and assault, although the records do not say against whom. Judge White ordered all four men arrested, but reported that Sheriff Head only arrested James X. Towles and some of his associates. Despite George and Thomas Brannen being at the courthouse when Judge White ordered their arrest, Head allowed them to leave town.[50]

This marked a turning point in the crisis, as it now appeared to Judge White, State's Attorney L.E. Roberson, and many others that Sheriff Head had taken a side in the feud. Roberson wrote to Governor Bloxham, arguing that if Head had arrested Thomas Brannen for Bump Padgett's murder when he had the chance, the fighting might have ended. As it stood, the Towles faction had decided to take matters into their own hands and were out hunting for the Brannens "with unlawful intent," as Judge White put it. "I am overwhelmingly of the opinion that Head should be removed," Roberson wrote. "There will be no improvement in the condition of affairs until it is done and he is succeeded by a competent and upright man."[51]

Having heard from county officials, local citizens, Judge White, and Roberson, Governor Bloxham's secretary David Lang wrote to Sheriff Head asking for an explanation. Head admitted he had a war on his hands. "There is two factions in this county and ... they have fell out," he wrote. He explained that he had chosen not to arrest the Brannens after their warrants were issued because he could not ensure their safety in the Taylor County jail. "I don't belong to neither side," he asserted, "and I am not for sail [sic]." He promised to arrest Thomas Brannen as soon as he could be sure of his safety, and even

Photo of J. Frank King, a prominent local land surveyor and one-time assistant state tax equalizer. King was believed by many to have been the member of Sheriff Lipscomb's posse who fatally wounded Thomas Brannen in 1899.

(Photo courtesy of the Taylor County Historical Society)

included a transcript of a letter from Brannen affirming that he would go quietly when the time came, as long as he could be sure that he would be held in Madison County, not Taylor. "All I ask," Head said in closing, "is [for you] not to take the lawless side of the case."[52]

Bloxham turned once again to Judge White and State's Attorney Roberson for advice, and neither man had anything good to say about the sheriff or his explanation. Judge White admitted that both sides were to blame for the fighting, but asserted that Head was incompetent and had to be replaced. "Both sides go armed all the time, and both in my opinion are capable of shedding blood without additional provocation," White wrote. "Each side fears the other side. A sheriff with a strong and courageous will will have all the backing he needs from the law-abiding citizens of that county to arrest any man in the county."[53]

Meanwhile, Taylor County's political leaders had reached a decision of their own that would ultimately make Bloxham's path forward much clearer. On October 24, 1898, the county's Democratic Executive Committee met and decided to ask the governor to remove Sheriff Head from office and install his deputy, Francis M. Lipscomb, in his place. State Senator S. Hiram Peacock forwarded this decision to Bloxham, adding his personal endorsement. Bloxham issued an order suspending Sheriff Head and appointing Lipscomb as the Taylor County officials had recommended.[54]

That still left the matter of what to do about the Brannens and Henry Horace. Judge White called a special session of the circuit court for March 1899, in which the grand jury once again indicted all three men for the murder of Bump Padgett. Horace was already in the Madison County jail, and Sheriff Lipscomb reported to Judge White in July that he had apprehended George Brannen. He added that he had been forced to kill Thomas Brannen after he resisted arrest, although many contemporaries and their children claimed local land surveyor Frank King was the member of Lipscomb's posse responsible for the fatal shot.[55]

George Brannen and Henry Horace awaited their fate in the Madison County jail, having requested and been granted a change of venue so that the trial would be held in Madison. They were represented by Hardee & Hardee, a duo which included the future governor Cary A. Hardee, a Taylor County native. The case was continued until the fall term of the circuit court in 1901, and by that time another Brannen, John, had been indicted. Witnesses for the state included Tom Morse, Colen Blue, Boyd D. Poppell, William Woods, N.R.L. Bowdoin, Frank King, and Dan Mathis. When the trial finally took place, the jury deliberated for more than a day before announcing it could not agree on a verdict. Henry Horace and George Brannen were released.[56]

This turned out to be the end of the Towles-Brannen feud, or at least the most dramatic phase of it. Thomas Brannen was dead, his brothers had spent time in jail, and Sheriff A.J. Head was no longer in office. Henry Horace moved to Brooksville and took up house painting and paperhanging. In a somewhat odd twist, he became mixed up in a bank robbery investigation after he and his son discovered $10,000 in stolen banknotes hidden in a hollow log. Having linked the robbery to another man, authorities did not charge Horace, but he did have to give back the portion of the money he had not spent. After his Taylor County debacle surfaced in his interviews with authorities, he told reporters the experience had been a rough one. "When I went into jail I had plenty of hair," he told one newspaper. "During the 21 months I spent there before being released on bail, my hair turned gray, and I grew bald."[57]

Thomas H. Stripling replaced Frank Lipscomb as sheriff following an election in 1900. A dispute between Lipscomb and Stripling in February 1903 ended with Deputy Sheriff W.W. Wilder killing Lipscomb. Jack Murray wrote in the "Flaming Six Guns" story that this was directly related to the Towles-Brannen feud, but the *Perry Herald* made no mention of a connection in reporting the incident when it happened. Walter Wright, interviewed about the feud by Gwen Faulkner in the 1960s, noted Murray's tendency to distort the timeline of events, and said it was difficult to say whether Lipscomb's death was directly connected or not.[58]

A New Era

While these dramatic events were unfolding at the close of the 19th century, preparations for big changes in Taylor County were taking place in the background. Interest in Taylor County's massive stands of yellow pine and cypress timber was increasing, especially since most of the trees stood on large tracts of land owned by investors ready to sell for the right price. The main obstacle preventing an immense timber and turpentine trade from taking shape in the county was the lack of a railroad for shipping out the products.

Two companies attempted to connect Taylor County to the state's growing rail network in the 1890s. The Florida, Georgia and Western Railway Company was the first, receiving a charter from the Legislature in 1891 to build a railroad from Gainesville through Lafayette, Taylor, and Jefferson counties to Tallahassee. The company and its successors built the road from Tallahassee as far as Covington near Eridu, with a short-lived extension to Waylonzo, but failed to reach Perry. Another company, the Live Oak, Luraville & Deadman's Bay Railroad, incorporated in 1893, but never finished building tracks beyond Dowling Park.[59]

Still, more companies were beginning to notice Perry and its potential for timber and turpentine operations. By 1900, Adel sawmill owner J.W. Oglesby had bought up a significant amount of acreage in Taylor County and was looking to extend his South Georgia Railway into the area. The Drew Lumber Company, based in Ellaville in Madison County, was also looking to build a line into Perry, which prodded the Drew family's competitors to do the same. All these companies would eventually build railroads into Taylor County, setting off an explosion of industrial activity that would set the tone for many decades to come.[60]

*Designed by Charles Herty, these clay cups were one half
of the cup-and-gutter system used to extract turpentine
from longleaf pine trees. It was supported by a nail
through the lip of the cup.*

(Photo courtesy of Joney P. Perry)

CHAPTER 5:

Timber and Turpentine

Once a logging company cuts a stand of timber, they usually let the remaining debris rot down for a while, and then plow it under to make way for a new crop of pine seedlings. Even after the young trees are planted, it can be a year or two before grass and weeds cover up the dirt. In the meantime, especially after a good, hard rain, those plowed fields often yield up all kinds of tiny treasures—railroad spikes, old bottles, rusty metal odds and ends, broken glass and ceramic of every imaginable color, and plenty of shards of terra cotta pottery.

These are the humble remains of a mighty timber and turpentine bonanza that defined Taylor County in the early 1900s. The glass and metal come from countless company houses, thrown up hastily by loggers and turpentine operators when they set up temporary camps near their land holdings. The terra cotta pottery bits come from thousands upon thousands of cups used to collect the sap dripping from "cat faces" cut into pine trees for turpentine. The spikes come from the multitude of railroads and makeshift trams the companies used to connect these satellite work sites with their factories, mills, and buyers.

Timber and turpentine transformed Taylor County from a strictly agricultural economy into a thriving hub of commerce. Although the nickname "Forest Capital of the South" did not come until after World War II, it would not have been much of a stretch to use it at the turn of the 20th century. At various times the county had the world's largest cypress sawmill, several of the largest pine sawmills in the South, and an annual output of many thousands of barrels of turpentine and rosin. One manager for the International Lumber Company said in 1908 that it would take his mill, processing 40,000 board feet of lumber per day, 20 years to exhaust all the timber in the county. The Burton-Swartz Cypress Company also illustrated the vastness of local timber resources by cutting, sawing, and shipping over 38 million board feet of lumber in its first year alone. This was business on an astounding scale for a small rural county.[1]

The old adage that you have to spend money to make money rang true during this turn-of-the-century boom. A few timber and turpentine businesses were built up by locals, but the larger, better known operations were bank-rolled by wealthy investors from all over Florida and as far away as New York, Chicago, and Minneapolis. Moreover, many of the capitalists who invested in Taylor County did so in more than one industry, buying and selling shares in companies as they saw fit. The Dowling family of Live Oak, for example, started out with lumber as their primary interest, but in Taylor County they also invested in turpentine stills and built one of North Florida's most success-ful lumber railways, the Live Oak, Perry & Gulf. Neill G. Wade, the engineer who contracted to build the Atlantic Coast Line Railroad from Old Town to Perry, was also heavily invested in the Southern Timber & Naval Stores Com-pany and the Wade & McNair Land Company, which collectively owned more than 100,000 acres of Taylor County territory for timber and turpentine pur-poses. Even the merchants who established stores in Perry during this era usu-ally included sawmills and turpentine stills in their articles of incorporation.[2]

Companies also tended to combine and invest in one another's stock, which can make researching their activities a bewildering task. As of August, 1908, for example, the Dowling Lumber Company was not even headed by a Dowling. Lumber magnate Henry Harding Tift (for whom Tifton, Georgia is named) was president, while the Dowlings held vice-president positions, and the company's treasurer was a former competitor in the naval stores side of the business, John H. Powell of Powell & McLean.[3]

Although outsiders controlled many of the largest companies, the devel-opment of these industries had profound local consequences. Taylor County's population more than tripled between 1900 and 1930 as newcomers moved into the area looking for work. Every corner of the county—from Clara in the south to Scanlon and Cabbage Grove in the west—was involved; new commu-nities popped up and disappeared regularly as companies moved from place to place to harvest their stands of virgin timber. Families that had relied strictly on farming and livestock for generations suddenly had new opportunities to make money, and many took advantage. Demand for consumer goods increased steadily during the early 20th century, and stores emerged in Perry to cater to these desires.

There were challenges, of course. Working trees for turpentine and log-ging them for lumber were tough jobs—difficult and dangerous in many ways. Government safety regulations were virtually non-existent in the early years of the boom, and the amount and nature of the pay often locked young workers and their families into the company's orbit for longer than they would have preferred. Still, the buzzing of the saws and the boiling of the turpentine vats became the natural rhythm of progress in Taylor County, a pattern that set the stage for much of the 20th century.[4]

Railroads

Establishing railroad service in the region was the first step in opening it up to large-scale logging and turpentine operations. The Legislature offered a major inducement to get the job done in 1891 when it passed an act incorporating the Florida, Georgia & Western Railway Company. The legislation specifically noted that "the Gulf coast counties of this State have not heretofore had the benefit of any railroad, or any aid from its Internal Improvement Fund to construct railroads therein." To make up for lost time, the Legislature granted the new company entire sections of land on either side of its railroad, as well as ten

thousand acres of land per mile of road constructed. The projected route stretched from the Florida-Georgia border through Tallahassee, Perry, Gainesville, and then south to Charlotte Harbor, over 350 miles. Had the Florida, Georgia & Western Railway completed every mile in their original plan, the state would have been obligated to grant the company more than 400,000 acres of public land.[5]

But there was a catch. To receive the state's generous land offer, the company had to start construction on the road within ten days of the law's passage, and twenty miles of track had to be completed within one year. The entire mainline, furthermore, had to be finished within three years. This timetable eventually proved unworkable for

Excerpt from a map of Florida published in the 1890s. The anticipated route of the Florida, Georgia & Western Railway through Taylor County is shown, but this particular track would never actually be constructed. Aside from a short-lived spur to Waylonzo for freight shipping, the road was never fully constructed past Covington on the Taylor County side of the Aucilla River.

(Map courtesy of the State Library of Florida)

– 79 –

the FG&W. The company managed to build a six-mile section of the road from Tallahassee southeast to Lake Como, but there it stopped. The Legislature granted the company an extension, but eventually it folded and its assets were sold at a sheriff's sale to railroad owner James M. Mayo of Ocala in 1895. Mayo reorganized the operation as the Tallahassee and Southeastern Railroad and convinced the Legislature to give him the same deal it had offered the FG&W. The new deadline for completing the railroad moved to 1903.[6]

Mayo sold the newly incorporated Tallahassee and Southeastern to Tallahassee railroad operator R.L. Bennett and Michigan lumberman R.G. Peters in 1897. By 1899, the company had extended the railroad as far as Wacissa along the route of what is now called Tram Road (County Road 259). The grading for additional track was also finished as far as Covington on the Taylor County side of the Aucilla River, just west of Eridu. Later that year, however, Bennett and Peters sold the road to the contractors that had been building it, the Florida Construction Company. The new owners applied to the Legislature for yet another extension, but this time it was not so easy.[7]

Two other railroads had been building toward Perry, including the South Georgia Railway owned by the Oglesby family of Adel, and the Suwannee & San Pedro Railroad controlled by the Drew family of Ellaville in Madison County. Both families owned large sawmill operations, and the vast amount of timber available in Taylor County attracted their attention. They protested the Tallahassee & Southeastern Railroad's bid for an extension, arguing that the company had done little to deserve such a massive land grant. Frank Drew, representing the Suwannee & San Pedro, implored the Legislature to "leave these lands open to be earned" by whichever company could actually construct the tracks.[8]

Taylor County citizens held a mass meeting in Perry on April 17, 1901, and resolved to ask their legislators to divide the land grant between the Tallahassee & Southeastern and the South Georgia Railway, giving whichever road reached Perry first the right to choose its land first. The citizens also asked the legislators to seek an extension of the construction deadline to 1902. The Legislature granted neither request, and the land grant offer expired at the end of 1901.[9]

Meanwhile, the Tallahassee & Southeastern's competitors had already sprung into action. By January 1, 1902, the Drew family's Suwannee & San Pedro Railroad had reached Mayo, and by June the line had reached the Fenholloway River over a route roughly parallel to the present-day Connell Grade south of U.S. 27. The completed route between Live Oak and Perry opened on

February 21, 1903, making it Taylor County's first through railroad connection. Two streets in downtown Perry still commemorate this achievement—Drew Street being named for the principal owners of the road, and Ellis Street named for its chief engineer, Robert Naudain Ellis, Jr. This was the same civil engineer who laid out the town of Fenholloway in 1902.[10]

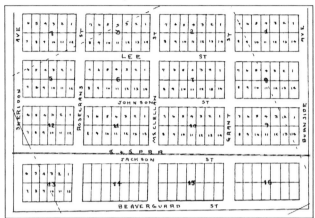

Robert Naudain Ellis's plat of the town of Fenholloway, dated 1902. The Suwannee and San Pedro Railroad is shown running right through the center of town, with 50-foot streets named for Confederate generals.

(Copy in the author's possession)

While the Drews' railroad reached Perry from the east, the South Georgia Railway was quickly approaching from the north. James Wood Oglesby and his brother Zenas had purchased a large amount of timber land in Taylor County around 1900, and by the time the Suwannee & San Pedro made it to Perry they had extended a railroad from just south of Adel to Greenville. In 1904, a subsidiary of the South Georgia Railroad called the West Coast Railway extended the line southward into Perry, opening it on September 1 of that year. J.W. Oglesby also invested in the nearby Hampton Springs Hotel. By 1911, he was president of the corporation that ran the hotel, and by 1915 he had extended his railroad out to it. In its heyday, the Hampton Springs Hotel received ten passenger and freight trains every day over this line. The route of the South Georgia Railroad and its West Coast Railway subsidiary are now owned by Georgia and Florida RailNet, and it is the last of Taylor County's original rail lines to remain mostly intact.[11]

For a while, Perry found itself in the unusual position of having two railroads directly linking it with Live Oak, a consequence of bad feelings between the Drew family and the giant Seaboard Air Line. The Seaboard had helped finance the construction of the Suwannee & San Pedro, and its officers expected the Drews to sign an agreement in return, specifying the Seaboard as their preferred connection at Live Oak. Frank Drew believed the Seaboard's rates for shipping lumber were too high, and he refused. This touched off a series of retaliations by both sides, including an effort by Seaboard's president, Skelton Williams, to convince the Dowling family, who owned a short line between Live Oak and Dowling Park, to incorporate their railroad and extend it on to Perry to compete with the Drews.[12]

The Dowlings incorporated their short line in October 1903 as the Live Oak and Perry Railroad, but just then the Seaboard changed its tune, having booted Skelton Williams and adopted a more conservative business approach. Another growing rail giant, the Atlantic Coast Line, sensed an opportunity and picked up where the Seaboard left off. In 1905, the Dowlings' railroad was rein-corporated once again as the Live Oak, Perry & Gulf Railroad, and by the end of 1906 it had completed tracks to Mayo and to Hampton Springs via Perry. Of the major railroads that eventually traversed Taylor County, the LOP&G, nicknamed the 'Lopin' Gopher,' handled the largest amount of timber and tur-pentine traffic. It offered a more direct route to Live Oak than the Suwannee & San Pedro (called the Florida Railway after 1905), and it eventually extended as far west as Flintrock in Jefferson County.[13]

The competition between the Florida Railway and the LOP&G was fairly one-sided from the beginning. The Dowlings controlled one of the Florida Railway's largest potential customers, the mill at Alton near Mayo, and had their own line to ship the lumber. When new leadership later took over the Dowling timber interests, they kept up the same policy of using the LOP&G for shipping. The Florida Railway limped along with revenue from transport-ing general merchandise, passengers, agricultural products, and phosphates from Luraville, but it fell into receivership in 1915, and by 1919 the road was abandoned. The LOP&G, however, would remain a vital route through Taylor County for decades to come.[14]

One final rail-road worth mention-ing is the Atlantic Coast Line's route looping from Jack-sonville southward to Newberry, over to Wilcox near Fanning Springs, and then up to Perry via Cross City. This line opened

Live Oak, Perry & Gulf Railroad Engine No. 100, photographed in Perry in 1938.

(Photo courtesy of the State Archives of Florida)

for traffic into Perry on January 18, 1909, connecting the southern part of the county with railroads heading to the north and east. This was critical to the success of the large timber and turpentine companies operating near present-day Salem and Tennille, including the Blue Creek Naval Stores Company, branches of the Putnam Lumber Company, Carpenter-O'Brien, and Brooks-Scanlon. Observers up and down the Gulf Coast, especially in Tampa, waited eagerly for the Atlantic Coast Line to build a link between Perry and Monticello. This would create a direct route from Tampa and points south all the way up to Atlanta and beyond, saving six to eight hours of travel time over the existing route, which required passengers and freight to jog east and pass through the busy rail hub at Jacksonville. This so-called "Perry Cut-off," was coming, but it would have to wait a few years.[15]

Turpentine

Timber companies may have built Taylor County's first railroads, but they weren't the only major businesses to use them. Even before the tracks were laid for the Suwannee & San Pedro and South Georgia railroads, eager businessmen were busily tapping thousands of pine trees to collect their sap and convert it into valuable turpentine. This was commonly referred to as the naval stores industry.

The term "naval stores" dates back to the era of wooden ships and boats, when tar and pitch were used to seal their hulls. European shippers obtained the majority of their naval stores from evergreen forests in Sweden and the surrounding region, at least until the British colonized North America. Colonists distilled pine sap in Virginia as early as 1608, and the industry quickly spread southward into the Carolinas and Georgia. Spanish subjects in Florida also produced naval stores. Over time, the turpentine created through this process became just as valuable as the pitch. It was used in making ink, medicines, paints and varnishes, cleaning solutions, and even patent leather.[16]

Taylor County's first commercial turpentine operations appeared around 1900. In December 1899, the *Tampa Tribune* reported that three firms planned to set up distilleries in the county, including McCormick & Company, Williamson & Company, and E.G. Brown Turpentine Company. Urban Potts, who had been involved in the turpentine business in Georgia for over a decade, purchased land in Taylor County in 1900 and began operating a still off the present-day Potts Still Road. Brothers Duncan and John Malloy, natives of North Carolina, arrived in 1903 and began buying up land and operating stills. The Malloy brothers' first still appears to have been east of Perry on property belonging to the S. Hiram Peacock family, although they were soon working trees at Boyd, Salem, Hampton Springs, and Fenholloway.[17]

Once the railroads arrived, more companies began leasing land and setting up turpentine stills. The Dowling Lumber Company, which built the Live Oak, Perry & Gulf Railroad to Perry, formed a separate corporation, the Dowling Park Naval Stores Company, to establish stills in the area and supplement the Dowling timber operations. Records show the company having turpentine sites at Athena, Spring Warrior, Lake Bird, Waylonzo, and Ewing Springs along the Fenholloway River. The Oglesby family, who built the South

Portrait of Urban Potts, one of Taylor County's earliest commercial turpentine producers. Potts Still Road is named for him.

(Photo courtesy of Ouida Allison)

Georgia Railway, partnered with some of their business associates in Quitman to establish the Perry Naval Stores Company, with a still located about a mile south of Perry. C.C. Rawls, who had previously been in the merchandise trade at Montbrook in Levy County, arrived in Taylor County around 1906 with his business partner, F.E. Crawford, and established the Taylor County Naval Stores Company. Rawls and Crawford appear to have operated out of both Perry and Stephensville. Powell & McLean incorporated in 1904 and established stills at Boyd, Shady Grove, and Hampton Springs. The Blue Creek Company set up operations at Thelma near present-day Keaton Beach. Blair and Hinley operated near Perry.[18]

Sometimes the naval stores operators tapped their own trees, but more often they simply leased the "turpentine rights" to property belonging to other owners, especially timber companies. Leases usually lasted three to five years and the price was often assessed as a set price per tree or thousand trees tapped, or sometimes as a percentage of the proceeds from the turpentine and rosin sold at market. The leases also usually laid down some ground rules for the turpentine operators to follow, mainly to protect the timber from damage. A lease might give very specific instructions as to which parts of a tract of land could be worked, how large the trees had to be before they could be tapped, how deep the turpentine crews could cut into the trees to make the sap flow, and even what kinds of vessels they used to collect the dripping liquid. The idea was to get as much sap from the trees as possible without ruining their value for lumber.[19]

Because their land holdings were often in remote locations, turpentine companies usually worked out of large camps far outside of town. In fact, the camps often became towns themselves, with everything the laborers needed to live and work without having to travel. Some of these camps were small and short-lived. Others, like Waylonzo in the western part of the county and Thelma near the coast, were larger and more permanent, enough so to have their own post offices.[20]

A still belonging to the Blue Creek Turpentine Company at Thelma near present-day Blue Springs Lake.

(Photo courtesy of the State Archives of Florida)

County records include a bill of sale recorded by the Malloy brothers that gives us a good idea of what the typical turpentine operation looked like. According to the document, the Malloy camp at Salem included a large still, 18 shanties, two nicer dwellings, a cooperage shop for making barrels, a sawmill, a storage building for the finished product, a barn for the horses and draft animals, and a commissary. Similar records for Andrew Poppell's still at Waylonzo list these features, plus a blacksmith shop and a vat for washing hardened sap out of the turpentine cups.[21]

The commissary was the main center of business for a turpentine camp. The workers received their pay there, half or more of it usually in the form of scrip or babbit. This was company money, usually coins made of wood or stamped aluminum. These coins were occasionally accepted at stores in town, but for the most part they were good only at the company commissary. These stores stocked everything a turpentine worker might need—clothing and cloth, food, fuel, medicines, tobacco, alcohol, and trinkets. The turpentine companies bought these goods wholesale, and often marked up the prices before selling the items to their workers. The companies also offered easy credit, with interest of course. Between the high commissary prices, the easy lending, and gambling, it was not hard for a worker to fall behind and get into debt. When the Malloy brothers sold their Salem operation, for example, they reported $911.04 owed to the company by the workers, with individual debts ranging from $2.07 to $328.24.[22]

The equipment for tapping the pines trees was not very sophisticated, but the process did have a lot of distinct steps. To do the work efficiently, turpentine operators generally assigned each employee to a very specific task, which they did over and over on hundreds or even thousands of trees. The first step was to make a "face" on each tree to provide access to the sap. A worker would use a broadax to cut off a slab of bark and a thin layer of wood at the base of the tree. Slanting cuts would then be made on each side of the open face, into which the worker would place metal gutters to guide the dripping sap into a single stream. A vessel, or "cup," was hung on a nail below the gutters to catch the sap, usually made of terracotta or sometimes metal. To make the tree produce, a worker called a "chipper" would create two "streaks" in the shape of a V on the face, usually about half an inch wide and ¾ of an inch deep. The worker

made these streaks with a hack, a specialized cutting tool with a two-foot handle and a heavily weighted notching blade at the end. Every week, a squad of chippers would visit each tree in their assigned area and add new streaks until they were too high to reach.[23]

Another specialized team, the "dippers," came behind the chipping squad after a short time to collect the sap—or "gum"—that had seeped out of the streaks and into the cups at the bottom of the faces. It generally took about three to five streaks to produce a full cup of gum. The dippers carried buckets to each tree, dumped the gum, and then replaced the cup before moving on. The buckets of raw gum were then emptied into large barrels in mule-drawn wagons. Once the barrels were full, a driver would take them back to camp, where the contents would be processed at the company's still.[24]

A worker cuts additional notches into the face of a pine tree to start the flow of sap into an aluminum cup below.

(Photo courtesy of the State Archives of Florida)

Yet another specialized task was "scraping," or removing hardened sap that had crystallized on the face of the tree rather than dripping down into the cup. "Scrape" tended to have wood shavings and other impurities in it, which resulted in a lower quality product, but it could still be used. Scrapers collected the hardened sap in buckets and took it back to the still separately from the higher-quality gum.[25]

Fire prevention was another key part of working a stand of timber for turpentine. Lightning, a smoldering campfire, or a cigarette butt flicked into a patch of dry grass could ignite a costly nightmare for a turpentine operator and the timber company that owned the trees. To minimize the threat, workers often spent the winter months clearing brush and grass away from the trunks of trees. Some operators also conducted controlled burns on the land, some-times in cooperation with state forestry officials. The state also helped establish fire lines, lookout towers, and fire-fighting crews.[26]

The still was a busy center of activity in a turpentine camp. Barrels of gum arrived by wagon and were loaded onto the second floor of the still building, sometimes called the "deck," where the thick liquid sap would be poured into a vat to be boiled. Ten barrels of gum could typically be cooked at a time. The still usually consisted of a copper boiler situated over a firebox. Workers stoked the fire and added fuel until the temperature reached about 290 degrees, holding it steady for about two hours. During that time, turpentine vapor and steam rose up from the boiling gum and forced its way into a copper tube that exited the vat and spiraled its way down through a cooling water tank before dumping out into a separator barrel. The water from this distillation process quickly sank to the bottom of the barrel, while the lighter spirits of turpentine remained on top and could be drawn off. The longer the gum was cooked, the less turpentine vapor it emitted, and eventually the still operator would deter-mine that the whole load, or "charge," had been fully cooked. The material remaining in the vat after the turpentine was distilled was called rosin, which had its own uses. The operators removed the rosin from the copper vat while it was still between 290 and 315 degrees—cool enough not to ignite on contact with the air, but hot enough to remain fully liquefied while impurities were strained out of it. The waxy material strained out of the rosin was called dross and could be used as fuel for fires.[27]

After straining, rosin went into pine barrels, often made onsite by the company's own coopers, or barrel makers. The spirits of turpentine were gener-ally shipped from the camp in 50-gallon oak barrels, or sometimes metal con-tainers. State inspectors rated the rosin based on its color and clarity, assigning each batch a grade. The palest and therefore purest batches of rosin received an N, WG, X, or WW grade, while the roughest product received lower letters from B through H. The higher the grade of the rosin, the higher the price it would bring at market in Valdosta, Jacksonville, Pensacola, or Savannah. In Savannah in December 1927, for example, grade WW rosin brought $10.50 per barrel, while grade B rosin only earned $6.50.[28]

The naval stores industry relied on an enormous labor force to execute this complex process. Chippers, dippers, scrapers, and many of the still workers tended to be African American, while the supervisors tended to be white. These supervisors were called "woods riders" after their habit of riding on horseback through the pines, checking to be sure each tree was properly streaked, that cups were in their correct positions, and that fire hazards were cleared away from the tree trunks. This was all tough work, which sometimes made it difficult to find enough hands to keep the camp fully staffed. Over time, however, Florida's Legislature passed laws that made this task a little easier for the turpentine operators.[29]

Woods rider J.B. Faircloth carrying the payroll around to workers, circa 1908.

(Photo courtesy of the State Archives of Florida)

For example, in 1891 Florida made it illegal for an employee who was indebted to his employer to leave his job without either repaying the debt or having just cause. If he did leave, he would be guilty of a misdemeanor and subject to a fine or imprisonment. Turpentine employees were frequently indebted to their company, usually because they had taken out advances on their pay to buy what they needed at the commissary. The prevalence of gambling, the high prices of commissary goods, and lost pay due to bad weather or illness all made this problem worse, as did the fact that workers were paid mostly in money that was useless outside the company. If an employee left the company while still indebted to it, local law enforcement officers would often track him down and either return him to the company or take him to jail to face the legal consequences. Sometimes, spurred on by the promise of a kickback from the turpentine company, even law enforcement officers from other counties would get involved. In 1905, for example, a deputy sheriff from Alachua County arrested John Clark at the still of Barber & Company near Archer and held him at Gainesville until a Taylor County deputy could come to collect him. Clark was charged with "jumping" his labor contract with a Taylor County turpentine firm.[30]

If a worker who jumped his contract or failed to pay a debt agreed to pay the resulting fine, his company would often pay it for him, with the condition that the worker return to the camp and work long enough to pay the new debt off as well as the old debt. If not, the worker was likely to be sentenced to a year on the county chain gang. Ironically, county officials often hired their prisoners out to local timber and turpentine operators, so it was possible for an indebted former employee to end up right back on the same turpentine farm he had left, except he would be in chains and not paid at all.

Florida law allowed both state and county prisons to lease convicts to private businesses, a boon to the turpentine industry. State prisoners had been hired out since the Reconstruction era as a cost-saving measure. The idea was that the convicts would contribute to Florida's industrial advancement while private enterprise shouldered the burden of caring for them. Companies interested in leasing state convicts would submit bids for the privilege, promising at the same time to maintain certain living and working standards in managing the prisoners. John H. Powell, for example, who was associated with both the Powell & McLean Company and the Dowling Park Naval Stores Company, submitted a bid in 1909 offering the state $237.50 per person per year for all of the available state convicts for four years. Just a few years later in 1913, the Blue Creek Company offered $280 per person.[31]

Leasing convicts from the state involved relatively strict rules and competition, so only the larger companies tended to bother with it. In 1908, for example, the only Taylor County companies leasing state convicts were the Blue Creek Company at Thelma, the Taylor County Naval Stores Company at Perry, and the Dowling Park Naval Stores Company at Waylonzo. Other companies leased convicts, but they obtained them from counties, rather than the state. They were not limited to just the local county prison; the law allowed a county to send its prisoners to companies far away if they so chose. One state convict inspector noted in 1913, for example, that the Dowling Park Naval Stores Company's camp at Ewing Springs contained prisoners from Jackson, Baker, Alachua, Taylor, Madison, Duval, Calhoun, and Hamilton counties.

Much like the state, county governments saw convict leasing as a revenue stream. When they hired out a prisoner, they benefited twice in that they did not have to pay for the prisoner's upkeep and they received a rental fee from the company that leased him.[32]

Life in a turpentine camp was no picnic for any worker, convict or free, but prisoners experienced especially tough circumstances on a daily basis. They typically worked between six and seven days a week, from "can't to can't," meaning from the time they could not see in the morning to the time it became too dark to see at night. To prevent escape, they were kept in a stockade when they were not at work, often chained together even as they ate and slept. They were under the constant supervision of a "captain," who meted out severe punishment to prisoners who failed to follow instructions or worked too slowly.[33]

The state set standards for the prisoners' health and welfare, and periodically sent inspectors around to make sure companies were following the rules. Records from these inspections reveal just how unpleasant the conditions in a prison camp could be. One inspector informed Governor Napoleon Broward in 1906 that the Malloy Brothers' camp at Spring Warrior was "in anything but good condition." The prisoners' sleeping quarters were only large enough to provide a space about 14 inches wide for each man. The convicts also complained of not having enough to eat, although the inspector said he could not find any evidence to support this claim. In 1913, a different inspector found the stockade at the Dowling Park Naval Stores Company's camp at Ewing Springs to be infested with bedbugs. The Blue Creek Company's stockade also came under regular scrutiny.[34]

Punishment was the most severe aspect of the convict leasing system. Prisoners could legally be whipped, although the practice was controversial even in the earliest years of the 20th century. The state required each company to keep records documenting when and how each prisoner was punished, down to the number of lashes. Reports from the Blue Creek Company at Thelma, for example, showed that prisoners often received anywhere from three to ten lashes for "disobedience," "laziness," or merely "bad work." As cruel as this system was in the first place, state inspectors did sometimes step in when the behavior of the "captain" took a clearly sadistic turn. One captain working for the Dowling Park Naval Stores Company came under fire in 1913 after prisoners died under questionable circumstances on his watch in two different camps. One prisoner was shot by a guard at Ewing Springs not long after complaining he could no longer work because of severe injuries to his hands. The investigation revealed the prisoner had asked his fellow prisoners to push him into the Fenholloway

River to end his suffering. Another prisoner took his own life at Athena by swallowing carbolic acid soon after that same captain was transferred there. State Convict Inspector J.B. Thomas detected something "radically wrong" in the captain's management and asked the Secretary of Agriculture to intervene. In another case in 1908, a Taylor County convict boss received six months of state prison for mistreating the men under his guard.[35]

Most of these dire conditions went unnoticed at the time, mainly because the camps and their prisoners were highly isolated from the outside world. Also, many of the prisoners were from other parts of the state, far away from the prying curiosity of friends and relatives. As a result, the most visible impact of the naval stores industry in Taylor County was the money it brought into the area. In 1914, for example, naval stores accounted for more than a third of the county's wages, and nearly half of the county's industrial workers. Turpentine operators, moreover, were crucial to the founding of many of Perry's most important institutions in the early 20th century. Duncan G. Malloy, for example, was the founding president of the Perry Banking Company, as well as president of the Perry Grocery Company and the United Hardware & Furniture Company. He was also a founding incorporator of the Perry Electric Company. His brother, J.H. Malloy, typically invested in the same corporations, as did other naval stores operators like Thomas Puckett and John H. Powell.[36]

Thomas B. Puckett, a prominent turpentine manufacturer in Taylor County, as well as a founder of the Perry Grocery Company.

(Image courtesy of the Taylor County Historical Society)

Taylor County's turpentine industry remained strong for several decades, although newer companies began to replace the original trailblazers in the 1920s. The largest of these was the Aycock-Lindsey Corporation, which first began buying up land and equipment in Taylor County around 1917. The company started out at Waylonzo, but quickly spread out, using Camp Nathan near Athena as its headquarters. At its peak in 1928, the company reportedly employed 1,400 men, operated 11 stills, and owned its own system of tanker cars for shipping its products to market. The operation produced a grand total of 54,358 barrels of rosin and 15,786 barrels of turpentine that year. In addition to working trees on its own land, the company also contracted with local lumber companies—namely Brooks-Scanlon and the Putnam Lumber Company—to tap the trees on their lands before they were cut for lumber.[37]

J.O. Huxford began buying and leasing land for turpentine operations in 1929, kicking off what would be a successful two-decade run in the south-central portion of the county. His main camp was located off the present-day Beach Road near its intersection with the Potts Still Road. The Holmes, Strickland, and Westberry families also had naval stores businesses during this period, followed up somewhat later by Andrew Dias Poppell, who used the long-standing turpentine town of Waylonzo as his headquarters.[38]

Timber

With railroads quickly penetrating Taylor County's enormous stands of virgin pine timber, it was not long before lumber companies began looking for opportunities to buy them up. "Everything is on a boom," the *Ocala Evening Star* said of the county in 1900. Perry M. Colson, a timber buyer from Gainesville, estimated in 1905 that Taylor and Lafayette counties collectively had more than five billion board feet of yellow pine. There were also massive stands of cypress and red cedar along the coast and around inland swamps and ponds.[39]

Much of the land was still tied up in the large tracts granted by the state to Sir Edward James Reed as part of the Disston-Reed agreement of 1883, although by this point most of that had passed to successor companies. This allowed interested timber magnates to buy up massive chunks of the county's territory all at once. The Wade & McNair Land Company, for example, bought about 100,000 acres of Taylor County land for timber and turpentine in late 1902. O'Brien & Irwin, an outfit based in Minnesota that would eventually spin off multiple lumber businesses in Florida, purchased 54,000 acres in 1903 for $378,000. The next year, J.S. Betts & Company of Ashburn, Georgia paid $240,000 for 40,000 acres, most of which later went to the Dowling lumber interests.[40]

The first commercial mills were small, and not much more complex than the water-powered sawmills that locals had used since the Civil War. The town of Fenholloway was an early site for mill development—it was the only sawmill site that made the Secretary of Agriculture's list in 1895, with an annual output of $2,000 worth of lumber. William L. Tedder of Live Oak built another mill at Fenholloway as early as 1904, and used the Drew family's Florida Railway to ship lumber out to the larger trunk lines.[41]

Boyd was another early center of lumbering activity. An early plat of the town filed with the county clerk's office in 1904 used the name "Nelray," but a post office application filed that same year by Mrs. Sonora M. Parker used "Boyd." The name may have derived from Boyette Poppell Blanton, who owned a quarter of the land on which the new town was to be situated. A relative, E.L. Blanton, owned the rest of it. By 1906, almost the entire town was owned by William E. Cox, who maintained a sawmill and supplied timber for trestles when the Oglesby family's South Georgia Railway came through. Unfortunately, Cox died in 1907 of complications from malaria. Two years later, three Weaver brothers—Thomas, Samuel, and John—teamed up with their brother-in-law John H. Loughridge, and established the Weaver-Loughridge Lumber Company, with their main mill at Boyd. The Weavers had previously operated lumber businesses in Georgia, Alabama, and Louisiana, and would later establish the Pinellas Lumber Company in St.

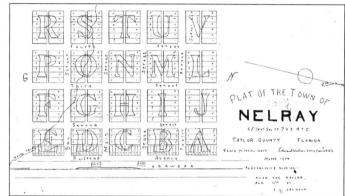

Original plat for Boyd, drawn in 1904 by Civil Engineer Edward Wilson. The name "Nelray" was apparently used in the early planning stages for the town.

(Copy of this map in the author's possession)

Petersburg. Weaver-Loughridge quickly began buying up land throughout the county, and by 1919 the mill at Boyd was sawing 100,000 board feet of pine and cypress daily.[42]

Thomas Dowling and his associates, who had been instrumental in bringing the LOP&G Railroad into Taylor County, shipped most of their logs back to their large mills at Alton in Lafayette County and Dowling Park in Suwannee County. In 1907, however, Dowling sold his North Florida logging interests and the railroad and invested in another concern farther south. The new owners included Henry Harding Tift, William Leroy Roach of Muscatine, Iowa, and Richard Warren Sears, co-founder of the mail-order giant Sears, Roebuck & Company. They immediately began expanding the former Dowling lumber empire, renaming it the Standard Lumber Company in 1910.[43]

Standard, with William Roach at the helm, began building partnerships with other investors and landowners, eventually gaining control of more than a million acres of land in Taylor, Lafayette, Suwannee, Wakulla, and Jefferson counties. The conglomerate generally marketed its products under the name Standard Lumber Company, but most of the actual millwork was done by subsidiary corporations. The largest of these was the Taylor County Lumber Company, a partnership between Roach and Peter Kuntz of Dayton, Ohio. The company built a mill at Springdale, located about halfway between Perry and Hampton Springs less than a mile north of the LOP&G. Just a year after opening in 1913, the mill was processing 100,000 board feet of cypress and pine daily. Despite being so close to the county seat, Springdale became a town all its own with a school, church, hotel, and company houses lined up along wide streets. A post office was established there in 1914, with the company's sales manager, John E. Graves, as the postmaster. Operations continued at Springdale until the mill burnt down in 1925.[44]

Sears and Roach teamed up with an eager young lumberman named Thomas Hamilton to co-found another subsidiary in 1913, the Rock Creek Lumber Company. The mill was located near Hampton Springs, and put out about 50,000 board feet of yellow pine lumber per day. A third entity, the Econfena Lumber Company, also came about in 1913, a joint effort between Sears, Roach, and the Weaver-Loughridge Lumber Company. The mill, completed in 1914, was located on the east side of the Econfina River about two miles southwest of the LOP&G, which had been extended to the logging camp at Econfena at milepost 62 in 1911. It consisted of a sawmill, planing mill, and shingle mill. The town that sprung up to serve the workers was named Loughridge— its post office opened in 1915 with Thomas W. Johnson as postmaster.[45]

Rock Creek Lumber Company Engine No. 1 near Hampton Springs, circa 1915.

(Photo courtesy of the State Archives of Florida)

The mill operated until it was destroyed by fire on June 13, 1917. The company chose not to rebuild, and the railroad spur linking Loughridge to the LOP&G trunk line was abandoned around 1921. Some residents appear to have stayed for a while after the mill burned, because mail continued to be delivered there until 1925. Eight of the young men from Taylor County who served in World War I listed Loughridge as their place of residence, including Jesse Sheffield, George Burney, Benjamin F. Callihan, Thomas Padgett, Ross Page, Perry Pitts, Pasco Young, and Capus Leggett. Evidence of the mill's existence can still be found at the site. Bricks from the mill buildings and company houses are still scattered through the pines and along the river, and that wide spot in the Econfina is still called the Mill Pond.[46]

While the Standard Lumber Company and its subsidiaries logged the woods west of Perry, another large timber operation was ramping up in the southern half of the county. William O'Brien, a millionaire Minnesotan who bought up thousands of acres in Taylor County at the turn of the century, partnered with fellow lumber magnate Samuel J. Carpenter in 1913 to establish the Carpenter-O'Brien Lumber Company. Although O'Brien's land holdings were concentrated in and around Taylor County, the new corporation built its sawmill at Eastport northeast of Jacksonville. The plan was to transfer the logs from the company's logging camps to the sawmill via the Atlantic Coast Line Railroad.[47]

Carpenter-O'Brien was mostly interested in logging yellow pine, but their land holdings contained a massive amount of virgin cypress timber. Rather than set up two separate mills, Samuel Carpenter invited colleagues from his adopted home state of Louisiana to help. The Burton-Swartz Cypress Company, which had been logging cypress in that state since 1905, was running low on timber at the time, and had recently begun acquiring land around the Everglades, mainly in Lee, Collier, and Hendry counties. Carpenter convinced William Burton and Edward G. Swartz to form a separate company in Florida to log and saw the cypress trees on the lands belonging to Carpenter-O'Brien. The new corporation—the Burton-Swartz Cypress Company of Florida—was chartered on December 12, 1913, with Burton as president, Swartz as vice-president, and Samuel Carpenter and William O'Brien as directors. Carpenter-O'Brien ended up controlling slightly less than half of their partner company's stock.[48]

Burton-Swartz originally planned to build a cypress sawmill alongside the Carpenter-O'Brien mill at Eastport near Jacksonville, but William Burton insisted on building at Perry instead. This put the mill much closer to the actual logging operation, and saved the company from paying the high rates the Atlantic Coast Line would have charged to ship the logs all the way across the state. Perry's town council was delighted to have the new plant as a neighbor. When Burton-Swartz began hinting that it might locate a plant within the county, the council members voted to extend the city limits to include the new mill site so they could exempt it from paying taxes.[49]

The sawmill was an enormous, sprawling 400-acre facility located west of Perry on land that had previously belonged to Judge Robert Henderson.

Huge cypress logs arriving by train at the Burton Swartz sawmill in Perry, 1925.

(Photo courtesy of the State Archives of Florida)

Ground was broken in March 1914, the first log was sawed on December 10 of that year, and the first shipment of lumber went out on October 1, 1915. The mill could process a stunning 120,000 board feet of lumber per day, plus 35,000 shingles and 35,000 lath boards. Logs arriving from the field were stored in a large pond covering nine acres, and more than three miles of standard-gauge railroad tracks carried logs and lumber wherever they needed to go within the complex.[50]

A force of 600 workers staffed the mill, a combination of locals and veteran sawmill hands from the Burton-Swartz mills in Louisiana. This migration of labor brought a number of new names into Taylor County, including Louque, Begue, Savoie, Borklund, McPhail, Heins, Rose, and many more. The company provided comfortable housing for its workers in what was called the Burton Swartz "quarters," which covered about twelve city blocks and featured indoor plumbing, sewers, and landscaping. There was also a boarding house and a hotel for visitors who came to observe what the *American Lumberman* called the "modern miracle" of the plant's efficiency and design.[51]

Like most timber and turpentine operations, Burton-Swartz had a company store, but locals convinced the company to put it in downtown Perry instead of near the mill. The Burton-Swartz Mercantile Company, as the store was called, was located in a stately two-story brick building at the corner of Jefferson and Green streets, southwest of the courthouse. It was as complete a department store as Perry had ever had up to that point, selling everything from hardware and farm implements to toys and clothing and ladies' umbrellas. Anyone could buy goods with cash, but mill employees also had the option of taking out an advance on their next paycheck. The company paid these advances in paper or aluminum scrip, which could only be used at the company store.[52]

Burton-Swartz also took steps to look after the workers' physical and spiritual health. The company supplied a doctor, whose salary was paid partly with deductions from every employee's paycheck. It also provided land for

Burton Swartz company store, located on the southwest corner of Green and Jefferson streets in downtown Perry.

(Photo courtesy of the State Archives of Florida)

churches, since at that time there were no Catholic or Episcopal churches in Perry, and many of the newcomers from Louisiana were of Episcopalian or Catholic faith. The original Catholic church, completed in 1918, was located at the western end of Main Street and called St. Albert's Mission. Itinerant priests from Tallahassee or Lake City said mass at the church periodically at first, but even without a permanent priest the Catholic community gathered every Sunday to pray and read the catechism. A few Episcopalians lived in Taylor County prior to the establishment of the Burton-Swartz mill, but they lacked a permanent building of their own. In 1921, William Burton donated a parcel of land on West Green Street to the congregation, on which was built St. James Episcopal Church, which still stands today.[53]

The arrival of Burton-Swartz accelerated the growth that had already begun with the railroads and turpentine industry. With so many new people relocating to Perry, the value of land jumped dramatically. Lots that had sold for nine dollars in 1870 were now priced in the hundreds. One visitor recalled seeing a large sign on a vacant downtown lot that read "This choice lot $800. Next Monday the price will be $900."[54]

Carpenter-O'Brien and Burton-Swartz jointly operated a large logging camp called Carbur, located near present-day Salem on the Atlantic Coast Line. When it came time to name the camp, the directors struggled to come up with something. William Burton already had a town named for him in Louisiana, William O'Brien had just been honored with a steamboat named for him, and Samuel Carpenter would not let the group use his name. Mark L. Fleishel, general manager of Carpenter-O'Brien until 1919, hatched the idea of naming the town "Carbur"—a contraction of the names of the two companies, Carpenter-O'Brien and Burton-Swartz.[55]

Edward G. Swartz laid out Carbur with streets and avenues on a 640-acre plot. It had everything the workers needed, including a barber shop, school, hotel, two churches, a doctor's office, and even a dry cleaner. The company store was called the Carbur Mercantile Company, and it operated on the same basis as its sister store in Perry, offering employees advances in the form of scrip. The company doctor usually traveled back and forth between Carbur and Perry, seeing patients from both the Burton-Swartz mill and the logging camp, plus non-company citizens. John Clement Ellis and J.R. Richardson were both company doctors at various times in Carbur, as was Walter J. Baker, who started there in 1922. When Louise Childers interviewed Dr. Baker in 1975, he recalled delivering his first baby, for which he was paid two deerskins, a venison ham, and the honor of having the little girl—Jo Baker Whiddon—being named for him.[56]

Employee housing was modest but comfortable. The houses were built of solid yellow pine and cypress. Like the Burton-Swartz quarters in Perry, housing was segregated, with houses for white and black employees separated by a wide avenue. All had running water, although most did not have flush toilets, at least not at first. Many of the homes had electricity, supplied for many years by the town's own power plant. There was also a boarding house for bachelors, nicknamed the "bull pen." The company deducted the rent from each employee's paycheck.[57]

During their off time, workers enjoyed a wide variety of amusements, including basketball, football, fishing, horseback riding, dances, movies on Saturday nights, and trips to Keaton Beach. The Carbur baseball team regularly traveled by car or train to other towns for games, and hosted their opponents at their own baseball diamond as well. Dowling Park, Otter Creek, Pisgah, Perry, and Tiger Ridge were some of the town's regular challengers. There were Methodist and Holiness churches, and Prissy Goodrich even started a bridge club. A Mrs. Nelson came from Perry periodically to provide piano lessons.[58]

As with any large settlement, there was occasionally trouble. Loggers who spent their days in a hot, dangerous work environment often liked to blow off steam, which sometimes took the form of drinking or gambling. Most of Carbur's heyday took place during Prohibition, but that did not stop the local juke joint from selling moonshine, most of which was produced by nearby farmers. Good times sometimes turned into bad behavior, leading to public intoxication, fights, and the occasional stabbing or shooting. The town had no police force, but it did have "quarter boss" Captain Henry Slaughter and

"Daddy Brown," the local justice of the peace. Slaughter's job was to make sure employees got to work on time every morning, and to handle cases of law breaking. There being no jail, he sometimes ended up handcuffing offenders to a porch rail to keep them in check until morning. Brown held court on Mondays to try cases, which usually ended with the culprit paying a small fine. Repeat offenders were taken to the county jail in Perry. In cases that resulted in a death, Slaughter would call one of the undertakers from Perry to get the body. If a deceased worker did not have any money or family members to claim his body, he would be buried in a "Boot Hill" cemetery near town.[59]

One of the brightest spots in Carbur's history was the development of its school. Before Carpenter-O'Brien and Burton-Swartz established the town, three different one-room schools served the area. In 1921, county school

Class at the Carbur School, circa 1920. Back row, left to right: Annie Kelly, Isabelle Martin, Ula Dilbon, Edna Raulerson, Thelma Borklund, Winnie Shaw, and Maxine Cannon. Middle row, left to right: Josephine Airline, Gracie Whitfield, Ruby Whitfield, Emily Livingston, Jessie Herrington [?], and Essie Raulerson. Bottom row, left to right: Verdie Ezell, Coal Slaughter, Buster Herrington, James Herndon, Cecil Poitevint, Richard Livingston, Myrl Richard, and Mr. Meeks (teacher). Billie Ellis is in the window.

(Photo courtesy of the Taylor County Historical Society)

superintendent W.T. Cash oversaw their consolidation into one facility at Carbur, and managed to get it accredited as a high school. It served the children of both the logging employees and their neighbors in the surrounding region. The new building cost $5,000 to construct, and had six classrooms on two stories, with an additional auditorium that seated up to 400 people. Alton H. Wentworth, who would later serve Taylor County as a state legislator and county school superintendent, was principal there for a number of years. During the 1926-27 school year Carbur had 265 students in first through eighth grades, and 35 in the high school grades.[60]

On November 5, 1917, the Carpenter-O'Brien Lumber Company announced that it had sold its sawmill at Eastport and all its timber holdings on the Gulf coast—including Carbur—to the Brooks-Scanlon Lumber Company of Minneapolis. Brooks-Scanlon had existed since 1894, when Michael J. Scanlon teamed up with three members of the wealthy Brooks family and a few other investors to go into the sawmill business in Minnesota. In 1905, the corporation expanded southward with the purchase of 40,000 acres of timber and a new sawmill at Kentwood, Louisiana. It also bought up timberlands in Oregon and the Bahamas, as well as a paper mill in British Columbia. By 1915, the supply of timber around Kentwood was dwindling, which led the company to go hunting for new forests to buy. Brooks-Scanlon had purchased thousands of acres of land from William O'Brien when he was still operating mainly in Minnesota, and Michael Scanlon was a stockholder in Carpenter-O'Brien's Florida operation. This close association, combined with the right price, made the buyout an easy transfer. Scanlon took over as president of Carpenter-O'Brien and changed the name to the Brooks-Scanlon Corporation in January 1918. The deal also included Carpenter-O'Brien's interest in the Burton-Swartz Cypress Company, which meant the old dual logging arrangement at Carbur could continue without interruption.[61]

In an effort to increase production at Eastport, Brooks-Scanlon established additional logging camps at Scanlon and Camp Hampton in Taylor County, as well as Broscan and Dixie Camp on company lands in Dixie County. Like Carbur, these were joint operations with Burton-Swartz Cypress Company, although none of them were ever quite as large. Scanlon, located just west of the Econfina River on the LOP&G, was the most prominent of the two Taylor County operations. It was active from about 1922 to 1942, and at its height had a workforce of about 500 men, both white and black. The workers and their families lived in segregated housing similar to Carbur, and had many of the same amenities, including a barber shop, commissary, company doctor, and church. Scanlon started out with its own school, although it was consolidated with the Waylonzo, Covington, Oakland, and Cabbage Grove schools around 1930 to form one school at Cabbage Grove. By then the county had built up the roads to a considerable degree, and the children could be transported by bus.[62]

In the early Brooks-Scanlon years, the company's directors were content to follow the old system, whereby cypress timber logged at the camps would be transported to Perry for milling by Burton-Swartz, and the pine would go to the big sawmill at Eastport. A small railroad dispute originating in Georgia in 1926, however, set in motion a chain of events that resulted in the whole Brooks-Scanlon mill operation moving to Taylor County. Since 1903, the Atlantic Coast Line and its predecessor railroad companies had based the shipping rates for logs on the "Cummer scale," a deal worked out with the Cummer Lumber Company that operated near Jacksonville at that time. Carpenter-O'Brien made a similar deal with the ACL in 1914, and over the next twelve years the railroad shipped approximately 700 million board feet of timber at the Cummer scale rates. In 1926, the Georgia Public Service Commission complained that these rates were harmful because it was so much more expensive to ship logs through Georgia than to send them to Jacksonville for export. The Interstate Commerce Commission agreed, and prescribed new rates for the ACL. Michael Scanlon and the heads of many other lumber companies fought to keep the Cummer scale, but lost out in the end. Furious, Scanlon declared that he would tear down the company's mill at Eastport and move it before he would let anymore timber be shipped across the Atlantic Coast Line Railroad.[63]

The railroad did not budge, and neither did Scanlon. On February 20, 1929, Vice-President Jeremiah S. Foley announced that Brooks-Scanlon would halt operations at its Eastport mill and transfer the entire facility to a brand-new town site about four miles southeast of Perry. The town would be named for Foley himself, who would oversee much of the planning and construction.[64]

Preparations for the new site had already begun. Brooks-Scanlon purchased land from Benjamin T. Whitfield, Harrison P. Padgett, and William J. Blanton in 1928, and hired Thrall-Shea of Louisiana as the contractors. While one team cleared the new site and laid the foundations for the new mill, another group painstakingly dismantled the old facility at Eastport, including a unique massive monorail system that moved logs and lumber from place to place within the complex. This herculean task took the company and its contractors only ten months to complete. By December, the machinery in the

A massive monorail system used to transport logs and lumber within the Brooks-Scanlon mill complex at Foley, photographed in 1936.

(Photo courtesy of the State Archives of Florida)

new plant was up and running, ready to process 275,000 board feet of lumber each day. Perhaps more importantly for the company's officers, very little traffic from Foley would have to travel over the Atlantic Coast Line. Brooks-Scanlon bought the Live Oak, Perry & Gulf Railroad from the ACL, who had bought it some years before from the Standard Lumber Company. Brooks-Scanlon also later bought the Oglesby family's South Georgia Railway, giving the company another option for transporting its products.[65]

Moving the mill also meant relocating a massive workforce of more than 2,000 people. Much like the transfer of Burton-Swartz to Perry from Louisiana, this move brought new families into Taylor County who had grown up in faraway places. Many of the Eastport workers had followed Brooks-Scanlon from its original home in Minnesota to Louisiana, and then to Florida in 1917. Now they would become Taylor Countians. They were joined in Foley by a number of workers from Carbur and Scanlon, as well as a few newcomers from the company's Kentwood, Louisiana operation. Just as William Burton had supported Catholic and Episcopal churches for his workers, Brooks-Scanlon provided for a Methodist church to be moved from Eastport to Foley, and the Foley family strongly supported the local Catholic church.[66]

The general layout of the mill town at Foley was similar to Eastport and Carbur, with a few improvements. The houses were painted and roomier, and had indoor plumbing, electricity, and screening to keep out the mosquitoes. A few of the houses were brought up to Foley from Carbur, since operations there were beginning to slow down, but most of the buildings were constructed anew under the supervision of Arndt Larsen. Rent was about ten dollars per month for a four-room house and $17 per month for a five-room house. Black workers were charged on a weekly basis rather than monthly; they paid $2.50 per week for a four-room house.[67]

The electricity and water came from the company's own turbines, and for a number of years the mill also supplied power to Perry. Employees received these services free in their company homes. Foley was also wired up for telephone service by the Gulf Telephone Company.[68]

Although the new settlement started out with dirt streets and sandy yards, the new residents took steps to beautify their homes and make Foley more attractive. Many families planted grass and rye, as well as flowers. The ladies formed a garden club, the Lantana Club, which had its own building and was a source of encouragement for the green thumbs in town. That building, incidentally, was moved to Forest Capital Park after the Brooks-Scanlon mill shut down, and it still serves as the headquarters of the Perry Garden Club.[69]

As with Carbur, a major point of pride in Foley was the local school, which opened in 1929. It operated for most of its three-decade existence as a junior high school, with the exception of the 1930-31 school year, when it was accredited as a high school. About 230 students in grades 1 through 10 attended Foley in its first year; the older pupils attended classes at Taylor County High School in Perry. Andrew E. Jackson served as principal for the majority of the school's tenure—22 years. Alton H. Wentworth was principal during its brief stint as a high school in 1930-31, and George A. Collins, Jr. filled the role in Foley's final seven years in the 1950s.[70]

Students at the school had a variety of extracurricular programs to choose from. During the first fall term Foley was open, local parents formed a parent-teacher association and hosted a Halloween carnival that became an annual event. The proceeds from the carnival went toward equipment, furniture, and supplies for the school, as well as funding for scout troops and other activities. Athletics were also a highlight. Foley had basketball teams for both boys and girls, with principal

Members of the 1940 Taylor County High School basketball team who won the state championship for their division. Front row, left to right: Ernest Jackson, Archie Swearingen, R.F. Ritch, Robert Williams, and B.N. Thomas. Back row, left to right: Coach Paul Worley, Ralph Massey, John Ritch, Fred Williams, June Bedgood, and George Reddick.

Andrew E. Jackson and Miss Georgie McCall as their respective coaches in the early years. Players from Foley often went on to supply talent to the Taylor County Bulldogs in Perry, including four members of the 1940 squad that won the State Class B Basketball Championship in Gainesville—Ernest Jackson, Archie Swearingen, Ralph Massey, and June Bedgood.[71]

By 1930, Burton-Swartz and Brooks-Scanlon were the major timber operators in Taylor County, with Weaver-Loughridge continuing to cut a significant amount as well. A few other companies are worth mentioning here, including the remarkable duo of the Wilson Lumber Company and the Graham-Paige Corporation, both based in Detroit. Graham-Paige was an automobile manufacturer, and used hardwood parts in making its car bodies. Wilson Lumber Company established a sawmill in Perry in 1928 and arranged to receive ash, maple, and magnolia logs over the Atlantic Coast Line and the Live Oak, Perry & Gulf. Graham-Paige followed later that year with a second plant next door that used the entire output of the Wilson mill. The Graham-Paige plant dried the hardwood cuts in large kilns and then shipped them out to the company's assembly lines in Wayne, Michigan and Evansville, Indiana. This setup only lasted about a year. The Great Depression and the auto industry's widespread move to all-steel bodies led Graham-Paige to close up shop. The plants were briefly leased to the radio maker Philco, who used them to manufacture wooden radio parts, which were then shipped off to Philadelphia for assembly. This operation also closed after just a year or so. Wilson Lumber Company took back over and continued operating as a hardwood sawmill until the mill burned in 1949.[72]

Another noteworthy if obscure company was the Blue Creek Logging Company, which operated at Thelma near Keaton Beach. It was no doubt connected to the Blue Creek turpentine producer that worked in the same area. The company's products reached the outside world using a railroad spur that snaked its way from the coast up to the LOP&G near present-day Foley. The entire Blue Creek operation suffered a serious setback on October 22, 1916, when a fire detonated 600 pounds of dynamite stored in one of the commissary buildings. The force of the blast destroyed buildings for hundreds of feet in all directions, windows cracked as far as seven miles away, and residents in Perry reported feeling the shock. The company went bankrupt the following year.[73]

The Putnam Lumber Company typically emerges in histories of Dixie and Lafayette counties, but it actually operated in Taylor County long before its mill opened at Shamrock near Cross City. Putnam was sort of a first cousin to the Carpenter-O'Brien Lumber Company, since both corporations were created to log timber on land belonging to William O'Brien. The Putnam entity was organized by O'Brien and E.B. Putnam in 1900, but it did not begin logging operations until 1919, when the Cummer Lumber Company decided to close its giant sawmill on the St. Johns River. Putnam leased the mill and began feeding it timber from the Big Bend region via the Atlantic Coast Line. One of the company's largest early logging camps was at Clara, located just northeast of present-day Tennille in Taylor County. The Shamrock mill came along later, in 1928.[74]

Clara had the dubious honor of being ground zero for the case that ultimately led the Florida Legislature to abolish the county convict leasing system. It started in 1921 when a 21-year-old man named Martin Tabert decided to take a break from his family's farm in North Dakota and travel around the United States, working part-time to fund his adventure. The trip went well until he ran out of money in Florida. A Leon County sheriff's deputy arrested Tabert on December 15, 1921, for riding a train without a valid ticket. The county judge found the young man guilty of vagrancy and fined him $25.00. Since Tabert could not pay his fine, the judge sentenced him to 90 days in jail.[75]

Portrait of Martin Tabert, who died in the Putnam Lumber Company logging camp at Clara in 1922. Outrage over his death led legislators to abolish the convict leasing system in Florida.

(Photo courtesy of the State Archives of Florida)

Leon County had an arrangement at this time with the Putnam Lumber Company, in which Putnam leased the county's convicts for $20.00 per month. Tabert, accordingly, was turned over to the company and taken to the logging camp at Clara. Shortly before his removal, however, he was able to send a telegram to his brother in North Dakota: "In trouble and need fifty dollars to pay fine for vagrancy. Please wire money in care of sheriff." The family sent money to Tabert in the manner he requested, but the sheriff sent the correspondence back unopened, saying the intended recipient was gone. The Taberts believed this meant Martin had secured his own release somehow, but then another letter arrived from the Putnam Lumber Company, stating that Tabert had died of a fever and other complications.[76]

The family had their attorney do some investigating, which ended with the Leon County sheriff and Putnam officials blaming each other for the situation. Then, an ex-convict named Glen Thompson wrote to the Taberts in July 1922 describing a far more sinister end to Martin's life. Thompson said he had seen a "whipping boss" named Walter Higginbotham deny Tabert properly fitting shoes, and then savagely beat the young man for working too slowly. Other former convicts also wrote, describing horrendous punishments and working conditions at the camp.[77]

After a state-sponsored investigation, the North Dakota Legislature passed a resolution calling on Florida lawmakers to launch its own probe and punish the responsible parties. The Florida Legislature appointed a joint committee to look into the matter, and determine if the convict leasing system ought to be abolished. The committee's findings confirmed that convicts were being abused at Clara and elsewhere in North Florida, and led lawmakers to abolish both the county convict leasing system and corporal punishment for state convicts. A jury found the whipping boss, Walter Higginbotham, guilty of second-degree murder, but upon appeal the Florida Supreme Court ordered a new trial, which never took place. Investigators determined that both Leon County and its sheriff personally benefited from a policy of arresting and convicting men for minor offenses and then selling them to the Putnam camp. The Florida Senate removed both the sheriff and county judge from office in 1923.[78]

In Retrospect

The timber and turpentine industries were major economic engines that pumped an unprecedented amount of capital into Taylor County. Even if the companies' shareholders exported much of the profits out of the region along with the logs and boards, the part they invested in local communities, families, and institutions was enough to effect major, permanent change.

Despite the hardships involved in laboring for these industries, the Taylor Countians who lived through the timber and turpentine bonanza years generally remembered them fondly. For many years, former residents of Scanlon would get together every November at the site of the old town to reminisce, see old friends, and show their children and grandchildren where all the buildings once stood. Former residents of Boyd who worked for Weaver-Loughridge began holding annual reunions in 1998. The organizers took the invaluable step of encouraging attendees to write down their memories of the community, which were then published in the reunion programs. These writings are now some of the richest available sources for understanding what life was like for everyday workers and their families in a North Florida lumber town in the early to mid-20th century. A common thread runs through these articles. Most of the authors, in their own ways, note that although their existence was a simple one without many luxuries, the strong bonds of family and community they enjoyed made life much sweeter. June Parker McLeod summed up the general attitude well in a short sketch published in the 1999 reunion program. "I remember many good times living in Boyd," she wrote. "I also remember some times that were not particularly good, but [they were] times that helped make me what I am."[79]

HOTEL DIXIE-TAYLOR — PERRY, FLORIDA

Postcard depicting the Dixie-Taylor Hotel at the corner of Green and Quincy streets in Perry.

(Image courtesy of the State Archives of Florida)

CHAPTER 6:

Perry: Gateway to Florida's West Coast

When Perry was incorporated by an act of the legislature in 1903, it had yet to pave its first street. The Suwannee & San Pedro Railroad was the only track in and out of town, and the only sidewalks were made from wooden planks. Cows and hogs still ranged freely in the streets. There was no sanitary sewer; only outdoor privies. Perry, and indeed all of Taylor County, was still very much part of the Florida frontier.

By 1930, however, virtually everything had changed. The streets were paved and illuminated at night by electrical lights, powered by the town's own power plant. Citizens communicated with one another by telephone, met one another downtown while walking along paved sidewalks, and shopped in dozens of stores. Automobiles, many bought from the town's own dealers, zoomed along the roads connecting the county seat with Fenholloway, Waylonzo, Carbur, and the world outside the county. Modernity was coming, and fast.

But the story of Perry's rapid transformation in the early 20th century was not just about growth or the arrival of new services and technologies. Local Taylor Countians and outside investors alike envisioned a new identity for the town—an exciting role in a state that was booming with activity. Real estate and tourism development were in a frenzy on the Atlantic coast, but many believed that with the right amount of capital, infrastructure, and promotion something similar could be achieved on the Gulf side. Businessmen in the Northeast and Midwest began taking an interest in Taylor County. Contemplating the growth of railway and road networks along the coast, these investors and local business leaders began excitedly referring to Perry as "Florida's West Coast Gateway." This enthusiasm spilled over into other projects seeking to turn even Hampton Springs and Steinhatchee into carefully planned developments rivaling Palm Beach and Miami.

In practice, many of these dreams were only partially realized, but the intense growth of Perry in the first three decades of the 20th century is undeniable. In addition to the new businesses that gave the local economy its vitality, new civic institutions emerged that gave the town character and distinction. Many of these institutions—and at least one or two of the businesses—still exist today.

Building Modern Perry

The rise of the timber and turpentine industries in Taylor County around 1900 brought a flood of new people, businesses, and construction, which necessitated a better system of organization for Perry. The county commission had managed the town's affairs in earlier years, but now it needed its own policies, oversight, and especially revenue to make much-needed improvements and accommodate the swift pace of change. The legislature assisted by passing an act in 1903 establishing Perry as a municipality with a mayor and town council. S. Hiram Peacock, Sr., John C. Calhoun, Jefferson L. Davis, J.T. Blair, and John O. Culpepper were appointed to hold the first election for these officers, plus a town marshal and town clerk.[1]

Even after transferring the responsibility of governing Perry to a new town council, the county government experienced growing pains during this period as well. The wood frame courthouse built in 1873 had already been replaced once in 1892, but as the county took on more residents and more statutory responsibilities the need for additional space persisted. On October 6, 1906, the county commissioners called for sealed bids for a new two-story courthouse of brick and stone. They selected a plan sketched by Montgomery, Alabama architect Benjamin Bosworth Smith in Georgian Revival style, and awarded the construction contract to Francis M. Dobson, one of Smith's associates. The original contract was for $54,000 and called for the building to be completed by September 1, 1907. Rather than demolish the 1892 courthouse, the commissioners had it

Taylor County Courthouse, completed in 1907.

(Photo courtesy of the State Archives of Florida)

moved to the side on log rollers, and later ordered the building sold to the highest bidder. The new building was briefly endangered by a fire in the spring of 1908 and sustained $123 in damage, but after that the building served admirably until it was torn down in 1969 and replaced with the current courthouse.[2]

The county was pleased enough with Smith and Dobson's work that they returned to these builders when the time came to construct a new county jail. The old structure had been built in the 1890s and was in dire need of repair or replacement. Governor Albert W. Gilchrist pushed the county commissioners to address the issue in 1910, which prompted them to call for bids and ship the old jail's prisoners up to Madison County until a new building could be completed. The county purchased two town lots at the corner of Washington and Lafayette streets for $350 and let the construction contract for $21,000. Dobson turned the new building over to the county on March 4, 1912. The jail has now stood for over a century and is listed on the National Register of Historic Places.[3]

At the turn of the century, Perry's white students attended school in a two-story wooden building located at the corner of Center and Lafayette streets. The structure had six classrooms on the first floor, an auditorium on the second floor, and a double-decker bell tower. Wood-burning stoves supplied the heat, and water came from a hand pump outside. The building's exact date of construction is unknown, but it was already in operation when the earliest surviving school board minutes were recorded in 1886. African American students attended a separate school, which at one time was located on the ground floor of the town's black Masonic Lodge on East Main Street.[4]

Fire destroyed Perry's white school on January 7, 1908, and the school board ended up renting a nearby building from John C. Calhoun for classes until a new facility could be constructed. Later that year, architect Benjamin Bosworth Smith of Montgomery once again came through with plans for a new seven-classroom school with an auditorium, which the board accepted with a few modifications. The new structure was completed by May 1909, and classes began the following school year.

Portrait of Nina Weaver, the sole member of Taylor County High School's first graduating class in 1913.

(Photo courtesy of the Taylor County Historical Society)

An annex was added to the building in 1914 and connected with the existing rooms through an arcade-like structure. The entire complex remained in use until 1957, when high school operations moved to a new facility at the east end of Lafayette Street.[5]

Perry's black school was also the victim of fire on at least two occasions in the early decades of the 20th century. School board minutes show that the building was damaged beyond repair sometime just prior to January 3, 1916, because on that date the board moved to furnish the materials to rebuild if school patrons would provide the labor. B.A. Williams received the contract to rebuild the school in August of that year, but not in the same location. Local black citizens donated a parcel of land across town on Bacon Street for the new school. This building stood until around 1922 when it was destroyed by arson. Classes for Perry's black students were held in privately owned buildings until a new school was constructed in 1931 with assistance from the Julius Rosenwald Fund.[6]

One of the striking features of Taylor County's education system at this time was the considerable gap between black and white schools in terms of the amount of funding and resources provided by the county. The county superintendent's reports to the state show that while the school board strongly adhered to the 'separate' part of 'separate but equal,' the 'equal' part was disregarded completely. During the 1918-1919 school year, for example, Taylor County reported having 75 total rooms in its white schools—for black schools there were only 2. That same year, the county spent $29.23 for each enrolled white student, while it only spent $5.93 for each black student. The county reported having 2,484 volumes in the libraries of its white schools, but not a single volume for black students. Black teachers received short shrift as well. The average monthly salary for all Taylor County teachers during the 1918-1919 school year was $72.65. Black male teachers averaged $58.33 per month for that same period, and black female teachers averaged $45.00. That $45.00, by the way, was the same rate as the lowest-paid white teacher in the district.[7]

Moreover, while Taylor County High School was growing in terms of attendance and the variety and quality of coursework it offered, none of these opportunities were open to black students at the time. Until the forerunner of Jerkins High School opened in 1931, no educational facility was available for black Taylor County students beyond the eighth grade. If a black Taylor County family wanted their child to receive a high school education, they had to send that child to one of the few high schools in Florida open to black students at that time—Jacksonville, Tampa, and Live Oak were popular options.[8]

As of 1900, no streets in Perry were paved, which made for a dusty down-town section. In 1911, the town council aimed to remedy the situation by ordering property owners to construct sidewalks between five and eight feet in width wherever their property faced the street. The county offered to construct sidewalks around the courthouse square, but only if the town council would do something to get the cows and hogs off the streets. This was a perennial problem in the old days of the open range. Since fences were not mandatory, live-stock often wandered around at will, including milk cows belonging to downtown residents. If a cow or pig became a nuisance, town officials could impound it, and the owner would have to pay a dollar to have the animal released. This issue surfaced at town council meetings well into the 1920s.[9]

An aerial view of Perry looking southward along Washington Street, circa 1912. No streets were paved at the time. The newly constructed county jail is in the foreground, with the 1907 courthouse in the background. The old Methodist Church building is seen on the left.

(Photo courtesy of the State Archives of Florida)

Paving was the most expensive part of improving the town's streets, and it took the longest to accomplish. Perry residents voted in 1917 to bond themselves for $75,000 to pave the town's main streets. The United States' entry into World War I squeezed off access to construction materials and capital, which delayed the work. By 1922, however, the town had made some progress. The Hutton Construction Company of Savannah had paved all of the streets surrounding the courthouse, and the town council had spent $150,000 connecting Perry's paved streets with the new Dixie Highway, which by that point was fully paved through Taylor County. Another contract was soon to be let for paving the residential streets, as well as portions of Main and Green streets. Pavement within the town limits was anywhere from 16 to 22 feet wide and composed of asphalt-macadam. C.E. Jackson was engineer for both Perry and the county.[10]

Sewage posed another problem that attracted the town council's attention. Outhouses or "privies" were the rule in Perry at the turn of the 20th century, but as the population grew this system was no longer feasible or sanitary.

By 1911 records show that a sewer system existed for at least some residents, and new sewer lines were included in a bond package put to the voters in 1917. Well into the 1920s, however, the system dumped into Spring Creek rather than using a drain field or treatment plant. In 1928, the town council voted to pay for a more sophisticated septic system.[11]

This was also the age of electrification for Perry. Electrical service first came in 1905, when T.J. Faulkner, C.A. Owens, and a Mr. Stanford established the Perry Ice & Power Company. The original plant was located at the corner of Faulkner and Lafayette streets, and depended on a steady supply of wood and sawdust to produce steam power. The company operated two wells, one of which was 10 inches in diameter and 76 feet deep. It served as both the public water supply and the source of the company's ice. The company went bankrupt in 1907, and service was temporarily halted. Joseph H. Scales of the Perry Banking Company and turpentine operators J.H. and Duncan G. Malloy resuscitated the plant in 1908 and renamed it the Perry Electric Company. As of 1911, the corporation had 52 customers; by the 1920s it had hundreds. Over time, control of the Perry Electric Company passed to outside investors, and it was renamed the Taylor County Electric Company. The town council contracted with this entity in 1925 to provide street lighting, and in 1929 the system was connected with Foley so the mill there could add power to the growing electrical grid. The Florida Power & Light Company, which still operates in Taylor County, took over the system in 1930.[12]

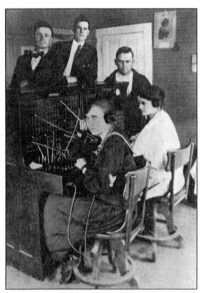

Operators working the Gulf Telephone Company's two new Stromberg-Carlson switchboards purchased in 1920. The equipment was located above Bloodworth's Drugstore. Standing are (left to right) Ward Hendry, Luther Cox, and Drew Hendry. Seated at the switchboards are (left to right): Pearl McCranie and Nannie Ross (later Shealy).

(Photo courtesy of the Taylor County Historical Society)

Telephone service began around 1904 when W.A. Hendry, J.T. Blair, and others established the Perry Telephone Company. Hendry bought out his fellow shareholders except Blair in 1905, and then reincorporated the firm as the Gulf Telephone Company in 1911. Wilson T. Hendry and Ollie

Williams were his partners in the new venture. The company's new charter reflected the directors' desire to expand—it called for an extension of the lines northwest to Monticello and southeast to Newberry. All service lines met at the company's central headquarters on the second floor of the Bloodworth's Drug Store building, where the switchboard was located until 1951. As of 1915, monthly service rates were set between $2.00 and $2.75 per line for customers in town. A second handset for home or office was an additional $1.00 per month. Rural rates were cheaper--$1.50 per month for customers living within two miles of the city limits—but only party lines were available.[13]

In 1911, W.A. Hendry hired a young man named Ernest Luther Cox as a night operator for the company. Cox quickly became a jack of all trades, collecting bills and making out statements in addition to his work as an operator. In 1915, he and his brother and sister bought Gulf Telephone Company from W.A. Hendry and his business associates. Cox was named president and general manager, and except for a brief stint in World War I he went on to serve as president for over six decades, continuing to work a standard 40-hour week into the 1970s. At the time of his death, Cox was widely believed to be the longest serving telephone company president in the history of the industry.[14]

Perry's population was growing as well. At the turn of the century, the town had a only about one hundred total residents. According to the census, that number had swelled to more than a thousand by 1910, and over 2,700 by 1930. The original street grid had to expand in order to make room for these newcomers. The Hendry family, led by brothers William Thomas and Wesley A., laid out subdivisions and sold lots through their newly established Hendry Abstract and Realty Company. In 1905, the company mapped out the "Hendry addition," located mostly south of where the old railroad depot is now located as far as Bacon Street, and bounded on the east and west by Center and Wilder streets. The following year, the company carved out another addition in the vicinity of where Main Street now meets U.S. Highway 19, and in 1908 the Hendry brothers teamed up with the Malloy family to create the West Brooklyn subdivision, located roughly between Spring Creek and U.S. Highway 98. A Jacksonville firm by the name of Brobston, Fendig & Company also laid out a few blocks in 1905 between Spring Creek and present-day Julia Drive, bounded on the east by Jefferson Street and on the west by Faulkner Street. Blair-Hinley, one of the main turpentine operators near town, opened up a new subdivision in the vicinity of their mill, which was bounded on the west by present-day Center Street and stretched east as far as Calhoun Avenue. More additions were established within a decade by the Faulkner family, J.C.

Curls, John C. Calhoun, and H.T. Wilder, over time creating the street grid that still serves Perry today.[15]

New Businesses and Institutions

More people meant a greater demand for goods and services, which helped transform downtown Perry into a major shopping center for both the townsfolk and residents of the outlying communities. General stores continued to thrive as they had for decades, offering everything from groceries to coffins and farming tools. S. Hiram Peacock's store, which he originally established in 1879, was one of the most prominent places to trade. It was originally located at the corner of Washington and Main streets, just across Washington from the courthouse. In 1909, Peacock's son Bud acquired the business from his father with the help of a partner, Gordon Kelly. The pair ran Peacock's store together until 1919, when Kelly died and Bud acquired full control. In 1923, Peacock's Store moved to the south end of the block, where it remained until Bud Peacock retired in 1946. Ione and Robert Prince operated the store briefly before selling it to the Emporium. Peacock's was an anomaly among buildings in Perry, as it had both a freight elevator and a basement.[16]

Quality and Service

Our Stock Of

Groceries Fruits Provisions Is Fresh

We Carry a well selected stock of

Dry Goods Shoes and Notions

We carry the largest and most complete line of Coffins and Caskets in the county. Funerals Directed.

R. H. Vereen

You can get us day or night. Day phone 29, night phone 157

Advertisement for R.H. Vereen in the December 13, 1918 edition of the Taylor County Herald. Vereen's was a true general store, selling everything from fresh groceries to coffins.

Several other proprietors operated general and dry goods stores in Perry during the early 20th century, including Robert H. Vereen, Henry T. Wilder, George R. Battle, Abraham Goldstein, David Mickelson, Louis V. Hester, and J.T. Horn. Grocers included Bird & Adams, Boyett P. Blanton, L.E. Caswell, Abner E. Morgan, Joseph A. Putnal, James G. Skipper, and Walter H. Slaughter. H.J. McMullen and H.C. Vick operated the Perry Meat Market.[17]

Two of the town's most resilient businesses were drug stores, located on either side of the courthouse square. Bloodworth's, at the corner of Jefferson and Green streets, was established in 1905 by Perry Franklin Bloodworth. Mr. Bloodworth was born and raised in Coopers, Georgia, not far from Milledgeville. He attended pharmacy school in Macon and worked at Holmes Drug

Store in Moultrie before marrying Miss Ella Holmes and moving to Perry to start his own store. O'Quinn's Drug Store was established by Barney O'Quinn, Sr., a native of Homerville, Georgia who trained in Atlanta and worked in Mayo before buying out the Tyson Drug Store in Perry in 1911. O'Quinn soon moved his store to the Blair Building at the corner of Jefferson and Main, where it still remains as of this writing. Other drug stores came and went over time, but for many years these two were the most prominent. They also fulfilled more than just pharmaceutical needs. Advertisements show that Bloodworth and O'Quinn sold everything from garden seeds to manicure sets, books, jewelry, flashlights, and electric irons in their stores. Their soda fountains were also popular places for young and old customers alike to find refreshment on warm days in town.[18]

Visitors arriving in Perry in the early 20th century had a variety of choices for lodging in the downtown district. The Peacock family operated a hotel at the corner of Main and Orange streets, and sent a carriage to meet every incoming train to meet potential customers. Just south of the Peacock Hotel, at the corner of Orange and Green streets, was the Vereen Hotel. The Palmetto Hotel operated on the west end of that same block, where the old post office building now stands. There were also a number of boarding houses for visitors who planned a longer stay, including the Wilder House on Jefferson Street just south of Drew Avenue. Segregated lodging for African Americans was available in a nearby boarding house at the corner of Drew Avenue and Quincy Street, as well as at "The Burt," located farther west along Drew between Calhoun and Faulkner streets.[19]

Gornto House, an early boarding house in Perry, circa 1900.

(Photo courtesy of the State Archives of Florida)

The Greystone Hotel, located across Jefferson Street from the Methodist Church, was originally built by Thomas Jefferson "Boss" Faulkner around 1904 as a private home, but in 1918 it was converted into a hotel, serving in that capacity until it closed during the Great Depression. The house, which still stands, has 13 rooms and 9 fireplaces, and the materials for the building's eponymous stone exterior had to be shipped in by rail at great expense. Nightly rates ranged from $2.50 to $3.00 when the hotel first opened.[20]

These lodgings served Perry adequately in the earliest years of the 20th century, but as the town's industries and railroad connections began to expand, local business leaders felt they needed something grander to offer the growing influx of visitors. A group of them formed the Perry Hotel Company in late 1925 and secured property at the corner of Quincy and Green streets. Frank A. Winn, an architect from Tampa, drew up the plans for a three-story building, which opened in late 1926 as the Dixie-Taylor Hotel, with 66 guest rooms and five stores downstairs. Griner Hotels, Inc. operated the hotel in its earliest days.[21]

A growing town also needed a bank. John L. Dew, a businessman from South Carolina, came into the area looking to start up a banking house in Perry in 1902. He pledged $5,000 toward the venture, but appears not to have succeeded in the end. The next year, however, a group of businessmen established the Bank of Perry, with Thomas Jefferson "Boss" Faulkner as president, S.H. Peacock as vice-president, and H.T. Crawford as cashier. George R. Battle, who had just arrived in town from South Georgia, was also involved with the bank, and became its vice-president by 1905. The new institution had an inauspicious start, taking up only a small corner of S.H. Peacock's store on the courthouse square. The safe had to be dragged up from Fenholloway by a team of eight mules, the Suwanee & San Pedro Railroad not having been completed just yet.[22]

View of the northwest corner of Main and Washington streets in downtown Perry, including the original single-story building of the First National Bank.

(Photo courtesy of the State Archives of Florida)

The Bank of Perry had a tumultuous first year. It was successful enough for the directors to construct a new brick building on the north side of the courthouse square, which it would occupy for just over a decade. Bad blood between Boss Faulkner and George Battle, however, led to Faulkner resigning his post and buying up a controlling interest in another bank that formed in 1903, the Citizens Bank. This bank's offices were located across the courthouse square at the corner of Green and Jefferson streets. The two banks' fortunes diverged in 1905. The Bank of Perry reorganized as the First National Bank and quickly began to grow. The Citizens Bank, by contrast, fell into hard times and reorganized in 1907 as the Taylor County State Bank. The new company did no better, and in 1908 the bank consolidated with its formal rival, the First National Bank. J.T. Blair was president at the time of the decision to consolidate.[23]

Some of the county's most prominent turpentine men joined forces in 1907 to establish yet another bank, the Perry Banking Company. Duncan G. Malloy was president, with John McLean of Powell-McLean and Thomas B. Puckett as vice-presidents. Joseph H. Scales, a Georgia native who had previously been cashier of the First National Bank of Tifton, was cashier of the new concern at first, though he quickly rose to the rank of vice-president and later president. Other directors of the bank included John H. Powell, president of the Consolidated Naval Stores Company in Jacksonville, R.L. Dowling of the Dowling lumber interests, and Morgan V. Gress, whose manufacturing company operated in Georgia, Florida, and Mississippi. The new bank set up shop in the building just vacated by the outgoing Taylor County State Bank. Several of these businessmen went on to form the Gulf Coast Investment Company, which constructed the Blair Building where the O'Quinn Drug Store has been located for over a century.[24]

These two banks would serve Perry through the remainder of the town's boom era leading up to the Great Depression. In 1916, the First National Bank constructed a new building in Greek revival style, which over the next few decades would house both the bank and a number of law and medical offices. The structure was on the verge of being demolished in the early 1970s, but a group of local citizens convinced the county commission to keep it, and it now serves as the headquarters of the Taylor County Historical Society.[25]

In an era before radio and television, Perry also needed a newspaper to keep citizens informed about events at home and around the nation. Taylor County has had at least one newspaper in operation continuously since 1895, although the names, owners, and at times quantity of papers have changed. When the 20th century began, Perry was served by the *Perry Herald*, owned by Thomas Jefferson "Boss" Faulkner. That year, John O. Culpepper and William Thomas Hendry bought the paper from Judge Faulkner, although Hendry only remained a partner in the venture for a short time. In 1903, Jefferson L. Davis, who back in the late 1880s had published the county's first newspaper, reemerged to establish a new sheet, the *Taylor County Advocate*. This lasted a few months before Davis decided to form a partnership with John Culpepper, their combined newspapers becoming the *Taylor County Herald*.[26]

But the dust had not settled just yet. W.T. Cash, who had been working his way up through the Taylor County school system as a teacher and administrator, established a new paper in 1904, the *Taylor County Topics*. "I

Portrait of William Thomas Cash, a Taylor County native who served as superintendent of public instruction and state senator before becoming Florida's first state librarian.

(Photo courtesy of the State Archives of Florida)

was lured into the newspaper game," Cash remembered, partly because the owners of the *Taylor County Herald* had been quarreling, and it was uncertain whether that paper could last. It was Cash, however, who threw in the towel a few months later, and Jeff Davis bought out the fledgling *Topics*, which he later sold to Culpepper. Another new paper, the *Taylor County Citizen*, appeared in 1905, the brainchild of Walter J. Lee. W.T. Cash became half owner of this paper the following year, but the *Citizen* ended up quickly selling out to J.E. Pound, who also purchased the languishing *Taylor County Herald*. After this last transaction, the newspaper situation in Perry stabilized for a number of years, although editors and owners continued to change periodically. In addressing the issue of Perry's volatile newspaper market, Cash quoted a man he once heard speaking on that subject in the office of the *Quitman Advertiser:* "There's not much money in newspapering, but there's more [damned] fun than anything else."[27]

Perry citizens formed a number of civic organizations during the early 20th century as well. One of the earliest of these was the Masonic Lodge, chartered in 1905. The Masons may have used the Perry Banking Company's building at the corner of Green and Jefferson streets as their first headquarters, as a Masonic emblem appears on the front. In 1921, they built a new three-story structure adjacent to the First National Bank on the north side of the courthouse square. The ground floor housed the Temple Theater, and the second floor was home to at least one doctor's office—that of Dr. George H. Warren. This building remained until it was destroyed by fire in 1944 and had to be rebuilt. Perry's African American citizens formed a separate Masonic Lodge sometime around 1907. Tax records from that year show the lodge owning a building located across Main Street from what is now the playground of the First Baptist Church.[28]

Another early civic organization was the Woodmen of the World, a fraternal society that offered tombstones, life insurance, and other benefits to its members. C.H. Dame of Ocala came to Perry in 1906 and established a chapter or "camp," with Perry mayor S.S. Sanford as the head. A separate camp called the Sulphur Spring Camp, was formed at Fenholloway sometime prior to 1919. The legacy of this organization can be seen in the large number of distinctive tombstones erected to the memory of deceased members in Taylor County cemeteries—usually shaped like a log with the organization's symbol on it.[29]

The Perry Rotary Club was chartered on May 11, 1923, at the Hampton Springs Hotel, with T. Joseph Swanson as president and R. Linton Thompson as secretary. Swanson and his friend Ernest Luther Cox had been sold on the idea of starting a Rotary chapter in Perry by Live Oak businessman Sid Hinley, who had recently become a member of the Rotary Club in his own town. The 16 original charter members were Clifford L. Cone, Ernest Luther Cox, Dr. John Clement Ellis, Homer L. Hays, Charles M. Jones, Thomas N. Jones, C. Frank Jones, W. Fount Kelly, A. Clifford Kirby, Charles W. Mathinson, Barney O'Quinn, James C. O'Rourke, John H. Parker, William S. Rose, T. Joseph Swanson, and R. Linton Thompson. The earliest known photograph of the Perry Rotary Club shows many of the charter members in 1927 in front of the Greystone Hotel, their usual meeting place in those days.[30]

The Perry Kiwanis Club formed in August 1924, also with a large group of local dignitaries on the original membership roster. Dr. Ralph J. Greene, Dr. George H. Warren, cashier Luther G. Blue of the Perry Banking Company, city clerk John E. Powell, Ben Lindsey, Captain W. Alston Brown, Perry F. Bloodworth, Bud Peacock, Dr. Wilson T. Hendry, John O. Culpepper, and Rev. H.F. Beaty of the First Presbyterian Church were just a few of the original charter members.[31]

Membership in these clubs was exclusively for men in the early days, but women had their own groups, especially the Perry Woman's Club. The club was founded on March 12, 1914, at the home of Mrs. J. Lee Ensign on Green Street, and immediately became affiliated with the Florida Federation of Women's Clubs. One of the club's first projects was to establish a reading room and public library, which they supported through subscriptions and later a membership scheme. Club members also personally worked on beautifying the courthouse square, planting St. Augustine grass and flowers, in addition to convincing the town council to pay for shrubs and palm trees to be planted around public buildings and churches. In 1920, the club reported providing equipment and supplies for Taylor County High School, including an encyclopedia.[32]

These were important contributions, but club members also took an interest in more serious matters affecting Perry's future, lobbying for causes they felt would improve the town's standing. The town ordinance penalizing owners of livestock that ran wild in the street was passed partly at the urging of the Woman's Club, as was the town council's action to improve its water system in 1915. The ladies of Perry also helped maximize the town's benefit from the burgeoning "Good Roads Movement," especially as plans were laid to put the Dixie Highway through Florida. Members of the club even traveled with county leaders to meetings of the Central Florida Highway Association, where the route for the new highway was being debated. "Our motto is 'We can, because we think we can,'" club reporter Daisy Culpepper explained to the press in 1916. "With this as our guiding star, we know that we are going to accomplish much for our club and town."[33]

In 1925, the Perry Woman's Club completed a new club house at the corner of Lafayette and Jefferson streets, where it still stands. Club members spent $150 on materials for beautifying the grounds, and furnished the kitchen with a stove, dishes, window shades, and silver. In his memoirs, Sam Register remembered the layout of the building causing a bit of a controversy among the club members during the planning stages. The proposed building was quite large, with more than enough room to hold public events. According to Register, some of the more conservative members were concerned that the new structure would be used to host dances, which their faith prohibited at that time. To prevent this, these members strongly favored an auditorium-style layout for the main room, with the floor slanting downward toward the stage. This would be excellent for meetings and lectures, but dances would be impractical. In the end, however, the club decided to go with a level floor, and it indeed has been used for many dances over the years. According to Register, a number of members did leave the organization because of this disagreement, but the remaining women continued their community work just the same.[34]

Youngsters also had the opportunity to get involved in community organizations. The county extension agent operated livestock and gardening clubs for boys and girls, the forerunners of today's 4-H and Future Farmers of America programs. In 1919, the county extension agent and home demonstration agent had 87 boys and 147 girls enrolled in Taylor County clubs, ranging in focus from cow and pig raising to canning and sewing. Children participating in these programs exhibited their work at the annual county fairs, and competed for prizes.[35]

Perry's first Boy Scout troop came along in 1917, most likely founded by Fred G. Warde, Secretary of the Taylor County Board of Trade at that time. Lacking funds for uniforms and other equipment at first, the new scout troop selected an unusual fundraiser to jumpstart their program. On June 7, 1917, troop leaders hosted a "fats versus leans" baseball game, all proceeds going toward uniforms for the scouts. All merchants and public offices closed at noon in support of the event.[36]

Scoutmaster Warde only lived in Taylor County a short time before relocating to Fort Myers, but new adult leaders took his place as the Boy Scout movement continued to grow in Taylor County. A. Clifford Kirby, a wholesale grocer in town, took over the troop in 1926, and a young lawyer named Claude Pepper also helped to keep up the program. Sam Register, a member of the Perry troop during the 1920s, remembered that local scouts seldom focused much on advancing toward the rank of Eagle Scout, which he said became apparent whenever the Perry troop attended regional meetings with scouts from other towns. The troop did, however, do a lot of camping, especially at the natural springs along the Fenholloway—Waldo, Ewing, and Iron Springs specifically. The boys would spend much of their time catfishing from the banks of the river, swimming, horse-playing, and enjoying plenty of good food, in addition to the occasional foray into activities their parents might have objected to. Mr. Register remembered, for example, that he and his fellow Scouts sometimes brought packs of cheap "Stroller" brand cigarettes out to their camping trips, enjoying them in secret along the creek banks.[37]

A variety of baseball teams, both in Perry and in the outlying communities of Taylor County, emerged during this period. While the schools sometimes organized teams of youngsters, the adults got in on the fun as well, and even traveled to nearby towns to compete. Such emphasis was placed on baseball that the Perry team and some of the lumber companies even hired semi-professional players to boost their star power. Sam Register remembered "imported" ball players making about $15.00 per week in the 1920s and 1930s, about double what a man could make doing other kinds of labor. Particularly good local men sometimes were paid as well, but not as much. The lumber companies paid for their ball players' salaries; the town teams usually paid their players with shares of the gate receipts.[38]

Perry had its own dedicated baseball diamond at least as early as 1916, but in 1920 Edward G. Swartz donated a plot of land for a new field, just across the Atlantic Coast Line tracks from the depot, roughly where the Skylark Motel now stands on U.S. Highway 19. As the prime season for playing baseball approached each year, chambers of commerce and other civic leaders would contact one another and try to form leagues. "We all love baseball," Tallahassee's chamber wrote to Perry and its other neighbors in 1920. "It makes the summers shorter and cools politics." Joseph H. Scales of Perry launched a similar campaign to establish a league in 1923, calling on teams as far away as Valdosta and Lake City to participate. In many cases, however, the matches between towns or lumber companies were arranged ad-hoc.[39]

In addition to the civic organizations named above, Taylor County business owners and professionals also had a few trade-related organizations that supported their work. Farmers and cattlemen had the Taylor County Livestock Association, which brought these citizens together to discuss issues of mutual interest, especially fencing policies and the state's efforts to rid Florida of scourges like the Texas tick fever. County doctors had the Taylor County Medical Association, organized as an affiliate of the Florida Medical Association around 1919. In addition to sharing knowledge about treatments and prominent health concerns, the members also set prices that they pledged to abide by. In 1919, for example, a standard house call within the city limits from 6:00 a.m. to 9:00 a.m. was $2.00. Outside of those hours the patient would pay $3.00. Residents located outside of town paid the same prices for the doctor's visit, but also had to pay mileage. Obstetric services cost $15.00 unless forceps were required, in which case the price went up to $25.00. Bone fractures fetched the highest price; treatment for those injuries could cost the patient as much as $50.00.[40]

The most dynamic group supporting the growth of business in Perry was the Taylor County Board of Trade, founded around 1915. This organization was the forerunner of the county's Chamber of Commerce, comprised of community leaders and business owners looking for ways to drive more people and companies to and through Perry. Several of its early leaders came from Tampa, including E.L. Williams and Fred G. Warde. Taylor County attracted the attention of these men because of the tremendous potential they saw in Perry, if only the Dixie Highway and a railroad link with Monticello or Tallahassee could be built. In addition to representing the county's interests at conferences and to the legislature, the Board of Trade also described Perry's virtues to the general public in glowing terms through advertisement. One brochure touted roads "as smooth as velvet," and crops never failing for lack of rainfall. There was no record of a case of sunstroke, the brochure claimed, and the city's water supply had a "very marked laxative effect," which at that time was considered especially beneficial for good health. "Perry is known as a Glad Hand Town," it said, "where the visitor is given a cordial greeting and made to feel at home."[41]

The Gateway to Florida's West Coast

The development of Hampton Springs was Perry's first major step toward becoming an important destination on a broader scale. The springs had been widely recognized for their medicinal qualities since before the Civil War, but at the turn of the 20th century, only primitive accommodations were available to visitors who came to drink and bathe in the famous waters. Some sort of hotel had been erected near the springs by 1902, however, because in January of that year the Madison newspaper reported that the hotel at Hampton Springs had burned. W.D. Smith had been the proprietor, according to the article, this likely being a relative of Sam B. Smith, who would soon marry Sallie Hampton, part owner of the springs property. By the spring of 1903, another hotel had been constructed, although visitors rated it poorly. "Everything there is in a state of crudity," sniffed a newspaper editor from Lumberton, North Carolina. "There is a hotel at it, one of the plainest of structures, with a capacity of about twenty-five people." The Lumberton delegation marveled at the springs themselves, however, commenting on the multi-colored mineral deposits left by the gushing water as it coursed down wooden troughs into the bathing pool.[42]

By 1904, the Hampton family had decided to do something more to develop the springs. Newspapers around the state announced that Captain Andrew Young Hampton would build a new hotel with modern conveniences, including hot and cold baths. It was completed by that summer, and included 27 guest rooms and a new bath house. By 1910, it was served by both the South Georgia Railway and the Suwannee and San Pedro Railroad. J.W. Oglesby, principal owner of the South Georgia Railway, had long been a fan of Hampton Springs, having camped there from time to time with his family since the 1890s. Sometime after the death of Andrew Young Hampton in 1910, Oglesby acquired a controlling interest in the hotel and began making improvements. Within a couple of years, the hotel had added steam heating for the dressing rooms at the bath house, a cement swimming pool, telephones, and other amenities. The parent company also began advertising Hampton Springs mineral water nationwide, promising it would help with everything from chronic stomach troubles to nervous disorders and even eczema.[43]

Hampton Springs quickly became one of the prime health resorts of Florida, drawing a large number of visitors throughout the year. Oglesby furnished the hotel with a high-class clientele in mind. It grew to 108 rooms under his leadership, with elaborate marble baths, fashionable wicker furniture, and a lobby floor of linoleum, which at that time was considered a real luxury. The entire building was steam-heated, and the running water and electricity available in every room came from the hotel's own plant. Guests could hunt in the surrounding forests, or fish in the Fenholloway River, aided by equipment rented from the hotel. Oglesby established a satellite camp on the Fenholloway closer to the coast for hunting and fishing, affectionately known as the "club house." With so much hunting and fishing going on, wild game and locally caught fish were frequently available on the hotel's menu. "You just ought to be here," wrote one Gainesville guest. "I am eating venison steak for breakfast and fine wild turkey for dinner every day … and I propose to stay here just as long as I can."[44]

Postcard advertising the Hampton Springs Hotel and the curative properties of its mineral water (circa 1930s).

(Image courtesy of the State Archives of Florida)

Perry citizens were rightly proud of having such a popular resort right on their doorstep, but they were increasingly aware of one serious shortcoming: there was no reliable automobile access. In fact, when J.W. Oglesby took over the Hampton Springs Hotel there were no paved highways anywhere in Taylor County, and only a handful of registered automobiles. This was a conundrum facing communities all over the state, and indeed the nation. Public highways had long been maintained by state and local governments during horse and buggy days, but up to this point they had been little more than wide trails with bridges. In other words, they were cheap and fairly non-controversial. The notion that governments would use tax money to pave public roads for automobiles, or that states might cooperate with one another to design and build hard-surface interstate roads, was still new and relatively untested. A few counties were already bonding themselves for "good roads," but there were also private groups attempting to build highways with tolls and subscriptions. It was an age of experimentation.

Taylor County's first attempt at paved highways began in 1911. John O. Culpepper, who represented the county in the Florida Senate at that time, introduced a bill granting Taylor and Lafayette counties the authority to issue bonds for building hard-surface roads. Soon thereafter, the county built three miles of crushed stone pavement at a cost of $5,180 per mile, but that was all.[45]

The real action began when Taylor County had the opportunity to be on the route of the Dixie Highway. Carl Graham Fisher, a Miami Beach real estate developer and co-inventor of the Prest-o-Lite headlight, hatched the idea for the Dixie Highway to get Northern tourists down to South Florida. He had tried a similar project—the Lincoln Highway—once before, with limited success. This time around, rather than seeking to build the road with private money alone, Fisher called on each community along the Dixie Highway route to pick up the tab for their portion of the roadway. The response was enthusiastic, and soon cities and towns from Michigan to Florida were clamoring to have the new road go through their neck of the woods.

Fisher and his backers organized a conference in Chattanooga in April 1915 to establish the Dixie Highway Association and decide on a route. The conferees called on each state governor affected by the new highway to appoint two commissioners to determine the best route for the road and then report back. Florida's governor, Park Trammell, appointed banker George W. Saxon of Tallahassee and Samuel A. Belcher, a road construction magnate from Miami. Fisher and many of the Dixie Highway's early supporters had long assumed the road would enter the state at Jacksonville and proceed down the Atlantic coast, paralleling Henry Flagler's Florida East Coast Railway. Gulf coast businessmen and civic leaders lobbied hard for a western option, however.

Perry was well represented in these discussions. The Taylor County Board of Trade sent delegations to Dixie Highway meetings in Orlando, Lakeland, and Madison, and asked the *Tampa Tribune* to help publicize the proposed western route. Joseph H. Scales of the Perry Banking Company was on the executive committee of the influential Central Florida Highway Association, which had members from Fort Myers to Tallahassee. W.B. Davis was on the Association's legislative committee, and John R. Kelly of Fenholloway was part of a team assigned to map out side roads connecting with the new highway.

These men all pressured Florida's Dixie High-way commissioners to recommend a split route through Florida, a loop that would serve both coasts.[46]

In the end, they won. By the summer of 1915, the Dixie Highway Association had approved both eastern and western routes through Florida, the western route leaving Tal-lahassee and proceeding southeast to Lamont and then to Sirmans, through Perry, and then off to Gainesville and points south. The remaining challenge was to figure out how to pay for the paving. Taylor County leaders, as in the other counties along the proposed route, had made big promises to get the new road routed through their area, but would the voters back them up? Joseph H. Scales and other highway enthusiasts formed a Taylor County Good Roads Association to lobby for a $600,000 bond issue to pay for the county's share of the work. The *Taylor County*

Portrait of Joseph Henry Scales, Sr., one of Taylor County's foremost business leaders in the early decades of the 20th century.

(Photo courtesy of the Taylor County Historical Society)

Herald helped by publishing figures explaining the costs and the potential benefits of having the Dixie Highway run through the county. When the bond election came on July 25, 1916, voters went two to one in favor of the proposal. Construction on bridges and culverts had already begun, and with the bond issue passed, Taylor County soon had its portion of the Dixie Highway completely paved.[47]

That left one major transportation problem unresolved. By 1910 Taylor County was well served by several major railways—the Seaboard came in from the northwest and terminated at Covington; the South Georgia came in from Adel and Quitman via Greenville and Sirmans; the Atlantic Coast Line looped in from the south; and the Live Oak, Perry & Gulf and Suwan-nee and San Pedro railroads came in from the east. Originally, the Seaboard was supposed to go through Perry and proceed south to the Suwannee River, and it was long assumed that the Atlantic Coast Line would complete the link between Perry and its terminus in Thomasville. Either of these "missing links" would have created a direct line connecting Perry with destinations all over the Midwestern United States, making the Gulf coast more attractive to investors and tourists from that region. By 1915, however, neither the

Seaboard nor the Atlantic Coast Line had completed the tracks that would close this vital gap. Instead, freight and passengers traveling north on the Atlantic Coast Line from Perry, Tampa, Fort Myers, and other points along the Gulf Coast had to first go through Jacksonville, adding several hours and over a hundred miles to the trip. It was widely believed that the two railroads had agreed to maintain the status quo on this issue, since it kept people and freight on their tracks longer, thus earning them both more money.[48]

After a while, business and civic leaders all along the Gulf coast realized what was happening, and vowed to find a way to force one or both railroads to finish linking Perry with the northwest. In 1917, the Taylor County Board of Trade sent a delegation to Tampa to meet with business leaders there and develop a strategy to approach the Atlantic Coast Line about finishing the so-called "Perry Cutoff." With the nation at war and the federal government controlling the railroads, however, the timing was all wrong. Gulf coast leaders and even Governor Sidney Catts approached federal railroad officials about compelling the Atlantic Coast Line to finish the road as a boon to the war effort, but got nowhere. ACL officials also showed no interest in changing course.[49]

Striking out with the Atlantic Coast Line, Gulf coast leaders considered a different strategy for compelling the Seaboard Air Line to finish its tracks from Covington to Perry. Although the Seaboard owned and controlled the Covington route, it was nominally the property of a subsidiary, the Tallahassee & Southeastern, which had long ago been given a franchise by the legislature to build all the way to the Suwannee River in return for grants of state-owned land. W.T. Cash, who was then representing Taylor County in the Florida Senate, suggested that if the company had received public land but not held up its end of the deal (i.e. finishing the road), it could be forced to either finish the missing link to Perry or give up its exclusive right to build it. The legislature passed an act a few months later giving the Seaboard until 1920 to build to Perry and until 1923 to finish its entire line to Gainesville or lose its franchise for the route.[50]

But the Seaboard continued to take no action in the matter, and when it came time to do something about it, proving that the company had forfeited its legislative charter was harder than previously thought. In 1923, the legislature passed an act directing the executive branch to take legal action against the Seaboard. When attorney general Rivers Buford reviewed the case, however, he publicly announced that there was no way for a court to declare a forfeiture. The very language of the law extending the Tallahassee Southeastern's franchise back in 1901 prevented such a measure. The Tallahassee Chamber of Commerce, which was deeply interested in the Seaboard extension, blasted this decision, and leaders even suggested that Buford was protecting the railroads at the Gulf coast cities' expense. Buford sent his correspondence to the newspapers and said that he could have easily filed a suit and let it drag on for years and made it look as though he was doing the Gulf coast a favor, but in his opinion it was better to just come out and tell the truth. The state could not force the Seaboard to finish its railroad to Perry while the Tallahassee Southeastern's charter was intact, and the legislature simply had not done its homework well enough to realize it.[51]

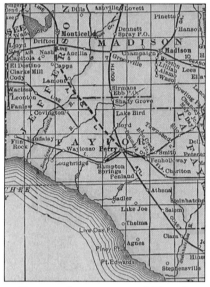

Excerpt from a map of Florida (circa 1922) showing railroads in Taylor County, as well as the anticipated "Perry Cutoff" connecting Perry with Monticello via the Atlantic Coast Line Railroad.

(Image courtesy of the State Library of Florida)

Sensing that the Seaboard might not be easily forced to act, Gulf coast leaders prepared to build their own Perry cutoff if necessary. In 1921, several of them formed the Florida West Coast Railway. Representatives from Fort Myers and Tallahassee were among the original incorporators, as well as potential investors from up north. Joseph H. Scales was their local contact in Perry. While the possibility of forcing the Seaboard to forfeit its franchise still existed, the company only contemplated finishing the short link between Covington and Perry. Once the state declined to even pursue a Seaboard forfeiture, however, Gulf coast representatives realized they might have to build the entire route from Tallahassee down to Tampa. To that end, the Florida West Coast Railway reorganized in 1924 with real estate developer M.D. Kelly at the helm. Kelly, a shrewd promoter from Tallahassee, immediately began selling the idea of a Gulf coast railway to Midwestern investors, using the slogan "Tampa to Chicago in 36 hours." "Big things are due in Western Florida," he told the *Milwaukee Sentinel,* "and the impetus will be felt in every city between Tallahassee and Milwaukee."[52]

Those Midwestern investors Kelly spoke to must have agreed, because within a few months several of them began quietly visiting points along the

Gulf coast and testing the feasibility of the railroad and other developments. Harper S. Hoover, a Chicago businessman who had been instrumental in developing the area around Grand Bay, Alabama, was one of the most interested. By early 1925, he had established a syndicate of northern and midwestern capitalists who quickly bought up more than 1.1 million acres of land along the Gulf coast, including 125 miles of coastline and river frontage. In June, the Hoover syndicate sent the most luxuriously equipped train of the Illinois Central Railroad down to Florida to bring its Floridian members up to Chicago for a big meeting at the Congress Hotel. There, the gathered businessmen formed the Florida West Coast Development Company, with plans to build a brand-new city at Homosassa and construct a new railroad down the Gulf coast. Another major railroad—though the company would not say which one—was also looking at purchasing the land and tracks necessary to connect with the new line at Perry and give it an outlet to the north.[53]

It is unclear whether the Hoover syndicate was bluffing about the new railroad along the Gulf coast just to prod the Seaboard and Atlantic Coast Line into action. The prospect had to have given the two railroads pause, since an entirely new line would have bypassed them both and left them without as much traffic from the western side of the peninsula. At any rate, engineers from the Atlantic Coast Line arrived in Thomasville in October 1925 to start surveying the route from there to Perry. In November, the company formally announced that it would finally build the Perry cutoff. The new line opened to tremendous fanfare on December 4, 1928. Representatives from railroads all over the eastern United States were aboard when the first Southland train arrived in Florida from Chicago over the line. A large reception committee formed at Perry the day before the big event, and met at the Hampton Springs Hotel to toast the new west coast gateway. Once the train made its inaugural stop in Perry on December 4, many members of the reception committee boarded the train and rode south to St. Petersburg. Perry representatives who rode the first train included John H. Loughridge, Joseph H. Scales, Claude Pepper, Mrs. May Plaskett, and Mrs. Willie A. Brown.[54]

Hoping to capitalize on a completed rail link with the north, several companies planned developments along the coast in much the same style as they were being built down in South Florida during the land boom. William F. Calhoun and Barney O'Quinn, Sr., for example, platted a town site at Steinhatchee in 1921, creating the street grid that is still in use today. The original plan called for 153 town blocks, with most of them divided into lots. Several of the avenues intersected at places where small springs emerged from the ground, with parks surrounding them. One park, called Riverside Park, was to be located roughly where State Road 51 now makes a westerly curve and becomes Riverside Drive. Another park called Royal Palm Park was to be located about where the Ideal and Sea Hag marinas are now located on the south side of Riverside Drive.[55]

Seeing that Steinhatchee was on the rise, two companies tried to build railroads directly into the new town. The first was the Perry and Gulf Coast Traction Company, chartered in 1919 by a dozen or so investors, including E.E. Sadler, William F. Calhoun, and Ellis and Lydia Bartholomew, the latter two being transplants from Ohio. Their plan was to build a railroad from Perry to Hampton Springs, and then down along the Gulf coast to Steinhatchee. It was clear they imagined a much more robust development, as they included in their corporate charter the right to build "hotels, parks, casinos and pavilions, and places of amusement." Not wanting to miss out on an opportunity, J.W. Oglesby's South Georgia Railway applied to the Interstate Commerce Commission for permission to build its own branch line down to Steinhatchee. The Commission rejected the company's request in 1926, saying there was insufficient evidence that Steinhatchee would ever become a significant port. If the War Department were to approve dredging and other improvements for the port, however, they might be more inclined to authorize a railroad. This decision would touch off a campaign to make Steinhatchee a deep-water port that would last into the 1930s.[56]

Neither railroad company succeeded in building a passenger rail line to Steinhatchee, but some of the investors quickly began working on another project farther up the coast. Ellis and Lydia Bartholomew, the Ohio couple who had invested in the Perry and Gulf Coast Traction Company, bought up some land near the mouth of Spring Warrior Creek and named it Boneta Beach. In 1926, they filed subdivision plats with the county commissioners, showing the coastal property carved up into a whole town's worth of lots separated by avenues with names like Buckeye, Western, and Seminole. Had Boneta Beach actually succeeded, it would truly have been a case of selling "land by the gallon," because many of the lots were located in the marsh. Eager to begin selling property to prospective buyers, the Bartholomews poured a concrete sidewalk along one of the would-be streets in the new subdivision. Tragedy struck, however, before the couple could realize their vision. The land boom began to falter in 1926, just as the Boneta Beach project was gaining steam, and Lydia Bartholomew fell ill and died in 1927. Facing these hardships, Ellis Bartholomew never finished developing Boneta Beach, and then he himself died in 1929. The only evidence of the grand project that still exists is the subdivision plats the Bartholomews filed with the county, the Boneta Beach Road, and one lonely strip of broken concrete sidewalk leading out into the marsh to a dead end.[57]

All that remains of the planned Boneta Beach subdivision is this single stretch of sidewalk in the marsh.

(Photo courtesy of the Taylor County Historical Society)

More investors from Chicago sought to use Perry's new rail connections to convert the popular Hampton Springs Hotel into an entire town, or even two. In 1925, a new corporation called the Hampton Springs Improvement Company filed subdivision plats with the county commission calling for hundreds of town lots and broad streets with names of the surrounding communities—Perry, Waylonzo, and Covington. Thomas B. Puckett, who by then had made a fortune in the turpentine business, platted a separate, smaller development he called Hampton Springs Villa. Rocky Creek ran through the middle of this proposed subdivision, and the street names were an eclectic mix of references to old Spain and American destinations like Fenway and Berkeley. Like Boneta Beach, these proposed developments fell victim to the collapse of the Florida land boom, and never got very far. Several of the four-inch iron pipes used by local surveyor Frank King to mark the exterior boundaries of the Hampton Springs Improvement Company site, however, are still in place and legally active today.[58]

In addition, a Chicago investor named Arnold Joerns went in with several partners and leased the Hampton Springs Hotel from the Oglesby family for 99 years starting in 1927. The syndicate planned to open the hotel for its normal tourist business, but to also build up the hotel's reputation as a hunting and fishing club. Charles Hesson, who had operated large resort hotels in Virginia, became the manager. Newspapers all over the eastern United States began advertising Hampton Springs water and the hotel again, with room rates of between six and ten dollars per night.[59]

Before the end of the Florida Boom and the onset of the Great Depression, there was one last major project designed to drive more traffic into Taylor County—the Gulf Coast Scenic Highway. The idea for such a road had existed since the days when the route of the Dixie Highway was being discussed. Since the Atlantic coast of Florida had a major artery linking Miami and Palm Beach and Jacksonville with the north, Gulf coast leaders wanted something similar funneling traffic into their region from the west. In 1925, a group of business-men formed the State Road No. 5 Association, named for the state highway that ran down part of the Gulf coast at that time. Their hope was to lobby the State Road Department and county governments to extend State Road 5 so that it would connect all the way from Tallahassee to Fort Myers. This would enable it to link up with the Tamiami Trail, which was already being built from Miami to the Gulf coast across the Everglades. There were also plans for a high-way along the Gulf coast in the Panhandle. Once completed, Florida would have a complete loop around the state, consisting of the Tamiami Trail, the Gulf Coast Scenic Highway (still Highway 5 at the time), and the Old Spanish Trail across the northern edge (later U.S. Highway 90). Joseph H. Scales of Perry was treasurer of the organization and a staunch advocate of maintaining State Road 5's line through Taylor County.[60]

In 1926, representatives from Gulf coast counties met at Panama City to form the Gulf Coast Highway Association. Joseph H. Scales was again named treasurer, and Thomas Puckett became a vice-president representing Taylor County. This new entity's goal was to get the Gulf Coast Highway built all the way from Pensacola to Fort Myers, hugging the coast as closely as possible to create a scenic drive for tourists. Some of the counties started the paving almost immediately, but getting the state involved proved difficult. The State Road Department did not initially put the Gulf Coast Highway on its list of high priority projects, and then once Governor Doyle Carlton was in office, funding for the project dried up almost entirely. The original plan for Taylor County's portion of the road had been for it to enter the county from St. Marks across the Aucilla River and follow the coast, crossing the Fenholloway well downriver of Hampton Springs and then passing through Steinhatchee before moving on to Dixie County. By 1928, the State Road Department had decided that this route would be too difficult and expensive to build, so they proposed moving it to higher ground through Hampton Springs and Perry via a road entering the county at Covington and roughly following the present-day Cabbage Grove Road. In the end, they routed the Gulf Coast Highway through Tallahassee and then along the existing Dixie Highway to Perry. The originally planned route linking Perry and St. Marks and Newport did not come to fruition until U.S. 98 was completed in the 1950s.[61]

* * *

In addition to its own growth, Perry also had the honor during this era of furnishing the state with some notable political talent. Cary Augustus Hardee, born in Taylor County in 1876 and educated in the local public schools, held several posi- tions of responsibility before ascending to the governorship of Florida in 1921. He taught in Taylor County, learned the law by reading his older brother's law books, became a state's attor- ney in 1905, was elected to the Florida Leg- islature in 1915, and served as Speaker of the House. He was also one of the organizers of the First National Bank in Live Oak. As governor, Hardee was most remembered for his strong stance against state income and inheritance taxes, as well as his role in shutting down the controversial convict leasing system.[62]

Portrait of Cary Augustus Hardee, a Taylor County native who served as Florida's 23rd governor from 1921 to 1925.

(Image courtesy of the State Archives of Florida)

W.T. Cash, who made a name for himself in Taylor County as an educator and newspaper publisher, also took an early interest in politics. He was elected to represent the county in the Florida House of Representatives in the 1909, 1915, and 1917 sessions. He also represented Florida's 12th Senatorial district in the state senate in 1918 and 1919. His most lasting contribution to Florida, however, came with his appointment as Florida's first State Librarian in 1927. Indeed, Cash had been a driving force behind the legislation establishing the State Library in the first place. Cash immediately set to work gathering and protecting a large collection of books and archival records documenting the history of Florida, which patrons continue to enjoy today. When the R.A. Gray Building was built in the 1970s to house the State Library and State Archives, the Archives' read- ing room on the first floor was named in his honor. Cash also wrote a history of the Democratic Party in Florida and a four-volume history of the state itself, both of which were meticulously researched and are still in use.[63]

Senator Cash, as he was called, sometimes shared rides home to Perry on the weekends with William Lawton Weaver, then representing Taylor County in the Florida House of Representatives, plus one unusual young politico for that time. Myrtice McCaskill, daughter of the McCaskill family that operated the Greystone Hotel on Jefferson Street, served as a reading clerk in the House for several legislative sessions, and became a very active participant in Florida politics. Educated at the Florida State College for Women, McCaskill honed her skills of oratory and persuasion as director of the YWCA's war fund campaign in Florida during World War I. She traveled all over the state urging women to support the war effort by conserving resources and buying war bonds. "She was virile, forceful, reproachful and persuasive by turns," the *Palm Beach Post* wrote in 1918, calling McCaskill "a wonderful little personage who rightly believes that she has a mission." Indeed she did. She was a vital force for achieving women's suffrage at the end of the 1910s, and then aimed to become a legislator herself. When she opened her 1922 campaign to replace Joseph H. Scales as state representative for Taylor County, no one opposed her at first. W.T. Hendry, however, joined the race at the last moment and was able to achieve victory in the Democratic primary, beating McCaskill by

Portrait of Myrtice McCaskill, Taylor County's first woman to run for a seat in the Legislature.

(Photo courtesy of the State Archives of Florida)

about four to one. After the election, Myrtice McCaskill was less outspoken in political circles, but she operated a successful insurance business in Tallahassee and Jacksonville.[64]

Perry and the World

Amid all this progress, Perry and Taylor County also became more interconnected with some of the biggest issues affecting Florida, the United States, and the world in general. One of the most prominent was the issue of liquor prohibition. Many Taylor County farmers had been making moonshine in illicit distilleries (or "stills") for years, mainly as a source of extra money. In a cash-poor society where the price of cotton and other produce sometimes dropped to perilously low levels, a crop of moonshine could make the difference between being able to pay taxes and general store bills or not. Nevertheless, the law was the law, and authorities at every level of government continued to make cases against moonshiners in local and federal court. In 1902, a group of revenue agents based in Birmingham, Alabama raided the county and shut down a number of stills. The moonshiners must have had a little advance notice, because some of them were able to hide the evidence of their work, just not quite well enough. Newspapers reported the revenuers finding at least one 30-gallon copper still in a Taylor County man's attic. He and two others were arrested.[65]

The related question of whether to allow alcoholic beverages to be sold in bars and saloons was a contentious one, and policy changed back and forth several times in Taylor County at the turn of the 20th century. When the town first incorporated, liquor could be legally sold by licensed bars, but the license tax was so high no one would pay it. There were, however, a few "blind tigers" in town—illegal bars. In 1907, after the town's charter was amended by the legislature, it was discovered that the town council was authorized to permit liquor sales by dispensaries, as opposed to bars. Anti-prohibitionists, called "wets," set to work trying to elect a town council that would actually allow one or more of these licenses to be approved. They were apparently successful, because over the next couple of years both a dispensary and several saloons opened up in Perry. Prohibitionists, called "dry," fought back and got the issue on the ballot in July 1909. They were disappointed, however, when the citizens voted by a slim majority to remain "wet." Moreover, a legal whiskey distillery opened in Perry later that year, dutifully paying the federal government $1.10 for every gallon it produced.[66]

The battle between wet and dry was far from over, however. In 1910, a statewide prohibition amendment was put on the ballot. A total of 151 Taylor County electors voted in favor of it, with 136 opposed. The amendment failed to get the necessary number of votes statewide, but local prohibitionists, seeing their likely advantage, put the issue on the local ballot in 1911. They won by a healthy margin, and Taylor County once again went dry. A few years later, the rest of the nation went dry with the passage of the 18th Amendment and the Volstead Act.[67]

Going dry meant the saloons in town were out of business, at least the legal ones, but there were plenty of locals willing to operate illicit stills deep in the woods. In 1924, a revenue agent named James E. Bowdoin came into Taylor County and destroyed eight stills in less than a week, and made ten arrests. Several young boys were apparently among those operating the stills, but Bowdoin reportedly let them off the hook after a stern warning not to assist with moonshining in the future.[68]

Prohibition enforcement was dangerous work, especially since revenue agents typically had to probe deep into woods and swamps to locate the stills they were after. Remarkably, only nine federal agents are reported to have died in the line of duty in Florida during the federal prohibition era. Two of those nine died in Taylor County in an episode that is sometimes referred to as the "Buchanan murders." Much like the case of the "Flaming Six Guns of Florida," the story has been clouded up a bit by rumor and selective memory, and some details may never be completely known. Still, court records and other documents can give us at least a basic understanding of what happened.[69]

On December 9, 1926, federal revenue agents Jacob P. Brandt and Walter D. Mobray drove out to the home of J.W. Buchanan, located about 14 miles from Perry. They suspected Buchanan of operating an illegal still, so they planned to try to buy some moonshine from him to justify getting a warrant to search his home. When they arrived, the two agents honked the horn, bringing Buchanan to the door. Buchanan and prosecutors had differing versions of what happened next, but suffice it to say the two revenue agents ended up shot to death.[70]

Buchanan, admitting he had shot the two revenue agents, surrendered himself to Sheriff Forrest Lipscomb and was arrested. The sheriff feared Buchanan's friends might try to spring him from jail, so he transferred the prisoner to the Duval County jail in Jacksonville, where he remained until the January term of the Taylor County court. The grand jury handed down three indictments against Buchanan, one each for the two slain revenue agents and a third for killing his son during an unrelated incident earlier in the year. At trial for killing Jacob Brandt, Buchanan claimed he had only fired on the revenue officers because they had shot first. The jury was not convinced, however, and found him guilty, recommending life imprisonment instead of the death penalty. The prosecutor offered to drop the other indictments as long as Buchanan did not appeal his conviction. A young lawyer named Claude Pepper, however, happened to be serving as counsel for Buchanan, and he believed the sentence could be overturned on appeal. Pepper took the case to the Florida Supreme Court, but he was not successful. The high court sustained the Taylor County court's decision, which triggered another trial for Mobray's death. This time, Buchanan received the death penalty.[71]

Having failed to save Buchanan's life through the appeal to the Supreme Court, Claude Pepper vowed to defend him as long as he could. Governor Doyle Carlton signed several different death warrants for Buchanan, but each time Pepper found a way to put off the man's execution. The case dragged on for a number of years, long after Pepper had become a legislator and then a U.S. senator. In the end, Buchanan died of natural causes in the state prison at Raiford.[72]

World War I, or the "Great War," as it was called before it had a sequel, was another momentous event for Perry and Taylor County. About 470 local men—including at least four officers—served in the military during the conflict. Enthusiasm for the war was high; many of these men enlisted for duty immediately after the call for volunteers went out from Washington. T.J. "Theo" Faulkner was among the first to sign up, but he was twice turned down for service on account of poor eyesight. Theo would not take 'no' for an answer, however, and on the third try he was finally accepted.[73]

While Taylor County soldiers trained for war in places like Camp Jackson, South Carolina and Camp Wheeler, Georgia, their families made adjustments on the home front to conserve resources and support the troops. Farmers dedicated more acreage to food crops, and Perry housewives grew large gardens in their backyards to satisfy the demand for food. More than 2,800 local citizens signed pledge cards promising to observe the "meatless" and "wheatless" days prescribed by Herbert Hoover's United States Food Administration. The *Taylor County Herald* joked that the price of eggs and butter had gone so high that local grocers were locking them up in their safes at night.[74]

The lumber mills continued to work at full speed, but much more of their product than usual went to shipbuilders in Tampa and Jacksonville, which were steadily turning out new boats for the war effort. Mill workers, who had the steadiest paychecks in the county at that time, also led the way in supporting the Red Cross and the government's Liberty Loan war bond program. F.H. Heins, superintendent of Burton-Swartz, led a fundraising campaign for the Red Cross in 1918 that earned more than twice its $4,000 goal. By October of that year, Taylor County citizens had purchased over $26,400 in Liberty Loan bonds, $10,500 of that amount having been raised by the Woman's Club led by Mrs. L.L. Lassiter.[75]

Taylor County was fortunately spared from high numbers of casualties during the war. Only 21 local men lost their lives during the conflict, with another 5 reported as severely wounded. Soon after the men began returning home after the Armistice in 1918, however, they and their families faced another dangerous foe—a series of devastating influenza outbreaks, which came to be called "Spanish flu." Public health statistics are unreliable for this time period, but it is clear Taylor County was seriously affected. Newspaper reports suggest Taylor County was hardest hit in the spring of 1920. A burst of new cases emerged following a lyceum performance at the Perry school in February of that year, prompting acting mayor Joseph H. Scales to close all schools, theaters, churches, and other public gathering places in town. The school board followed this up by closing schools throughout the county. Many students missed so much school that spring that they had to be held back a grade, and the high school in Perry only graduated one student that year—Stanley McCaskill. Overall, the cases of flu in Taylor County seemed to be milder and less often fatal than in other parts of the United States, but the epidemic still had serious effects for locals. Joseph H. Scales was called to Chattanooga in March 1920 on account of illness in his family, and during his visit he lost a brother, a sister, his mother, and a brother-in-law to influenza and pneumonia—all in two weeks' time. Scales himself was ill for part of that time, but he recovered and returned to Perry.[76]

One of the most violent episodes in Perry in the early 20th century occurred in December 1922 when Ruby Hendry, a young schoolteacher, was found dead along the South Georgia Railway tracks just north of town. The train crew who discovered the body immediately returned to Perry and alerted Sheriff Forrest Lipscomb, who went to the scene and quickly determined that Ruby had been murdered. Four suspects were detained shortly after the sheriff began his investigation, but their alibis checked out and they were released without any charges being filed. As authorities continued to examine the evidence at the crime scene, their attention turned to Charlie Wright, an African American man who had reportedly escaped from a stockade in Dixie County. Sheriff Lipscomb found several items hidden near the crime scene that he had reason to believe had been stolen by Wright. Lipscomb also had information that the man might be headed north toward the Georgia border, so he and an armed posse of more than 100 men left Perry to attempt to capture him.[77]

As the sheriff and his men closed in on their suspect, racial tensions were on the rise in Perry. At least four buildings in the African American sections of town were burned during the week following Ruby Hendry's death, including the Masonic Hall, a school building, and Springhill Missionary Baptist Church. Several African American families were reportedly told to leave town, and one man was shot to death and his home burned down after he was accused of writing an "improper note" to a white woman. Newspapers reported that African American residents, angered by these violent acts, warned white storekeepers to leave their section of town by nightfall on December 6, and that some business owners did so. Local authorities responded by having a group of armed white men patrol the neighborhood.[78]

Charlie Wright was arrested in Madison County, while an alleged accomplice, Arthur Young, was arrested in Kinderlou, Georgia, west of Valdosta. Sheriff Lipscomb took custody of both men on December 8 at Madison, but it quickly became clear that a growing crowd of locals planned to take justice into their own hands rather than wait for a trial. Lipscomb announced at the courthouse in Madison that his suspects were already in the county jail in Perry, and that deputies were barricaded along with them for their protection. Hardly anyone accepted the sheriff's story, and when he tried to return to Perry with the two prisoners, he found himself surrounded about seven miles north of town by a large group of angry locals.[79]

Heavily outnumbered, Lipscomb and his deputies turned Charlie Wright and Arthur Young over to the mob, who took the men to the scene of Ruby Hendry's murder and questioned them. Wright reportedly confessed to killing the young woman while another man robbed her. He did not give his accomplice's name, but he said it was not Arthur Young. Satisfied that Wright was indeed Ruby Hendry's murderer, members of the crowd gave Young back to Sheriff Lipscomb. They tied Charlie Wright to a stake, piled wood and grass at his feet, and set it on fire, the flames consuming Wright's body in minutes. Newspapers and attendees reported that more than a thousand people witnessed this event, and even the high school had been closed that day so students could attend.[80]

Once the lynching of Charlie Wright was complete, the mob began to disperse. Local officials and an undertaker went to the scene early on the morning of December 9 to remove the body and prepare it for burial. Arthur Young remained in custody at the Taylor County jail, but officials doubted he was safe there. Hoping to head off any additional violence, Sheriff Lipscomb quietly attempted to move Young to another jail on December 11. Just as had happened three days before, however, locals stopped the sheriff's car outside of town and demanded that he turn over his prisoner. Lipscomb complied. The crowd hung Young from a tree and riddled his body with bullets. No charges were ever brought against anyone associated with either lynching.[81]

* * *

As the 1920s drew to a close, it was clear that Perry was emerging as a vital center of commerce in North Florida. Trains rolled through town every day filled with visitors wanting either to try out Hampton Springs or do business with the local timber and turpentine operators. The woods still had trees and sap to spare for keeping these industries going, and they continued to generate a payroll that supported both longstanding families and newcomers. Still, there were limitations. Events like the Martin Tabert and Buchanan debacles and the Wright-Young lynchings laid bare the fact that the prosperity touted by local leaders was not experienced evenly by all citizens. Moreover, there were vague signs that Florida's broader economic boom of the 1920s was slowing down. Few could have imagined just how badly the boom would bust, or how deeply it would affect the people of a place like Taylor County. Everyone was about to find out.

Front page of an issue of the Pine Knot Journal, a newsletter published by members of Civilian Conservation Corps company 1410 while encamped at Shady Grove in 1935.

CHAPTER 7:

Depression and War

We often think of the stock market crash of October 1929 as being the starting point for the Great Depression. It was certainly a dramatic moment. The leading industrial stocks lost 40 percent of their value in just a few days, hemorrhaging billions of dollars at a time when 'billions' was not even a measurement that seemed real to most people. Still, the economic rot that triggered the Great Depression set in well before the crash—a toxic mix of high tariffs, loose regulation of banks and stock trading, and overbuilt industries for which there were not enough customers buying the products.[1]

For Florida, the downturn came even sooner thanks to a combination of factors. South Florida was building new subdivisions and businesses so fast in the 1920s that the demand for supplies overwhelmed the railroads and ports. Florida East Coast Railway cars packed with building materials sat for days on their sidings, making the company no money as they waited to be unloaded. Finally, the railroad had had enough. In August 1925, the company placed an embargo on most nonperishable cargo, cutting off supplies for the contractors who had been building all those new homes. There was the Port of Miami, of course, but it was still a young facility with nowhere near enough capacity to pick up the slack. Ships sometimes waited for weeks to offload their cargoes, which translated into big losses for everyone involved. To make matters worse, a ship called the *Prinz Valdemar* sank in the middle of the channel in January 1926, effectively closing the port for two months. Investors began to pull out their capital, construction got behind schedule, and land sales began to drop off.[2]

Mother Nature added insult to injury by hurling not one, but two devastating hurricanes at South Florida in two years. The Great Miami Hurricane of September 1926 killed 392 people and leveled large swaths of its namesake city. The damage was valued at around $100 million, comparable to more than

$1.3 billion in today's money. The region hardly had time to catch its breath and regroup before the Okeechobee Hurricane came roaring in almost exactly two years later at West Palm Beach, bringing a death toll in the thousands and another hefty price tag. If investors had been uneasy about pouring more money into Florida before, now they had plenty more reasons to think twice about it. The famous Florida boom was over.[3]

Taylor County did not sustain damage from those two hurricanes, nor did it lack for building supplies to meet local demand. The burst of Florida's real estate bubble had far-reaching effects, however, that put a damper on developers' plans for transforming the Big Bend. With investors doubtful about the wisdom and profitability of building up Florida any further, the money necessary to make these ideas a reality simply was not there. The subdivision at Boneta Beach failed, save for that one lonely sidewalk leading into the marsh, and Steinhatchee did not take off as expected. The plans to build entire towns out of the woods surrounding Hampton Springs came to nothing. This did not affect most Taylor Countians that much, of course. There were still plenty of pines to tap or cut, and plenty of land for raising crops and cows.

By 1931, however, the situation had gotten serious. One of the local banks had failed, prices for lumber and farm products were dropping, and families were feeling the squeeze. One newspaper plea from the Woman's Club urged citizens "who are fortunate enough to be employed or have sufficient money to not be in need for the comforts of life, to make liberal subscriptions to the Red Cross and Community Welfare Drive … Many of our citizens are unemployed or only part time employed; others have made crop failures thru no fault of their own, many are sick and unable to secure proper food. They merit our help and sympathy."[4]

The depression years that followed tested the resolve of Taylor County families and leaders, especially when natural and manmade problems threatened to make matters worse. Even in the darkest moments, however, there were acts of individual generosity and creative community-minded solutions that helped ease the burden for many citizens. And, when Taylor County joined the rest of the United States in facing the challenge of winning World War II, that same spirit of community cooperation energized local efforts to support the war and secure the home front.

Calamity

Taylor County's local economy was already getting sluggish by 1930, but it really became obvious that trouble was brewing when the First National

Bank closed its doors in October of that year. Bank president John H. Loughridge and vice president W.S. Weaver blamed "silent withdrawals" as the main reason for the bank's failure. This was a common pattern during the Great Depression. Many banks closed when their depositors began to fear the declining economy and pulled all their money out at once, draining their bank's cash reserves. No system of depositor's insurance like today's FDIC existed at this time. Your life savings might be on the bank's books, but if they had no cash to pay it out to you, you simply lost that money, or received only pennies on the dollar.[5]

The First National Bank never reopened. Its assets were sold at auction, and G.O. Hingson acquired its stately building on the courthouse square. Many depositors lost the money they had put in the bank, but perhaps no one faced more trouble than James R. Jackson, clerk of the courts for Taylor County at the time. The county had deposited its tax revenue in the bank, and owed a

John Hendrix Loughridge, part owner of the Weaver-Loughridge Lumber Company and president of the First National Bank when it closed in 1930.

(Photo courtesy of the Taylor County Historical Society)

significant amount of that money to the state. Legally, Jackson was on the hook for it, and it took a special act of the legislature to relieve Jackson from having to pay it out of his bond for public office.[6]

The county's major industries also took a hit, including one of the oldest—cattle. Ticks and the diseases they spread to cows had been a problem in North Florida for decades, but the situation reached serious proportions in the 1920s, forcing the state to act. In 1923, the legislature enacted a compulsory tick eradication program requiring cattle ranchers—even the smaller ones—to dip their cows in an arsenic solution every two weeks to kill the ticks. Taylor County farmers obeyed the law for the most part, and by 1928 there were 69 "dipping vats" in use around the area. These were concrete basins with sloping sides that allowed a farmer to drive his cattle through a chute, down into the arsenic solution, and out the other side.[7]

The dipping system beat back the disastrous tick fever, but it was expensive and time-consuming work. When the Great Depression began, Taylor County was still an open range, which meant farmers had to ride for miles to round up their cattle and get them to the nearest dipping vat every other week. In many cases, by the time all a cattleman's cows had had their bath, it was time to start over. Moreover, dipping could be dangerous. Animals sometimes fell and were injured or killed while making their way through the vat, and if the arsenic solution stayed too long on an animal's hide it would dry it out

A cow makes its way across a dipping vat filled with an arsenic solution intended to kill ticks.

(Photo courtesy of the State Archives of Florida)

and cause it to crack. Rain right after a dipping made this problem worse because it caused the arsenic to run down the cow's sides and gather around its belly.[8]

The results of the state's tick eradication program were mixed in Taylor County. Many cattlemen chose to get out of the business altogether because it became very burdensome to stay within the law. At one point in 1927, according to the Madison newspaper, Taylor County farmers were shipping between one and four thousand head of cattle every couple of days, saving only the best stock. Many of these cows were purchased by Zach Miller for his 101 Ranch in Oklahoma, sometimes at prices as low as six or seven dollars a head. The cattlemen who did manage to hang on slowly began to transform the ranching business. They imported bulls to improve their herds, planted grass to fatten them up, and in some cases even voluntarily fenced their land to keep the cows close by for better management. By 1949 all cattle owners in Florida would be required to fence in their cows.[9]

One final plague hit the cattle industry during the worst phase of the Great Depression – the screw worm. No one is sure exactly when this new pest came to Florida for the first time, but it likely spread from Texas, where it had been a problem for decades. Screw worm flies laid their eggs in open wounds on cows and other animals, which then hatched and wreaked havoc on their host, often killing it in days if left untreated. Scientists eventually slowed the infestation by releasing sterile screw worm flies into the environment. In the meantime, Taylor County farmers and their cohorts around the state had to monitor their cows constantly to treat even the slightest scratch in their skin.[10]

The timber industry also had its share of problems during the depression years. Not only was the demand for lumber diminished by the slump, but the supply was starting to run dry as well. Carbur, which had boomed during the 1920s, shrank during the depression years as the seemingly boundless stands of cypress and yellow pine nearby turned out to have bounds after all. By 1940, the population of Carbur had dropped to just over 100 persons. Operations continued at other logging and milling sites, but often with reduced hours and wages. J.H. Tedder recalled working at Scanlon for $1.15 per day during the 1930s, reaching $3 per day only once he became a foreman. Weaver-Loughridge reduced its number of layoffs by furloughing workers one day a week.[11]

Perhaps the worst blow to the timber interests came in 1935 when a devastating hurricane came ripping through the area. The infamous Labor Day Hurricane, the same one that killed hundreds in the Keys and blew a Florida East Coast Railway train right off its track, swung northward in the Gulf and struck the Florida mainland just south of Taylor County on September 4. The destruction was widespread. One of the train depots and the Peacock Building lost their roofs. Carnival workers who had just set up in town wisely took down their Ferris wheel, but it was no use. After the storm passed, they found all their equipment twisted and scattered. A church in Boyd collapsed in the wind and killed a whole group of cows that had taken shelter nearby.[12]

The American Red Cross determined that 441 Taylor County homes were damaged or destroyed by the storm, including 80 in Perry and 61 in Steinhatchee. About 80% of the commercial timber in the county was also wiped out, creating a serious crisis because the wood had to be harvested and sawed before it ruined. The sawmills ran day and night for months to process the logs, and more went over to the Kraft paper factory in Panama City. This emergency kept the mills running and the paychecks flowing in the short term, but it also added to the uncertainty of the timber industry's future in Taylor County. Turpentine producers suffered as well since they too depended on the trees for their trade. Company officials estimated they would only be able to employ a tenth of their former labor force after the hurricane, which only added to the misery of the depression years.[13]

Mother Nature certainly had her way with North Florida during this era, but there were manmade problems as well. Widespread moonshining and illegal liquor sales were perhaps two of the biggest ones. Although Prohibition had been in effect since 1920, locals reported that liquor was being served all over the county. One anonymous letter to Governor Dave Sholtz in 1933 named off a whole list of "disorderly houses and liquor joints" in Carbur, Boyd, and Perry, one of which was within two blocks of the courthouse. "If any town in Florida needs attention in those lines," the unnamed authors wrote, "it is Perry."[14]

Rum-running was a problem as well. Smugglers took advantage of Taylor County's maze of tidal creeks and marshes to secretly bring in large amounts of liquor and transport it northward to sell. Law enforcement officials occasionally caught up with the rumrunners and made some spectacular stings. In one bust in 1929 near Keaton Beach, revenue agents arrested eight men riding in four motor trucks loaded down with extra license plates, a boat, and liquor—all valued at about $100,000.[15]

Prohibition came to an end with the ratification of the 21st amendment in 1933, and local voters chose overwhelmingly the following year to allow the sale of liquor within the county—683 in favor to 261 opposed. This helped alleviate the county's trouble with smuggling and illegal consumption, but it did not solve the other major alcohol-related problem, moonshining. Taylor Countians had been distilling their own liquor for decades, but it was even more popular during Prohibition because it was a good way to make extra cash. The Great Depression only added to the temptation to get in on the bootlegging game

Boiler and other typical equipment for a moonshine still.

(Photo courtesy of the State Archives of Florida)

to support the family income. One time in 1930, federal agents raided the county and destroyed five stills, 35 gallons of whiskey, and 2,000 gallons of mash in less than a week. They also made 13 arrests.[16]

But even with the revenue officers on patrol, many local citizens feared that bootleg whiskey was corrupting their county and damning their young people. One anonymous letter to Governor Sholtz in 1934 claimed even the sheriff and his deputies were in on the liquor trade, and that if state officials did not do something soon the author was planning to appeal directly to the President. "It is ruining our young boys and girls," the letter reads. "They are going down the road to destruction." A citizen of Fenholloway offered to take state law enforcement officials to some of the stills he knew about, just so long as he could do so anonymously. "I don't want my name used in it any further than you and myself and the officers," the man said," for you know it would make enemies and I might be destroyed." Law enforcement officials did make raids into Taylor County from time to time and bust moonshiners, but bootlegging continued for many years after the Great Depression was only a memory.[17]

Sponge fishing was probably one of the strongest industries in Taylor County during the depression years, but it too had problems, mostly stemming from disagreements between the sponge fishermen themselves. In the early 20th century, Rock Island sponges gathered off the Taylor County coast commanded some of the best prices anywhere, prompting a number of Greek spongers to come up from Tarpon Springs and establish headquarters at Steinhatchee, Keaton Beach, and Jug Island. There were two kinds of spongers, "hookers" and "divers." The hookers operated in shallow water and plucked the sponges from the bottom using long poles with hooks on the end. The divers operated in deeper water and used underwater breathing equipment and weighted boots, which allowed them to walk across the seafloor and gather sponges by hand. The hookers generally lived full-time in Taylor County, while the divers often traveled back and forth between Tarpon Springs and the sponging area off the Taylor County coast. Both groups spent time in Perry and at the beaches, but relations could be tense. According to Sam Register's recollections, they even ate in separate restaurants.[18]

The tension stemmed mainly from an ongoing conflict over territory. The law required divers to work outside of territorial waters, meaning they could operate anywhere more than three leagues, or nine nautical miles, from the shore. Hookers were entitled to work in any of the shallower waters closer to land. Hookers frequently accused the divers of coming too close to shore, taking sponges from their territory, and damaging the delicate sponge beds with their heavy weighted boots. As the sponge market became more profitable in the 1920s, these disagreements became more serious because every sponge lost or gained affected the spongers' bottom line. It was not long before the hookers turned to county and state officials for help.

In 1929, Claude Pepper wrote a letter to Governor Doyle Carlton on behalf of the hookers at Keaton Beach, complaining about the divers' intrusion into territorial waters and the failure of Thomas R. Hodges, the state shellfish commissioner, to do anything about it. Pepper suggested hiring a local man trusted by the hookers to patrol their sponging territory, and recommended an employee of W. Alston Brown, who was working turpentine and running a business at Keaton Beach at that time. Hodges claimed that he and his deputies were patrolling the area plenty, and they had not seen any sign of law-breaking from the divers. Carlton wrote Pepper back saying he could only enforce the law through the shellfish commissioner, and did not see how anything more could be done. Having hit a wall with the state, Pepper had three owners of the sponge diving boat *Liberty* arrested and brought before Judge John O. Culpepper for a hearing. According to Pepper, Hodges arranged for attorney O.C. Parker of Tallahassee to go to Perry to represent the divers, suggesting that Hodges had taken their side in the ongoing spongers' dispute.[19]

Before the case against the owners of the *Liberty* could be settled, Governor Carlton decided to replace Hodges with E.C. Strickland, who Pepper believed would be more attentive to the problems plaguing the Taylor County sponging industry. Pepper wrote to the three accused ship owners, saying he would recommend that the county drop the charges against them if they would pay the hookers' court costs and not allow any further violations of the sponge law to take place. The three spongers complied, and for at least a few months there was a period of relative peace.[20]

In the fall of 1930, however, a new conflict developed when Taylor County sponge hookers decided to open up their own sponge exchange instead of shipping their catch to the exchange down at Tarpon Springs, where the divers usually sold theirs. Tarpon Springs spongers claimed this was an inefficient system

and that the "hooker sponge" was inferior to what the divers brought in anyway. Still, they still felt compelled to boycott Taylor County sponges unless they were brought to Tarpon Springs "in the regular sales manner." It did not appear to matter. The new local sponge exchange sold $15,000 worth of product at its first sale in December 1930, and another $7,500 at the next one.[21]

The sponge boat Liberty in port at Saint Marks. This particular boat became embroiled in a legal battle between two groups of spongers in 1929.

(Photo courtesy of the State Archives of Florida)

Meanwhile, the turf war between the hookers and divers continued. Acting on the pretense that that state was refusing to enforce the law, Taylor County officials themselves patrolled the Gulf and arrested divers they said were illegally operating within the nine-mile limit. Tarpon Springs-based divers secured a federal injunction in 1931 against the county, the sponge hookers, and even the state, ordering them all to halt any court proceedings against the divers and let them do their work. The injunction was only temporary, however, and even after careful study no clear agreement was reached on how to resolve the issue completely. When Governor Dave Sholtz took office in 1933, he ordered the nine-mile boundary to be patrolled more frequently off the Taylor County coast, eventually appointing a Tarpon Springs sponger, Arthur Kaminis, to do the job himself in one of his own sponge boats. Taylor County spongers objected to Kaminis's appointment, but the new constant patrol did seem to quiet down the controversy for the moment.[22]

Meeting the Challenge

As the depression sapped away their jobs, savings, and buying power, Taylor County families found a variety of ways to stretch their dollars and make ends meet. Taking odd jobs was a common solution; even people with steady employment sometimes found a side gig here and there to help pay the family bills. Ray Evans, for example, remembered his father doing all sorts of tasks after his logging business dropped off—everything from clearing right of way for what would eventually become U.S. 221 to wrangling gas tanks near the train depot. Women sometimes took in sewing and laundry or cleaned houses for the better-off residents in town. Families pooled their resources and sometimes even moved in together to minimize their expenses.[23]

People also began watching their tax bills much more closely, looking for ways to reduce the amount they had to pay. This was especially true in town where the taxes were higher and folks were on the hook for more public services like water and sewage. The town council regularly faced a flood of taxpayers asking to have their property reassessed or parts of their business licenses revoked in order to decrease the amounts they owed. In January 1930, for instance, several local business leaders came before the town council and asked to have their taxes retroactively adjusted all the way back to 1925. Some residents who were told they had to connect to the town sewer system said they simply could not afford it. They asked to be allowed to build outdoor privies instead. The council voted to permit this, pending inspections.[24]

Citizens outside town tried similar tactics. In 1933, the county's school bus drivers sent a petition to Governor Dave Sholtz asking that they be allowed to pay their truck taxes in installments rather than all at once. The state did take action in this regard; the legislature reduced the rates for license plates and allowed citizens to pay their taxes over a period of time. That did not stop some people from trying to make the process even cheaper by illegal means.

That same year, a man was arrested in Taylor County for selling fake auto tags at reduced rates to consumers.[25]

Knowing the financial trouble many families were in, local government officials helped their constituents take advantage of as many tax breaks as possible. This helped in the short term, but it also forced the town and county to get creative with balancing their own budgets. In 1930, the town council attempted to renegotiate its contract with the Florida Power and Light Company for street lighting services. After haggling for more than a year, the town finally instructed Florida Power to cut off all streetlights except the ones around the courthouse square. "This means a step backward for Perry," lamented the *Taylor County News,* pointing out that this came just as two new state highways into town were being completed.[26]

More cuts soon followed. In 1932, the town council slashed the salaries of its employees—even firefighters and police—by as much as 25 percent. As more citizens defaulted on their taxes, the town ran into debt, which led the council to pass an ordinance authorizing paper scrip to be used to pay its obligations. These certificates were given to town employees and others who provided services to the town, and they could be turned in as payment for municipal taxes in lieu of real cash. This system had almost immediate drawbacks. Town employees complained that local merchants charged more when they paid with scrip instead of real cash, and the council ended up backtracking on its salary cuts to make up the difference.[27]

At the county level, roads and schools were two of the biggest expenses, so they received some of the deepest cuts. Many roads that the county had adopted as public highways were dropped from county maintenance lists, which reduced the amount of revenue needed for upkeep. The school board voted for stinging salary cuts in 1932 and 1933, eventually settling at about 18 percent for teachers and five percent for bus drivers. Superintendent L.R. Moore cut his own salary by $300 and agreed to pay expenses for his own car and his assistant. The board also stopped allowing students from outside the county to attend local schools without paying tuition. These measures added to the hardship already faced by many educators and their families, but unlike other counties in the depression-stricken state, local schools were able to remain open for a full eight-month term instead of closing early.[28]

Private organizations and businesses found a number of ways to help families cope with the financial crisis. The Woman's Club collected toys for needy children at Christmas, put on plays, and operated a soup kitchen for the local school children. Mrs. Ben Lindsey and Mrs. M.A. Maxwell headed this last project, which was feeding 116 students as of March 1933. The Landry Ideal Market and Piggly Wiggly donated groceries and meats, Mrs. J.E. Powell donated milk, the local newspaper donated the tickets, and Perry's two main bakeries donated the bread. Baskets in the local grocery stores provided a way for other local citizens to contribute. The Foley school had its own soup kitchen run by the Parent-Teacher Association. Mrs. Jeremiah Foley herself donated a two-burner electric stove for preparing the soup each day.[29]

Others donated the means for local families to grow more of their own food. The Kiwanis Club encouraged school children to grow their own gardens and gave away prizes for the best produce. In February 1932, the town council voted to allow citizens to plow vacant lots in town and grow community gardens. The following year, turpentine magnate Thomas B. Puckett and Mary Goza donated land north of Perry that local welfare officials had cleared and plowed for food crops. The government provided the seeds and fertilizer, and unemployed workers took turns providing the labor in exchange for a share of the produce.[30]

The Taylor County Farm and Livestock Association offered a unique solution to keep the food supply going for local families while also supporting local businesses. The association built a canning plant on East Drew Street in 1933, and members could bring in their vegetables and can them professionally for home use or for sale. Locally grown products were specially labeled, and grocers agreed to stock them at reduced prices. This allowed local farm families to use more of their own produce and earn a little cash for the surplus. This plant remained open throughout the depression and was eventually taken on as a project of the Federal Emergency Relief Administration.[31]

Access to health care was another major concern during this era of tight budgets. Taylor County's chapter of the American Red Cross stepped in to help by directing some of its funds toward helping people pay their hospital and doctor bills. Those bills were drastically lower than what we regularly see today, but they were still too expensive for the unemployed. The Red Cross also gave away free garden seed, barrels of flour, and other food supplies. A full-time county health unit opened in 1930, the first such unit in the state. It started out by helping with malaria control and sanitation, but as the depression worsened it stepped in to help people take care of their basic health and hygiene needs. In 1932, the health unit sponsored a county-wide "toothbrush drill" for school children. At the beginning of that school year, health experts surveyed the students and reported that one in four said they had no toothbrush at home. Many said they were unable to afford one. Some had been doing the best they could with rags. The Perry Rotary Club paid for every student in the county to receive a toothbrush and samples of tooth powder, and the health unit staff made their rounds to the schools to show films about proper brushing habits.[32]

Local merchants, although they too were hurting, took steps to help their customers, not least because they wanted to keep as much of their business as possible. They began allowing customers to barter for some items, and advertised big sales in the newspaper urging folks to take advantage of "depression prices." In Foley, R.M. Callihan dropped the price of admission to movies at the Royal Theatre to fifteen cents Tuesday through Friday. The one catch, he announced, was that no one was allowed to mention anything about the depression in or around the building. The *Taylor County News* encouraged people to keep their valuable dollars circulating locally by buying from local businesses instead of from catalogs

We Are Prepared

To Do Everything in the ——
PHOTOGRAPHIC LINE

Prompt Attention To——
KODAK WORK

Prices to Suit the Times. See——

"DAD" HOWER

Studio East Main Street   Perry, Florida

Acknowledging the financial crunch imposed on families by the Great Depression, photographer "Dad" Hower promised "prices to suit the times" in this advertisement in the Taylor County News.

(Image courtesy of the Taylor County Historical Society)

or merchants in other towns. In September 1932 the newspaper organized a "Good Will Sale," and gave away prizes to citizens who purchased the largest volume of goods from participating local stores.[33]

Federal Aid

These tactics went a long way toward meeting people's most vital needs, and the strong sense of community spirit must have been heartening in such tough times. In the big picture, however, the economy was still miserably bad. When President Franklin D. Roosevelt was sworn into office in March 1933, the people of Taylor County held a mass prayer meeting in the courthouse, asking God to guide the new president and Congress as they attempted to break the nation's economic stalemate. They did not have to wait long for action. Armed with the innovative insights of his so-called "Brain Trust," Roosevelt embarked on what historians call the "Hundred Days," a flurry of new legislation and emergency policies that completely transformed the federal government's response to the depression. Local observers were impressed. "The

President has shown the people what can be accomplished if you pull off your coat and go to work," beamed the *Taylor County News*. "Timidity has cost the people millions of dollars and many a man his job."[34]

One of the first "New Deal" agencies that came to Taylor County was the Civil Works Administration (CWA). Authorized in November 1933, the agency aimed to put unemployed men and women back to work by constructing or upgrading public buildings, roads, sanitary sewers, and the like. C.L. Brandon was appointed to administer the CWA program locally, and within a month there were 466 men and 110 women registered in the county. Over the next year, the CWA spent more than $80,000 in Taylor County, mainly on road construction.[35]

CWA was a temporary measure, so in the spring of 1934 it began to wrap up its work and shut down. The depression was far from over, however, so Roosevelt and Congress worked out new programs to put people back to work. In January 1935, government representatives met with the Perry Rotary Club and encouraged the members to draw up a list of potential projects that might qualify for funding. Local officials formed a county planning board to take on this task. Sewage and garbage disposal facilities for Perry, a county hospital, a new high school, a park along Spring Creek, repairs to the courthouse and jail, a paved road to the beaches, new schools at Stephensville and Carbur, and a hangar at the Perry airport were high priorities on the list.[36]

Some items were accepted outright, others were rejected, and many more were accepted in a modified form. By late summer 1935, the government had approved funding for a new schoolhouse at Carbur, some road work, and a project to rebind and repair some of the books in the high school library. In 1937, the Works Progress Administration (WPA) agreed to provide labor and materials to help build the "rock building" at Perry Elementary School. Two years later, more approvals came for a community recreation center, a swimming pool, and new sewer lines.[37]

Perry post office, constructed in 1935 by the Public Works Administration. The building was added to the National Register of Historic Places in 1989.

(Photo courtesy of the State Archives of Florida)

The WPA built plenty of buildings, but it also funded other creative ways of getting folks back to work. In the late 1930s, the agency opened a sewing room in Perry so local women could earn money making garments that were then distributed to needy families in the area. This project lasted until 1941, when a Burton-Swartz official came up with something even better. The company began employing these same women to assemble cypress-slat soft drink bottle crates. The women made more money working for Burton-Swartz than they did working for the WPA, and it reduced the amount of public funding needed to support the county.[38]

The WPA also supported several "white collar" projects, such as a historical survey to inventory all of the old records stored in the courthouse, as well as a church survey to compile data about every church in the county. There was also a veteran's grave registration program, designed to locate and record the site of every veteran's burial. One worker had some trouble locating a particular grave in Taylor County and began asking around for help. Locals informed him that the veteran he was looking for had died overseas and was shipped home in a sealed copper casket, which was later dug up by moonshiners and fashioned into a still.[39]

Perhaps one of the most inspiring WPA projects in Taylor County was the community band led by Everett J. Evans. Members furnished their own instruments, but sheet music and Professor Evans's time were paid for with government funds. According to Ray Evans, the band originally practiced above Tom Abdoo's grocery store at the corner of Jefferson and Green streets, and sometimes gave impromptu concerts on the sidewalk. The high school later "adopted" the community band, which evolved into what we now know as the Pride of Taylor Marching Band. Evans said the first uniforms consisted of solid blue coats with brass buttons and an orange braid on one shoulder, plus a blue cap with orange braid and a white visor. The pants were white with blue braid, but to save money the students bought regular pants and the braid was sewn on by volunteer mothers.[40]

Another federal relief program that had a significant local impact was the Civilian Conservation Corps (CCC), which many folks shortened to just "the CC's." It put young, unmarried men to work building roads and bridges, planting trees, and doing projects to prevent forest fires. In most cases, the CCC did not assign men close to home, but sent them elsewhere to camps established close to where the work was needed. They earned $30 a month, most of which the government sent directly to their families. The CCC camps had a military-like look and feel, partly because they were operated by the War Department. The men wore uniforms, stayed in barracks that were regularly inspected, and practiced drill for flag ceremonies and special occasions.[41]

Taylor County's first CCC enrollees left Perry in May 1933, including John L. Wood, Secil Platt, Wilson Culpepper, Herbert Knight, Albert Sistrunk, Roland Slaughter, Homer Pittman, Wilson Hightower, and T.M. Denmark of Perry; Harvey Kirk of Hampton Springs; Tye Massey of Shady Grove; Eulee Lewis of Eridu; James Green of Carbur; Nathan Odom of Fenholloway; Vannis Shaw of Steinhatchee; and C.B. Wilder and E.E. Mattair of Athena. By 1937 there were 77 young men from Taylor County in the CCC, earning a total of $2,210 monthly.[42]

While the locals went elsewhere to work, men from around the South came to Taylor County to join CCC camps established at Foley, Shady Grove, and Carbur. They planted pine seedlings, built roads and bridges and fire towers, and strung telephone lines. Like virtually all public institutions in the South at that time, the CCC was segregated. Camp 1410 in Foley and Camp 4448 in Carbur were staffed by white enrollees, while Camp 4451 in Shady Grove had black enrollees. This did not change up the program much, although it affected how the men interacted with the public. White camp members usually went into Perry for entertainment during their off-time; black members more often went to local black churches.[43]

A bridge over the Econfina River, built by workers from the Civilian Conservation Corps camp at Shady Grove.

(Photo courtesy of the State Archives of Florida)

The men did more than work—they also had a wide variety of activities to enjoy back in camp. Many of the enrollees had left school to support their families, and some could not even read. The government required each man to take at least one course while they were in the CCC. They could choose from academic subjects like reading, history, or arithmetic, or skills like photography, first aid, radio, surveying, and woodworking. There were also sports—baseball, diamond ball, boxing, and even volleyball. Every camp had its own reading room, and most had a camp newsletter. Camp 1410 in Foley called its newsletter the *Pine Knot Journal*. The men of Camp 4451 in Shady Grove called theirs the *Hurricane Chronicle*, since the camp had been hit by the Labor Day Hurricane almost immediately after opening in 1935.[44]

World War II

The Great Depression had not ended by 1940 by any means, but Taylor County families were beginning to see some improvements in the local economy. New businesses had emerged, especially at the beaches. Funding from both the state and federal governments had helped improve the roads to the coast, and as more Taylor Countians purchased automobiles the beaches became an easy trip to make for the day or the weekend. Restaurants and guest houses sprung up at Keaton, Dekle, and Adams beaches, plus Jug Island. Thomas Puckett, the turpentine operator, established a hunting and fishing lodge at Mandalay on the Aucilla River in 1934, catering to politicians, wealthy businessmen, and other upper crust Floridians looking to get away from their hectic offices. It was an isolated outpost—Mandalay visitors traveled to Scanlon on the L.O.P.&G. and then were chauffeured the rest of the way on a handcar. Supplying these rustic resorts earned other local businesses a little more money, and even inspired a few new ventures.[45]

Just as things were beginning to look up at home, however, events in faraway Europe and Asia threatened to draw the United States into a new global war. Dictatorial regimes in Germany, Italy, and Japan had forcibly annexed territory from their neighbors and demanded more. The United States had pledged itself to a policy of neutrality, but a growing number of Americans, including President Roosevelt, believed the nation would eventually have to get involved. Walking a tightrope between these political realities, Roosevelt looked for ways to help the Allies—led by Great Britain and France—without violating the United States' neutral status. He also pushed for measures that would prepare the United States in case the war made its way across the oceans into the Western Hemisphere.

Taylor County's first real experience with these preparations came in 1940 when Congress passed the Selective Training and Service Act, which required men between the ages of 18 and 36 to register for the draft. Governor Fred Cone appointed Judge Byron Butler to be head of the county's local draft board. When the time came for registration, more than 1,500 Taylor Countians signed up. J.H. Parker, Ben McCracken, and R.F. Chesser took over draft board functions after the initial signup period. J.F. McCall was the appeal officer, and Colon Blue was the clerk.[46]

Cleo Simmons, Willie Lee Clark, and Garland Griffin were the first three Taylor County men called up for military service. They left for Camp Blanding on December 10, 1940 after a big send-off at the bus station. More men were called up in 1941, and others volunteered, especially after the Japanese attack on Pearl Harbor. Soon there were Taylor Countians serving all over the world from Africa to Australia. Brooks-Scanlon paid for every Taylor County soldier to receive a copy of the *Taylor County News*, which helped locals keep track of where their friends, neighbors, and relatives were located on the globe. As of July 1943, at least 92 Taylor County men were receiving the paper—56 in the Atlantic theater of operations and 32 in the Pacific.[47]

Portrait of Donald Grant, one of several Taylor County boys who left high school to volunteer for military service during World War II.

(Photo from the Taylor County High School yearbook for 1943)

Family members often submitted letters from their loved ones overseas for publication in the *Taylor County News*, and sometimes service members sent letters directly to the editor, especially if their address was changing. Reading these letters from the front gives a sense of what it was like for these young men and women to leave the relative comfort and simplicity of rural North Florida to face the difficulties and uncertainties of war. "Here in the dark jungles you hear a twig snap and wonder what it is," Marvin Lee wrote from New Guinea in 1944. "You strain your eyes looking through the dark until they hurt, trying to see what's there when you can't."[48]

Sometimes the letters were more light-hearted, especially when the writer had had the good fortune of seeing someone from home. Joseph W. Newsome, for example, was driving down a street somewhere in Italy when a man in another jeep waved and yelled at him as they passed one another—it turned out to be a childhood friend from Foley, Jenks Sumrall. Across the globe in the Pacific Theater, June Bedgood wrote that he had seen Roy Chesser, Ray Hazelwood, Bobby Parker, and William Winstead while serving as a mail censor on an undisclosed island. Two brothers from Steinhatchee, Luther and Laurence Ross, served in different infantry divisions but ended up seeing one another for the first time in 15 months in Lauterbach, Germany.[49]

A common theme in almost all the letters was a fervent desire for the war to end and to get back to Taylor County as soon as possible. "There is no place like old Taylor," Broward Jackson said in a 1944 letter. "Just think of all the good hunting and fishing I am missing. I can smell salt water trout and mullet frying right now."[50]

Crucially, it was not only men serving in the armed forces—far from it. A large number of Taylor County women also enlisted for service in the Women's Army Corps (WAC) and the Navy's Women Accepted for Volunteer Emergency Service (WAVES) program. Willie B. Lyons, Ollie J. Baggett, Ida J. Horvath, and Frances Durahimer were some of Taylor County's first WAC recruits, while Lucile Cogburn, Mary Louise Novia, Elizabeth Collins, Marguerite Huxford, and Marie Crouch were some of the first local WAVEs. Katherine Corbin and Martha Sharpe were among the first local women to become Army nurses. Carolyn Culpepper received her wings from the Atlanta Air School in 1943, the same day as her brother Jack, and she became a Ferry Command pilot for the Army. Plenty more local women served in civilian capacities on military bases around the country.[51]

A few of the county's older citizens also put their skills to work for Uncle Sam in the armed forces. Byron Butler, who had been county judge for several years, was called up in 1942 to serve as a lieutenant in the 67th Tank Division. The Army soon took advantage of the judge's legal training and experience by moving him into the role of judge advocate. Governor Spessard Holland appointed Butler's wife Louise to finish out his unexpired term as county judge, which worked out well considering she had worked in her husband's office for years. The new Judge Butler told the press she occasionally called on attorney friends for advice, but otherwise felt comfortable with her duties.[52]

While these Taylor Countians served their country overseas, others stayed busy organizing the folks on the home front to support the war effort and keep an eye on the coast and skies. Even before the United States was officially in the war, local leaders established a defense council to coordinate these tasks. The Taylor County Defense Council took its marching orders from the Florida State Defense Council, which in turn got its instructions from the Office of Civilian Defense in Washington. Together, these agencies helped distribute information and organize groups of citizen volunteers to do all sorts of war-related work.

As of December, 1941, when the U.S. officially entered the war, John Rowland was chairman of the local defense council, with T. Joseph Swanson as his vice-chairman and J.W. Weidler as secretary. More than a dozen committees operated under their watch, each chaired by someone with relevant skills and experience. The council's transportation and communication committee, for example, was chaired by railroad official J.H. Kansinger and E.L. Cox, president of Gulf Telephone Company. Grocer R.W. Vereen headed up the food committee, and local physician Dr. John Clement Ellis managed the health committee. As new programs and guidelines came down from Washington and Tallahassee, these groups helped translate the ideas into action.[53]

The war put an unprecedented strain on the nation's supplies of food, rubber, wood, paper, and other raw materials, which made conservation and recycling a critical part of the home front agenda. Tires were rationed as early as January 1942, followed by automobiles, gasoline, and even typewriters and bicycles. Sugar was rationed starting in May 1942, and within a year almost all processed foods were under some form of government-imposed restriction. Consumers and restaurants alike were allotted ration points that had to be turned in along with the purchase money to buy the items they needed. The idea was to ensure a steady flow of food and supplies for the military and home front alike, and to control price inflation.[54]

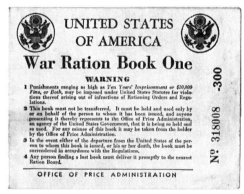

A typical booklet of ration stamps issued by the federal government during World War II.

(Image courtesy of the State Archives of Florida)

Taylor County residents felt the pinch from not being able to buy as much of their favorite processed foods as they would have liked, but they generally had plenty of local produce to make up for it. In April 1942, home demonstration agent Manilla Welles reported that 80% of the county's 1,500 families had already planted so-called "victory gardens." Moreover, 278 pressure cookers were at work helping housewives can extra fruits and vegetables for their families. Perry's town council helped out as they had during the depression years by allowing locals to plant gardens on vacant lots owned by the town.[55]

To conserve crucial non-food supplies like metal and rubber and paper, the local defense council partnered with businesses and institutions to set up scrap collection drives. In 1942, for example, President Roosevelt called for a nationwide effort to turn in scrap rubber so it could be reconstituted for war purposes. Taylor County citizens turned in some 62,000 pounds of the material, which was then carted off to collection sites for recycling. The drug stores, meanwhile, encouraged buyers to turn in their aluminum ointment and toothpaste tubes once they were empty so the metal could be melted down and reused. The grocers did the same for cans. School-age children likely did more than anyone to collect scrap metal, mainly because local and state officials wisely turned it into a high-spirited contest. In one 1942 drive alone, Taylor County schoolchildren collected 223,736 pounds of metal. The school at Steinhatchee turned in the largest amount of scrap per capita—15,000 pounds collected by only 49 students.[56]

Young people also proved adept at selling war bonds and stamps to support the war effort. Just days after the attack on Pearl Harbor, the Key Club at Taylor County High School began selling defense stamps to both teachers and students. Colon Blue and Lawrence Wilson headed up the committee managing the sales. Local businesses took out advertisement space in the newspaper encouraging readers to invest more of their money in bonds and stamps. By October 1942, citizens had already raised $175,646, exceeding every monthly goal set for the county by the U.S. Treasury Department. Thomas B. Puckett, who was county chairman for bond and stamp sales, noted that these results would be especially gratifying to the locals serving overseas when they saw the numbers published in their copies of the *Taylor County News*.[57]

In addition to helping out Uncle Sam, Taylor County citizens also donated money and goods to organizations that served soldiers and refugees overseas. The public library, for example, established a Victory Book Campaign, encouraging people to turn in gently used books that could be sent to military posts for the soldiers' enjoyment. Joe Foley headed up an effort to send over free packets of cigarettes—his committee placed jars at businesses all over town where shoppers could deposit money to support the plan. Each packet cost only five cents, and Taylor County distinguished itself as the top donors in the state for this scheme, raising enough money to send 888,000 packets of cigarettes. The local chapter of the American Red Cross collected a wide variety of goods for refugees and set up a sewing room in Perry to make clothing for their use.[58]

Some residents got directly involved in civilian defense by patrolling the beaches and watching the skies for enemy aircraft. Taylor County's cooperation in this kind of work was considered especially important since it was on the coast and could potentially have the first opportunity to spot enemy ships, submarines, or aircraft coming in from the Gulf of Mexico. Men and women alike served as aircraft observers, watching from fire towers and the tops of tall buildings at Perry, Hampton Springs, and elsewhere. Vera Hall and Ellen

Jenkins had the honor of being the first ground observers to take a shift at 6:00 a.m. on August 7, 1942. The next year, the Coast Guard established a volunteer beach patrol unit at Dekle Beach, with Gus Dekle as commander and Earl Loughridge as junior commander. Eighteen members made up the volunteer force when it first emerged, including Mrs. Don Cameron and Mrs. Louise Butler. The unit was in charge of patrolling the coast between Dekle Beach and Steinhatchee.[59]

Taylor County citizens were proud of their home front accomplishments, and in February 1943 local officials organized a Civilian Defense Day celebration to recognize the time and money people had put into supporting the war effort. George Burr, executive director of the State Defense Council, came down from Tallahassee to make a speech and present the schoolchildren with a pennant for their scrap collection performance. More than 1,600 students greeted Burr after marching around the courthouse square with the Foley Junior High School and Taylor County High School bands at the head of the group. Representatives from Dale Mabry Field arrived with a large machine gun, trucks, and other military equipment for display. Six planes from Dale Mabry's auxiliary field in Cross City flew over the downtown section and dropped colorful leaflets bearing the message, "Keep us flying – buy war bonds!" People took the message to heart—$26,000 in war bonds were sold during that single event. It was a banner day for a small county that had responded to the wartime emergency in a big way.[60]

Had the Civilian Defense Day celebration been held a little later in the year those planes might have come from just south of town rather than Cross City. On May 2, 1942, the Army Air Forces' site selection board chose a 1,200-acre parcel of land just south of Perry on which to build an air base. This new airfield would serve as an auxiliary base for Dale Mabry Field up in Tallahassee. Construction of three runways and several buildings began late that summer and was completed by the beginning of 1943 at a cost of around two million dollars. Even before the work was finished, airmen from Dale Mabry Field began arriving in Perry to staff the base and begin training for dive bombing operations. At its busiest phase during the war, the base was home to more than 200 officers and more than a thousand enlisted men.[61]

Perry Army Air Field's role was to provide flight training for replacement pilots. New recruits first received 120 hours of ground training at Dale Mabry Field, then they were transferred either to Perry, Cross City, or one of Mabry's other auxiliary bases for 60 hours of flight training. After that, the newly trained airmen returned to Dale Mabry Field for reassignment to the units that

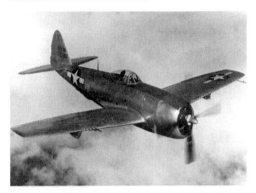

A Republic P-47 Thunderbolt, the first aircraft used by pilots training at Perry Army Air Field during World War II.

(Photo courtesy of the United States Air Force)

needed them overseas. In the early days of the Perry base's existence, airmen trained on the Republic P-47 Thunderbolt, although in mid-1944 these aircraft were replaced by the Curtiss P-40. In the final months of the war the airmen trained on the P-51 Mustang.[62]

More than 3,000 pilots passed through Perry Army Air Field during the war, in addition to a host of support personnel who maintained a whole city's worth of services at the base. Aside from the barracks and buildings for tending the planes, there was a gunnery range, weather office, base hospital and dental clinic, post exchange, theater, and communications center. The base also had its own newspaper, the *Take Off.* Enlisted men and most of the officers lived on the property, although some officers had their families in tow and lived in Perry. The sudden influx of people stretched the town's boarding houses to their maximum capacity, and the problem was only solved when several Taylor County residents offered to host soldiers and their families in their own homes.[63]

Overall, the Perry base put up an impressive training record, but there were a number of crashes, including some dramatic mid-air collisions. A trio of these tragic crashes occurred in the summer of 1943, starting with a collision between two P-47's near Jug Island on June 26. One of the pilots survived, but the other airman, Lt. Norman R. Messier of Pawtucket, Rhode Island, was killed. Another incident happened days later at Horse Pond, just inland from Keaton Beach. Again two P-47's collided, and again only one of the two pilots was able to bail out before the planes crashed into the ground. The other pilot, Lt. Marlin M. Moore of Kentucky, died instantly. Another crash occurred a month later, although one of the pilots in that incident was able to fly his damaged plane back to base.[64]

Hosting the base also meant hosting hundreds of newcomers who wanted a little time away from work every now and then. The airfield had its own officer clubs, but Perry also provided places for service members to relax and enjoy their time off. The American Legion home opened its doors, as did the Perry Woman's Club, which had a library and writing room set up for soldiers to use. The Junior Woman's Club regularly hosted dances on the weekends, and movies at the Foley and Temple theaters were a popular attraction. A fire in the Temple Theater in 1945 put a temporary damper on the fun, but proprietors George and Kay Porter solved the problem by erecting a makeshift tent theater on South Washington Street, complete with silver screen, seats, and a sawdust floor, until the building could be rebuilt. All these activities brought base personnel in regular contact with the young ladies of Perry, and more than a few marriages resulted. Judge Louise Butler reported record-breaking numbers of marriage licenses being sold in late 1943, a pattern that was only amplified by the close of the war.[65]

As Taylor County's young men and women began returning home following the Allied victories in Europe and Asia, it was clear that a lot had changed and more change was on the way. More than 20 local men had been killed, while others carried wounds and injuries that would stay with them for years to come. A number of service members and civilians alike had found their life partners while away from home and were either married or aiming to get that way. Some had already started families, marking the beginning of the postwar "Baby Boom" that would swell Taylor County's population to unprecedented numbers. Often, these young people had left home with a limited education and little knowledge of the world outside North Florida, but they returned with training and experiences that changed their lives forever. Lieutenant Wilson Gordon put a fine point on it in a letter he wrote home to the *Taylor County News* while he was stationed in New Guinea in 1944. "I have seen a lot of the world since I left Perry and have done many things that the censor will not allow me to tell," he wrote. "I can say that this war is no fun, and it isn't easy, but we are winning."[66]

Taylor County itself was changing as well. When the war began, the Great Depression had yet to be fully stamped out. Relief projects were still active, and unemployment and underemployment were still major problems. By 1945, the war and its unceasing demand for goods and labor had put many people back to work, but it remained to be seen what those workers would do when things returned to normal. The vast stands of virgin timber that had sustained the county's growth in the early 20th century were almost gone. New industries and new ideas for building the region's prosperity would be needed, and it would largely fall to the new generation of young leaders emerging from these difficult years to make it happen.

A portion of the new Buckeye Cellulose Corporation mill at Foley under construction (1953).

(Photo courtesy of the State Archives of Florida)

CHAPTER 8:

Becoming the Forest Capital

E arly in 1948, officials at Brooks-Scanlon announced what many had known was coming for a long time—that they would soon have to close down their enormous sawmill operation at Foley. Since the 1910s, the company had focused strictly on lumber, harvesting yellow pine timber on a "cut out and get out" basis, just as its Oregon and Canada divisions were doing. It had been a real moneymaker as long as the timber lasted. At peak operation, Brooks-Scanlon had been able to saw a million board feet of lumber every month, generating a $20,000 monthly payroll, a critical lifeline for the community.[1]

But it was not sustainable. The company's chief forester, John McCain, admitted that it had awakened too late to the fact that a reforestation plan was necessary to avoid a complete collapse of the local timber industry. "If we'd started our forestry work back in 1909 we wouldn't be closing down the big mill in another few years," he told reporters. "We won't be able to stop the mill closing, but we've started soon enough so that we won't shut down operation in Taylor County altogether."[2]

McCain was referring to the company's new emphasis on proper forest management—replanting trees, preventing forest fires, and perhaps most importantly, finding uses for younger trees that in earlier years would have been considered too small to bother with. The widely favored solution was to turn these trees into pulpwood, meaning they would be chipped up and processed to extract their cellulose fiber instead of being sawed for lumber. That fiber could then be used for making paper, cardboard, and a wide variety of other products. Since a pulpwood mill could use smaller trees, the lack of virgin pine growth would no longer be a problem as long as a steady enough supply of planted pines was available.

As it turned out, pulpwood did become the dominant industry in Taylor County in the post-World War II years, although Brooks-Scanlon ended up not being the company to make it happen. This was a different kind of timber industry, one that relied much more heavily on scientific management and planning. It also impacted the local environment in ways that the sawmills had not done, something that would pose new challenges as the years went by.

The pulpwood industry was valuable both locally and regionally, and combined with other postwar-era changes it helped forge a new identity for Taylor County as the "Forest Capital of the South." This new title was inspired by the progressive turn in local forestry, but from a marketing standpoint it also captured how much the county was growing in other ways, including as a waypoint for tourists. The postwar decades were not always smooth sailing, but in many ways the changes that occurred set the stage for what Taylor County is today.

From Lumber to Pulp

The end of World War II marked a much-welcomed return to normalcy, but it was no secret that the old way of life that had existed before the war and the depression would not come back entirely. It simply was not viable. Population figures tell the tale as well as any other measurement. During the depression years of the 1930s, Taylor County's population decreased by 12 percent, dropping from just over 13,000 to about 11,500 people. In the 1940s, despite the Baby Boom, the population fell another 10 percent.[3]

Jobs were the culprit. The local population had mushroomed in earlier decades because of the vast number of workers it took to run both the timber and turpentine industries. But turpentine was taking a dive locally, as it was across the state. County Forester Erdman West noted shortly after the war that Florida's turpentine production numbers had been on a downward trend since 1923. That year Florida had produced 40 percent of the nation's turpentine, but as of Erdman's writing in 1947 the state's share was down to 18 percent.[4]

Lumber production was falling as well. Almost all of Taylor County's marketable cypress had been cut. Burton-Swartz, which had been milling the so-called "wood eternal" locally since 1914, closed the sawmill in Perry and liquidated its assets at the end of 1942. The Lee Cypress Company bought the mill and resumed operations a year later, but had to get its logs from 400 miles away in the Everglades. Virgin yellow pine was still available in some parts of the county, but the supply was getting dangerously low. When Brooks-Scanlon announced its impending closure in 1948, company officials said the only reason they had not closed sooner was because they had purchased additional timber lands in Madison County to have enough wood for the mill.[5]

The problem was not that the company had completely ignored the need for reforestation. Brooks-Scanlon began experimenting with replanting methods as early as 1934, establishing a tree farm called "Timbuctoo" on its cutover land. By the end of World War II, 60% of the company's acreage was set aside for reforestation projects. In addition to planting pine seeds and seedlings, Brooks-Scanlon applied new management techniques to protect its fledgling forests—fire breaks, observation towers, telephone lines, and roads that allowed firefighters easy access to any potential fires. The Florida Board of Forestry and Parks qualified more than 80% of the company's territory for "tree farm" status in 1947, posting signs to raise awareness of the value of the work.

A fire-fighting truck at Brooks-Scanlon's Timbuctoo tree farm.

(Photo courtesy of the State Archives of Florida)

Brooks-Scanlon ran its own advertisements in the local newspaper explaining the new way of managing forests. "As we refine … our methods of processing wood from the forests, we can use younger trees," one ad read. "TREE FARM trees of tomorrow will go to work at an earlier age."[6]

The point of all this was to get Taylor County citizens to think of timber as a renewable crop—and a worthwhile investment. Many of the county's largest landowners did choose to get in on tree farming, and in 1946 a group of them formed the Taylor County Timber Growers' Association. Ben Lindsey was the first president, H.J. Westberry was vice-president, and Gus Dekle was secretary. Joe H. Scales, Jr. and Marvin Gamble were two of the first board members. The association purchased the county's first tree planter in 1947, and took advantage of a new program in which a county could have its own professional forester with the majority of the salary paid by the state. Taylor County was the first county in Florida to take the state up on this offer. Erdman West, a graduate of the University of Florida's forestry school, was the county's first forester under this program.[7]

Within a couple of years, tree farming was taking off in a big way, but locals knew they would not be able to grow their crops fast enough to save the sawmill at Brooks-Scanlon. Company officials knew this as well, and they gave strong consideration to establishing a pulp and paper mill, which would be able to profitably use smaller trees. Foley had most of the right features for a mill of this type, although it would be a costly construction project, and the Fenholloway River was really too small to handle the amount of wastewater that would be produced. As of 1947, with wood supplies running out, the company was still on the fence about making the big switch. Locals began to get nervous because Taylor County was far from the only community in the southeast vying for a pulpwood plant at this time. The Chamber of Commerce decided to publicly invite other companies to consider the area for producing pulp. "We hope to see a paper mill installation by local interests," president Joe H. Scales, Jr. said. "If not, we will cover the country until this development matures."[8]

The small size of the local rivers was one of the county's main drawbacks in attracting an industrial suitor. The territory along the coast was far too marshy and swampy for a mill, so it would have to be located inland. Local leaders knew the volume of wastewater discharged from a pulp and paper operation would likely overwhelm any of the local streams, but there seemed to be no other alternative if there was to be a mill at all. Taking that view, Taylor County's representative in the Legislature, Gus Dekle, proposed a bill declaring the county a "manufacturing industrial area," and further stipulating that any industrial concern could legally dump sewage or chemical waste into the Fenholloway River as long as it created no obstruction. The bill passed, and within a year Brooks-Scanlon was already drilling wells to supply a potential mill.[9]

The company ultimately chose not to go into the pulpwood business, however, and in September 1951 officials announced that Brooks-Scanlon had sold its mill site and 440,000 acres of timber acreage to the Buckeye Cellulose Corporation. Buckeye was a subsidiary of Procter & Gamble, the consumer goods giant that had originated Ivory soap and Crisco. Established in 1901, Buckeye's first role in the company was to produce cottonseed oil for use in Crisco and other products. In the 1920s, Buckeye researchers discovered that linters—short cotton fibers that cling to cottonseed after the ginning process— could be used to produce high-quality cellulose pulp. The company established a mill in Memphis, Tennessee, and became one of the nation's leading pulp producers.[10]

By 1950, the demand for cellulose pulp was skyrocketing, but the supply of cotton linters was dropping as Southern farmers diversified their crops and relied less on cotton production. Buckeye researchers in Memphis developed a process for extracting cellulose pulp from pine trees, which prompted company officials to begin searching for a place to build a new mill. They considered sites all over the United States and Canada, but the one they ultimately settled on was in Taylor County. It had everything the company was looking for—good railroad connections, a supply of workers, a designated place to dis-charge wastewater, and—thanks to reforestation efforts—a hefty supply of pine trees.[11]

Construction began on the $20 million plant in February 1952. Engineers on the project were from J.E. Sirrine Company in Greenville, South Carolina. Duval Engineering and Constructing Company of Jacksonville and H.K. Ferguson Company of Cleveland handled the construction. The mill's massive machinery came from the Sandy Hill Iron and Brass Works of Hudson

A portion of the new Buckeye Cellulose Corporation mill at Foley under construction (1953).

(Photo courtesy of the State Archives of Florida)

Falls, New York. Forty flatbed rail cars were required to transport the parts down to Foley once they were finished.[12]

The new mill was constructed almost exactly where the Brooks-Scanlon sawmill had been. As part of its sale agreement with Buckeye, Brooks-Scanlon retained the right to temporarily continue operating its sawmill and cutting the trees large enough for lumber off the property it was selling. By running the sawmill right up to the point when construction on the new plant was getting underway, the two companies prevented local workers from being unemployed during the transition period. Lester Foley, son of the Jerry Foley for whom Foley was originally named in the 1920s, managed the sawmill during this final phase. The last log was processed by the old mill in February 1953. The company houses that Brooks-Scanlon had built for its workers were put up for sale, but buyers had to move them away. Many are still standing in other parts of the county today.[13]

Constructing the new mill took more than two years, partly because a series of steel workers' strikes slowed down the arrival of critical building materials. The plant sprawled across about 50 acres of land and originally consisted of four main buildings, including a 688-foot-long two-story structure that housed the pulp drying equipment. Massive pumps were installed to draw 5,000 gallons of water from the ground every minute, plus generators powerful enough to supply a small city with electricity. The plant finally opened in the summer of 1954, shipping its first load of pulp on July 9. Four out of every five employees in the 500-person workforce were from Taylor County. Gil Tougas was the first plant superintendent, while W.D. Smith was the first forester, and Marshall Courtney was the first head of wood procurement.[14]

Buckeye began expanding its Florida operations almost as soon as the original plant was finished. In 1956, the company bought 177,000 acres in Franklin and Liberty counties, plus 20,735 more acres locally. The Weaver-Loughridge Lumber Company sold its 67,000 acres of timber land in Taylor County to Buckeye in 1967. Another 52,000 acres came in 1971 from the estate of Leonard P. "Pete" Gibson, who for several years represented the county in the Florida Senate. Much of this acreage was located west of U.S. 19 in what is still known as "Gibson's Pasture." In 1959, the plant doubled its capacity by integrating a second mill into the complex at Foley. That put the plant's output at 315,000 tons of cellulose pulp annually, and the number of employees at more than a thousand.[15]

Celebrating a New Identity

Pulpwood was a profitable industry, but it was also fragile. Forest fires, both natural and manmade, could wipe out thousands of acres of valuable timber in a matter of days. This was a major problem during the transition to pulpwood production, partly because burning the woods had been a traditional practice of local cattle owners for generations. In earlier days, most of the county's forests had belonged to faraway landowners who seldom even laid eyes on their property. The woods were widely considered a public resource, open to everyone, especially for hunting and cattle grazing. Cattlemen allowed their cows to range over this unfenced territory at will, and would set fires every spring to burn off underbrush and allow tender new grasses to grow and give the cows something fattening to eat. The landowners generally said nothing, even when the timber industry perked up in the early 20th century, because there were plenty of trees and the fires seldom caused much harm to the enormous yellow pines that dominated the local forests.[16]

By the 1940s, however, circumstances were different. The county was more heavily populated, the timber companies were more hands-on in their approach to land management, and an increasing amount of acreage was being painstakingly replanted in slash pine. These smaller, younger trees were far more vulnerable to destruction by fire. Cattle owners continued burning in the spring, even when the fires jumped onto neighboring property and damaged timber and turpentine operations. Large landowners like Brooks-Scanlon had to protect their investment in reforested pines, but they had to choose their methods carefully. Attempts to fence in timberland and keep the cows away usually ended with the fences being cut, and arresting the woods-burning cattlemen only soured relations between the company and the community. Timber was important, but so was cattle raising. The county needed a solution that respected both industries.[17]

A combination of practices helped solve this riddle. Some landowners, including Pete Gibson, joined forces with local cattle owners and scheduled controlled burns—setting small fires into the wind so they would burn slowly, with volunteers and firefighting equipment on standby in case any flames spread too quickly. Gibson burned portions of his land that already had well-established trees, which meant the cattle owners got grass for their cows without damaging the younger stands of pulpwood timber.[18]

Brooks-Scanlon came up with another method that emphasized cooperation rather than conflict. The company leased out grazing rights to local cattle owners, charging them a fee based on the acreage and the taxable value of the land. If less than one percent of the land had been damaged by fire at the end of the lease term, the company refunded half of the fee to the cattleman. The program was an instant success, and soon most of the lessees were getting refunds every year.[19]

Around the time Buckeye Cellulose entered the picture in the 1950s, woods-burning emerged once again as a major problem, but this time cattle owners were not the prime suspects. Florida Forest Service officials reported evidence of outright arson, including intricate fuses designed to start fires slowly, giving the perpetrators time to get away undetected. The results were devastating. One fire in 1951 in San Pedro Bay damaged 5,500 acres of timber in two days. A 1956 fire in Lafayette County burned more than 50,000 acres before firefighters brought it under control. Buckeye estimated it could have operated the mill for more than two years on the timber that was destroyed, and pegged the total cost at around $2.5 million. Forest Service investigators determined that both fires were intentionally set.[20]

Arsonists in these cases were seldom caught, leaving their motives something of a mystery. People speculated that some of the so-called "firebugs" did what they did because they were angry at the big timber companies for restricting access to the local woods, or because a company had not given them a job. The Taylor County grand jury recommended in 1955 that the legislature send a message to potential arsonists by increasing the penalties for setting forest fires. Local timber owners backed this plan as a step in the right direction, but at the same time pursued a softer approach—one that focused on the positive impact of the pulpwood industry on the local economy.[21]

In October 1956, the timber owners teamed up with the Chamber of Commerce to hold the first annual Pine Tree Festival. Taylor County had had at least one forestry "field day" before this, but the Pine Tree Festival was larger, and it aimed spe-

cifically to link good forest stewardship with the county's identity. Doug Powers was general chairman of this first festival. Bands from Taylor, Madison, and Jefferson counties led the parade at noon on Saturday, October 13, which included color guards from the local veterans' organizations and Moody Air Force Base. Floats from Buckeye, the Weaver-Loughridge Lumber Company, and the Florida Forest Service showed off firefighting equipment, while

The Taylor County Marching Band passes through the intersection of Main and Jefferson streets during the annual Florida Forest Festival parade (1971).

(Photo courtesy of the Perry-Taylor County Chamber of Commerce)

nearly 100 rodeo performers rode their horses down the street.[22]

Judge Hal Adams gave a keynote address, calling on all Taylor County residents to do their part to protect the local forests. "The timber industry in and near this county means the very lifeblood of the community," he said. Following Judge Adams' speech, Chamber of Commerce president Henry Dorsett crowned Carol Smith the first-ever queen of the Pine Tree Festival. She was selected from a field of 22 contestants from Perry, Salem, and Foley. Members of her court included Miriam Janeway, Pat Brannen, Charlotte Strickland, and Virginia Ezell. Once this inaugural honor court had been announced, more than 50 servers began dipping up plates of free barbecue. The event closed with the annual Taylor County Rodeo, held at the old rodeo ground on South Jefferson Street.[23]

The festival was a resounding success, although it had one tragic element. Donald Carroll, a state wildlife specialist, was bitten by a five-foot rattlesnake while he was exhibiting it to the crowd. Ed Timmons, his colleague, caught the snake and helped Carroll administer first aid. The injured man was taken first to a local doctor's office and then to Tallahassee by ambulance, but despite doctors' best efforts he died the following day.[24]

The Pine Tree Festival was instantly popular, and helped establish Taylor County's reputation as a community dedicated to forest conservation and industry. The event grew larger each year, and by the tenth annual festival in 1965 the crowd was estimated at 50,000 visitors. That year, Governor Haydon Burns signed a proclamation declaring Taylor County the "Tree Capital of the South," and personally visited Perry to speak during the festivities. New events like fireworks, forestry competitions, and dances had become part of the program by this time, and the barbecue had morphed into a fish fry, a tradition that continues today. The parade in 1965 included a large number of legislators and state officials, including Governor Burns, congressmen Billy Matthews and Don Fuqua, Secretary of State Tom Adams, State Forester Hux Coulter, Randolph Hodges of the State Board of Conservation, and state senators Pete Gibson and Doc Melton.[25]

Governor Haydon Burns brands his signature onto a slab of cypress inscribed with a proclamation declaring Taylor County the "Tree Capital of the South" (1965).

(Photo courtesy of the Perry-Taylor County Chamber of Commerce)

During his remarks before the parade, Governor Burns called for Taylor Countians to rebrand their successful festival as a statewide celebration of forestry. "I do not view the annual Pine Tree Festival as something that is peculiarly the property of Taylor County," he said. "I consider it an all-Florida event in recognizing the value of one of our vital crops." Burns's suggestion won him a round of applause and, sure enough, the following year the event was billed for the first time as the Florida Forest Festival. More than half a century later, that is still the name.[26]

Growth and Expansion

The postwar era brought growth and activity in a number of other areas, some related to Buckeye and some not. Coming out of World War II, for example, one of the main projects was to convert the Perry Army Air Field for commercial air service. The War Department had spent some two million dollars on the base, but it was not slated to be kept open after the conflict ended. County officials applied in 1946 to use it for a commercial airport. The War Assets Administration allowed a permit on a temporary basis, but also looked at the possibility of eventually tearing down the buildings and selling the land. The Taylor County Chamber of Commerce, which reorganized in 1946 with Joe H. Scales, Jr. as president, offered the federal government salvage material roughly equal in value to what they would make from scrapping the buildings if they would give or sell the base to the county or city.[27]

The War Assets Administration eventually deeded the airport property to the county in February 1947, but getting and keeping commercial air service proved to be a challenge. The Chamber of Commerce successfully wooed Florida Airways into putting Perry on one of its routes, and sent local businessman Thomas Leonard to Washington to lobby the Civil Aeronautics Board to approve the change. The board agreed, and Perry's first commercial air service began on April 7, 1948. For about a year, four daily flights aboard all-metal, twin-engine Beechcraft Airliner planes connected Perry with Tallahassee, Lake City, Gainesville, and Leesburg. This new luxury was short-lived, however, as Florida Airways closed down operations in 1949. Other airlines picked up some of the former Florida Airways routes, but the Perry stop was omitted.[28]

Despite the setbacks with commercial air service, the airport continued to get plenty of use. For a time, the barracks served as apartment housing, and several businesses set up shop in the other buildings. B.E. Tucker of Live Oak established a small factory making new mattresses and adding inner springs to old ones. E.S. Eisenman and his wife established Taylor County Novelty Industries, using pinecones and other forest products to make holiday decorations and toys. Henry Dorsett established a shop for building and repairing furniture. And, to keep the runways in shape, there was the Perry Flying Service, which ran the actual airport and offered training for pilots. Roland Fisher, Harley Huxford, and Huel Wheeler were the organizers of the company, and Stanley Davis of Bainbridge was the first instructor.[29]

Building a hospital was another top priority after the war. Shortly after the Chamber of Commerce was reestablished, Ben Lindsey was tapped to chair a new committee to study ways of using federal funds to make the hospital a reality. Sam Grubbs, Nathan Fleet, E.W. Crouch, and Barney O'Quinn were also on the committee. Congress had passed an act appropriating money to help rural communities build hospitals, and the State Improvement Commission had given Taylor County top priority. Finding the local matching funds was still a major hurdle. By mid-1948, after a year of fundraising, about $100,000 had been pledged by local private sources, but even with federal matching grants it just was not enough to start construction.[30]

Momentum picked up in the 1950s with the arrival of Buckeye and a faster-growing population. In 1955, the state approved an allocation of $225,000 in federal funding toward a 30-bed hospital. A county board was established to administrate the project; J.H. Kansinger, Roland Fisher, Eva Loughridge, T.W. Stackhouse, G.W. Clark, Sam Register, and Buckeye's Paul K. Honey were among the earliest members. Once the federal funds were secured, the hospital board put out a call for bids, but ended up rejecting them all because they were too high. About $450,000 was available for construction and equipment, but the lowest bid for construction alone was $464,000. The board simplified the plans for the new facility, which cut costs enough for construction to begin. The building, named Doctors Memorial Hospital and located at the corner of Center and Ash streets, was finally dedicated on September 1, 1957.[31]

Doctors Memorial was a welcome addition to the community, but it was quickly outpaced by the growth and needs of the local population. In 1965, the county commission voted to use some of the county's share of state race track revenue to expand the hospital. Forest Capital Hall, located near the airport, was approved for funding out of this same source at the same time. More funding from the federal government became available in 1968, and by July the hospital board began calling for bids to construct the new addition. Within a year, the two-story, 48-bed hospital was complete.[32]

The original hospital continued to function as an annex to the newer building, but in 1972 disaster struck. Around 10:30pm on August 15, a patient in the new section of the hospital smelled smoke and sounded an alarm. A fire had started in part of the original hospital building used for storage and physical therapy. Firefighters acted quickly to control the flames, while Buckeye employee John Cruce plowed his company bulldozer through a connecting walkway to prevent the fire from spreading to the new hospital. In the end, the original hospital building was a total loss, but the new hospital escaped damage. According to hospital administrator James Arnold, the incident was thought to be the largest hospital fire ever seen in Florida.[33]

Just as the number of people living in Taylor County increased in the postwar era, so did the number of people traveling through it. Perry was already accustomed to serving a few transient tourists and travelers by virtue of its role as a waypoint on western leg of the old Dixie Highway system. After World War II, however, circumstances made Perry the meeting point for four U.S.

highways—five if you count the designation of U.S. 19 and U.S. 98 as the "alternate" route for U.S. 27 heading south toward Ocala. With the interstate highway system yet to come, that made Perry a critical control point in Florida's transportation system, especially for travelers rounding the Big Bend to get to or from points along the Gulf coast.

The highway linking Perry with Newport (U.S. 98) was one of the county's most important new roads in the postwar era. Before it was completed, a traveler wanting to get to Apalachicola from Perry on a main road had to drive up to Tallahassee on U.S. 19 and then back down to Medart on U.S. 319 before turning due west to follow the coast. Business and civic leaders across the region had been calling for this Newport-Perry shortcut since the 1920s when the Gulf Coast Scenic Highway was being built. This time, with persistent urging from local citizens and legislator Gus Dekle, the state finally agreed to build the long-awaited road. The Newport-Perry cutoff was officially designated by the legislature as an extension of State Road 30 in 1947. It took the state six years to build up the roadbed and construct the necessary bridges across the St. Marks River, Aucilla River, and other waterways, but the new highway eventually opened in late 1953. Federal highway officials included the shortcut in their new routing for U.S. 98 from Apalachicola all the way to West Palm Beach, making Perry one of the key waypoints.[34]

Looking east at the intersection of Hampton Springs Blvd. and Byron Butler Parkway in 1953.

(Photo courtesy of the State Archives of Florida)

U.S. Highway 27 was extended from Tallahassee south to Miami in 1948, mostly over existing state roads. In Taylor County, the route overlapped with U.S. 19 as far as Perry, then turned east toward Mayo via Fenholloway. Although establishing this route did not require any new roadway to be built, the designation encouraged travelers coming into Florida from western Georgia and Alabama to go through Perry on their way to Ocala or Miami. U.S. Highway 221, which was officially extended to Perry in 1953, worked much the same way. The road itself already existed, but once the signs went up they clearly identified a route funneling travelers all the way from Roanoke, Virginia, down to Taylor County via Valdosta, Quitman, and Greenville.[35]

As the traffic volume on these roadways increased, the state opted to four-lane the most heavily used highway, U.S. 19. A 15-mile section entering Perry from the northwest via Eridu and Iddo was finished in 1956. A portion of U.S. 19 south of town was four-laned around the same time, while the in-town section—what is now Byron Butler Parkway—was begun in 1960 and finished the following year.[36]

Even before the state expanded U.S. 19 to four lanes, Perry's position in the federal highway system made it an ideal place for motels, restaurants, trailer parks, and other facilities for tourists passing through the area. Motel construction picked up especially during the early 1950s as a small army of specialized workers arrived to outfit the new plant at Buckeye. By 1960, more than 700 motel rooms were available in Perry, many at places with colorful names like the Skylark, the Sun-n-Sand, or the Bambi. Officers of the Perry Motel Association, formed that year by the owners of these establishments, included Morton Mencher of the Kingswood Motel, Fred Santora of the Bambi Motel, Frank Bolton of the Skylark Motel, Tom Kirkland of the Perry Motor Lodge, and O.W. Jones of the Perry Motor Court, among others.[37]

Business was picking up at the beaches as well. Before the war, Jug Island and Dekle and Keaton beaches had mainly been the province of the sponge fishermen. Local residents went for picnics and to fish and camp, but these were rustic outings. The roads were sandy and there was no telephone or electrical service. In the postwar era, all of that began to change. The Tri-County Electric Cooperative began running electrical lines to the beaches, including Steinhatchee, in 1946. That same year, the State Road Department finished paving the Beach Road as far as Keaton Beach. The spur to Dekle Beach was completed the following year.[38]

These improvements made it possible to develop the beaches into more of a residential area. In 1959, a group of investors purchased the land around Keaton Beach and began subdividing it into lots. For $100 down, a family could buy a "waterfront lot," which usually meant it was on one of the newly dug 100-foot canals, and pay the balance off in $25 monthly installments. This was to be an upscale neighborhood, at least by the standards of those days. No metal roofs were allowed, and all houses had to be a minimum of 600 square feet.[39]

The founders originally planned to carve 3,000 lots out of 500 acres of land, and used all sorts of tricks to sell them. They held a "Miss Keaton

A 1961 advertisement for the "Miss Keaton Beach" contest.

Beach" beauty contest, as well as boat races, to get people down to see the new development. For the 1961 race, the second place prize was a boat and trailer; the top prize was a waterfront lot. In the end, Keaton grew, just not at the ambitious rate imagined by the developers. By 1970 there were about 35 homes there, along with a boat ramp, a store, the much-beloved Johnny Knight's restaurant, and a shortwave radio station, KBL 4690.[40]

Dekle Beach was originally sort of an offshoot of the Jug Island community, owned and named for Taylor County's representative in the Legislature, Gus Dekle. Cottages and a café operated there under the supervision of Lonzo McCall as of 1947, and a handful of locals built houses. After Gus Dekle died in 1961, his widow sold the beach property to Janie and Lewis "Ham" Hamilton and Willie Joe and Ann Moody, who formed a new corporation to run the place. They expanded the cottages, built a fishing pier and store, and divided up the remaining land for residential lots. Dekle Beach is shaped like a ring with a large marshy area in the middle. Originally, the developers had planned to fill in some of that marsh to create more residential property, plus an open area to be called "Sable Park." This expansion never came to fruition, though.[41]

Steinhatchee was already a little farther along, having been partially developed by Barney O'Quinn and the Oglesby family before the war. Sponging was beginning to drop off sharply in the postwar era, but mullet fishing was still a going concern, and so was tourism. Colonel John Rives of Birmingham operated an outpost called the Tennala Lodge as late as 1947, then sold it and opened up another called the Shangri-La. Broward Cooey opened up a similar lodge that operated for a number of years. The Karageorge family arrived in Steinhatchee in 1941, and focused mainly on serving the Greek spongers at first. When Roy Karageorge returned home from the military in 1947, the business expanded to include commercial fishing, and in 1969 the family opened Roy's Restaurant, which is still around as of this writing half a century later.[42]

In 1960, the State Road Department finished paving the highway between

Keaton Beach and Steinhatchee, which opened up the territory in between for development. Ben Lindsey subdivided both Cedar Island and Dark Island, having acquired at least the Dark Island portion of the property from Buckeye Cellulose, which in turn had gotten it from Brooks-Scanlon when they sold out in 1951. Buckeye had a direct role in marketing Dark Island—the company gave away 34 lots to employees in a lottery in 1959. The only catch was that the winners had to invest in the new central water system. The company made it easy, though. Up to $250 could be taken out over time as a payroll deduction, and the remainder could be paid off in annual installments over 10 years.[43]

Rough Patches

The 1950s and 1960s were a prosperous period for Taylor County over-all, but not entirely without problems or controversy. In fact, the main engine driving the county's growth, Buckeye Cellulose, ended up being responsible for one of the most pressing issues that came to a head in the 1960s—the Fenholloway River.

It was impossible to say that no one saw this coming. After all, the county's leaders had urged the legislature to make the Fenholloway an industrial river years before Buckeye arrived on the scene. By 1960, however, the effects of mill pollution on the river were obvious and distressing. Fish became scarcer as industrial wastes reduced the amount of oxygen in the water. A strong odor emanated from the river, and on days when the wind and humidity were just right the smell drifted all over the county.

Even in the early years, some residents tried to force the mill to clean up its act. A pair of landowners sued Buckeye for more than $25,000 in the early 1960s, claiming the pollution had ruined their land. The case made it as far as the First District Court of Appeal but was dismissed. Around the same time, citizens began circulating a petition protesting the mill's pollution, claiming it

View of the Fenholloway River.
(Photo courtesy of Susan Moody)

was contaminating the wells from which nearby residents pumped their drinking water. Buckeye hired Thornton Laboratories, a chemical analysis firm in Tampa that worked mainly with the phosphate industry, to test water from 89 of these private wells. General Manager Paul Honey announced that the tests showed "no scientific proof that any wells even in the immediate vicinity of the river are being contaminated by mill effluent." He promised, however, that the data would be made available to interested parties as the company searched for ways to reduce pollution of the Fenholloway.[44]

Confronting this issue put Taylor County residents in a tough spot. The damage to the river was unmistakable, but so was the degree to which Buckeye had lifted the community out of the economic doldrums. So many families depended on the mill for their jobs and livelihood—were the benefits worth the cost? A good indicator of where public opinion rested on the matter came along in 1965, when State Senator Pete Gibson proposed a law giving Rocky Creek and Spring Creek the same industrial status as the Fenholloway. Governor Haydon Burns vetoed the bill, but he agreed to a revised version that called for Taylor Countians to vote on the question. When the referendum was held later that year, local voters approved the plan to allow industrial pollution in Rocky and Spring creeks by an overwhelming margin—1,482 in favor and 394 against.[45]

Neither of those creeks ended up as the dumping ground for a pulpwood mill, but the Fenholloway continued to be a problem that drew the attention of environmentalists and state health authorities. In 1967, Buckeye announced a plan to "unpollute" the river by removing more particles from its wastewater and aerating it before sending it downstream. Engineers cautioned that this would not be a 100 percent fix, and they were right. The smell abated to some extent, but not entirely, and parts of the river still lacked enough oxygen to support marine life. Environmental standards have tightened even more since those days, but with pulpwood and related industries firmly in place as the lifeblood of the county, the focus has remained on keeping the mill open while finding ways to mitigate pollution and restore the Fenholloway as much as possible.[46]

* * *

The school system went through some challenging years during the postwar period as well. As of 1950, there were 15 schools in the county, eight for white students and seven for the black students. The eight white schools were Taylor County High School and Perry Elementary in Perry, Salem High School,

Homer J. Smith, principal of Jerkins High School from 1943 to 1950.

(Photo courtesy of the Taylor County Historical Society)

Foley Junior High School, and smaller rural schools at Shady Grove, Cabbage Grove, Pleasant Grove, and Steinhatchee. Black students from all twelve grades attended Jerkins High School in Perry, led at that time by Principal Homer J. Smith. There were also black schools in the outlying communities, mainly near timber and turpentine operations. Foley, Hampton Springs, the Huxford community off the Beach Road, Canal, Boyd, and North Perry all had black schools in 1950.[47]

The arrival of Buckeye and its growing workforce quickly filled the schools in Perry to capacity. In 1954, county freeholders bonded themselves for $900,000 to build a new high school, which was completed in 1957. The following year, voters opted to shell out another $325,000 to build a new elementary school on the northwest end of town. Classes began there in the fall of 1959. School officials named the new facility for Gladys Morse, who had just retired after 43 years of service to the Taylor County school system.[48] With these new facilities in place, the school board began closing some of the smaller schools in the outer communities. Foley Junior High closed in 1959; Cabbage Grove followed in 1961. Salem High School held out the longest. In 1965, the school reverted to an elementary school as part of the school system's racial integration plan. Five years later, the school board closed the Salem site down entirely and sold it. The building burned in 1980.[49]

In 1954, the United States Supreme Court ruled in the case of *Brown v. The Board of Education of Topeka, Kansas* that racial segregation in public schools was unconstitutional. Local and state leaders vowed the decision would never take effect in Florida, but by the mid-1960s it was clear that school systems would either have to integrate or lose their valuable federal funding. In 1965, the state's Department of Education informed the Taylor County School Board that it stood to lose thousands of dollars in federal assistance, mainly from school lunch and vocational programs, if it did not submit an acceptable plan to integrate both the students and faculty in the district. The board established a new policy in which a student could apply to attend any school in the county, but assignments would be based on space availability, test scores, and other criteria. This approach resulted in some degree of integration, but federal authorities pressed the board to move faster.[50]

In August 1968, federal officials informed the school board that it would lose $175,000 in funding if it did not comply with the terms of the Civil Rights Act within a month. Jerkins High School was the main sticking point. While school officials had moved about 20 percent of the county's black students into previously all-white schools, they would not assign white students to Jerkins, which kept it essentially a segregated school. The Taylor County Education Association held a mass meeting of local teachers and suggested turning Jerkins into a junior high school or some other kind of institution—whatever was necessary to satisfy the federal mandate and avoid the loss of funding. The group also contemplated seeking a court order to force the board's hand.[51]

The school board ended up in court first, asking for an injunction to stay the cutoff of funds. Board attorney Don Dansby argued that federal officials had initially approved the county's desegregation plan and then changed their minds without giving a reason. A federal judge ordered the Department of Health, Education, and Welfare to reconsider the matter, but the funding stayed bottled up until the county submitted a new plan in 1970 that finally met with approval in Washington. Jerkins High School was closed, and its students were distributed among Gladys Morse Elementary, Perry Elementary, and the old wooden school building on Faulkner Street, plus the junior and senior high schools. Salem and Shady Grove schools were also closed as part of the deal.[52]

*   *   *

One of the most bizarre episodes in the postwar era came in 1958 when Perry briefly had two police forces, each claiming to be the legitimate officers. It all started when a group of the city's policemen complained to Mayor Willard Carmichael about Police Chief Walter Hamby. They said he treated them poorly and gave them contradictory orders on how to deal with gambling and moonshine. Carmichael called a special meeting of the city council that week and had the policemen present their case. The council members heard the policemen, then had a conversation with Chief Hamby. The chief said it was not that his orders were confusing, but rather the officers simply did not want to do as they were told.[53]

Ultimately, the council decided not to take action against Hamby, which prompted five police officers to resign. Two more officers went on leaves of absence. For several days, Chief Hamby was the city's only law enforcement officer, although he had help from the county sheriff's deputies. City firemen helped man the police station, since they shared the force's radio equipment. The city council instructed Mayor Carmichael to hire a new slate of police officers.[54]

The mayor chose, however, to side with the officers who had resigned in protest. He used his authority to suspend Chief Hamby and ordered the five resigned officers to return to their posts. He appointed one of them, Floyd Odom, to serve as acting chief of police. The council, meanwhile, established its own police force, including an acting chief, Sam Blue, who was one of the two officers who had gone on a leave of absence rather than resigning.[55]

This resulted in a peculiar situation in which there were two sets of policemen patrolling Perry. The officers backed by Mayor Carmichael wore dark blue and white uniforms and drove the city's black and white police car. The council's officers wore powder blue uniforms and drove a civilian car fitted with an emergency light. The mayor, who also served as the city judge, said he would dismiss charges brought before him by the council's policemen. The council, in turn, ordered the fire chief not to allow the mayor-backed policemen to get fuel from the city's gas pump. The council also refused to pay the mayor's officers, saying their own policemen were the only legitimate city law enforcement officials.[56]

The city charter stipulated that Chief Hamby's suspension by Mayor Carmichael had to be either sustained or overturned by the city council. At the next council meeting, the members asked anyone wanting to come forward and testify regarding the charges against Hamby. The mayor himself did not appear, saying his attorney was not available to be present. No one else offered to testify, so the council reinstated Hamby and once again declared the mayor's police force to be illegitimate. Mayor Carmichael suspended Hamby once again, as well as the council's police force, but council members instructed their men to ignore the suspension order. With no solution in sight, Perry's two police forces went on about their work, each pretending the other did not exist.[57]

Seeking to break the impasse, both sides went to court. Mayor Carmichael asked the circuit court to rule on which police force was legitimate. The city council asked for that suit to be dismissed and for the mayor's policemen to be forced to turn their equipment over to Chief Hamby. The mayor's policemen, meanwhile, sued the council for their wages. While these battles played out, state's attorney W. Randall Slaughter prepared to summon the Taylor County

Portrait of Walt Hamby, Perry's chief of police.

(Photo courtesy of the Taylor County Historical Society)

grand jury and determine whether there really was a problem with rampant gambling and moonshine.[58]

Finally, after more than two months of Perry having two feuding police forces, Judge R.H. Rowe ordered the mayor's policemen to disband and turn their equipment over to Chief Hamby. Shortly thereafter, the grand jury determined that while there was indeed a gambling and moonshine problem in town, it was nothing like the "wide open" situation Mayor Carmichael had described. Given how acrimonious the dispute between the mayor and council had gotten over the issue, however, the grand jury recommended that the legislature make the chief of police an elected position, and revise the city charter to clarify the chief's relationship with both the mayor and council.[59]

Hamby remained in office as chief for another year, but was asked to resign in 1959 after new council members came into the picture and Carmichael remained mayor. Carmichael himself resigned the following month over new disputes with the council.[60]

*   *   *

A similar spectacle took place about a decade later, although this time it was the county commission under fire rather than the chief of police. In May 1967, Governor Claude Kirk ordered an investigation into the Taylor County commissioners after receiving allegations of bribery, gambling, and attempts to influence members of the grand jury. The *Perry News-Herald*, edited at that time by Pete Osborne, had been part of the push for a probe. More than fifty locals testified before the grand jury and special state's attorney William Hopkins. The jury returned no indictments in its June 14 presentment, but did declare all five commissioners guilty of using county funds and equipment to enhance private property, mainly hauling fill dirt and building roads and canals around the beaches. For this, the grand jury recommended that Governor Kirk suspend the commissioners.[61]

Kirk opted to build up his evidence first. Jack Ledden, the governor's chief assistant, hired engineers from two different firms to come to Taylor County and assess the private property the grand jury said had been improved using public resources. The engineers' report estimated that $163,045 in work had been done on the sites in question. Ledden forwarded the report to Governor Kirk on August 10, along with the news that one of the county commissioners had been arrested following an altercation with Pete Osborne, who was aiding the investigators. Ledden's advice was to follow the grand jury's recommendation and suspend the entire slate of commissioners, although he was careful to suggest that this be done after the legislature had adjourned. At that time, the Democrats controlled both houses of the legislature, while Kirk was a Republican governor, the first since the 1870s. Politically divided as they were, relations between the legislative and executive branches had been tense, and Ledden likely feared the Senate would immediately reverse Kirk's suspension order.[62]

The governor waited until the following spring, and then suspended all five county commissioners—William Nelson Wood, William H. King, Robert L. Edwards, E.J. Tedder, and Johnny A. Livingston—on April 1, 1968. Two days later, he appointed Marvin Fleming, Don Everett, H.S. Mauldin, James A. Rawls, Jr., and Jack Burke, Jr. as replacements. When the legislature convened later that year, the ousted commissioners testified before the Senate, claiming that while they might have made some errors in judgment, on the whole their improvements around the beaches had been in the public interest and there was no evidence of graft. The Senate eventually chose not to take action on the governor's suspension order, which meant the commissioners were automatically reinstated once the legislative session was over.[63]

A bit of political theater ensued at this point. Governor Kirk suspended all five Taylor County commissioners for a second time on July 9, citing the same charges of malfeasance. He also re-appointed the same five replacements he had used before. The ousted commissioners challenged the governor's actions in court and won a favorable judgment in January 1969. Judge Sam Smith said they had suffered "double jeopardy" when Kirk re-suspended them on charges the Senate had already declined to uphold. Smith's ruling allowed two of the commissioners, R.L. Edwards and William King, to serve out the two years remaining in their terms. W.N. Wood was re-elected in the midst of this debacle, so he merely succeeded himself. Johnny Livingston and E.J. Tedder had run for re-election and lost, but the judge awarded them back pay for the time they were improperly suspended.[64]

Governor Kirk responded by suspending the entire county commission for a third time in less than a year, including the two newly elected members,

Bert Fife and Bob Millinor. He initially skirted the double jeopardy issue by basing his actions on the commission's decision to stop work on a new county courthouse near the jail on U.S. 27 and put it on the site of the old courthouse instead. Kirk accused the commissioners of resuscitating old contracts to make this sudden change rather than advertising for new bids as the law required.[65]

Hoping to bring some order to the chaos, Representative Ken Smith and a number of Taylor County citizens sought help from Florida Senate President John Matthews, who ended up calling an unprecedented special session of the Senate to settle the matter once and for all. Governor Kirk, meanwhile, appealed Judge Smith's ruling, which allowed him to amend his latest suspension order and include the old malfeasance charges, which he claimed the Senate would now have to consider. When the senators met in special session in February, a committee heard evidence from both the governor's team and the embattled commissioners. The committeemen ruled that while there was evidence of the commissioners' wrongdoing, Kirk's latest suspension order was improper because it was based partly on events that took place in an earlier term of office. As a result, the Senate rejected the suspensions and the commissioners were once again reinstated.[66]

*   *   *

That ended the bizarre cycling of county commissioners, but there was still one painful problem left to solve—the old courthouse. The debate over what to do about the iconic but aging building had been going on for several years before it became mixed up with the commissioners' drama. The building was well-loved by the public, but it was too small for the growing range of services the county provided, and the structure itself was beginning to have serious problems.

In 1966, Sheriff Maurice Linton polled county officials about whether they favored building the new courthouse on the present site or someplace else. All reportedly favored building on the existing square, and on May 2, 1966, the county commission voted unanimously to make that plan a reality. They hired architect Robert Maybin of Tallahassee to work out a design, and prepared to float a bond issue secured by the county's share of state racetrack revenue over a period of years.[67]

Here the project hit some turbulence. A sluggish bond market in the fall of 1966 forced a delay, and the Merchants Division of the Chamber of Commerce began pushing back against the idea of putting the new courthouse on the original square. If the new building were built elsewhere, the merchants argued, the city could expand parking and attract more business downtown. Commissioner Johnny Livingston also noted that tearing down the old building and putting up a new one would block traffic for as much as 18 months, complicating the slump downtown businesses were already facing.[68]

A separate group called the "Save the Courthouse Committee," led by Mrs. John Dyal and Ned Brafford, also objected to the commissioners' plan, saying the old building ought to be saved as a historic landmark. They asked the county to take a straw poll to gauge public opinion on the subject before taking any further action. The commission agreed to the poll, provided Brafford and Dyal's group paid for the ballots to be printed. "Save the Courthouse" did pay for the printing, and county election officials took the poll on March 28, 1967. The vote was 1,623 to 967, favoring renovation of the existing courthouse.[69]

Demolition of the old courthouse (1969).

(Photo courtesy of the State Archives of Florida)

It was about that time, however, that Governor Kirk launched his investigation into the county commission, which slowed the project to a crawl. At its spring 1968 term, the Taylor County grand jury urged the commissioners to move faster on the courthouse project, but Kirk suspended them shortly thereafter. The new commissioners appointed by the governor then voted to scrap the existing plan and build a three-story building out by the county jail on U.S. 27 instead.[70]

A group of 30 citizens, including three commissioners-elect set to take office in January 1969, went before the appointed commissioners and blasted their decision to ignore the results of the 1967 straw poll. The citizens sued for an injunction to stop work on the U.S. 27 site, which Judge Sam Smith granted on a temporary basis. Smith refused, however, to make the injunction permanent without a more compelling reason, and the appointed commissioners received the go-ahead to let contracts once the temporary order expired at the end of November. A.P.I. Construction of Tampa came in with the low bid at $682,400, and excavation began near the jail in December.[71]

Very little was accomplished before January, when election results and Judge Smith's double jeopardy ruling once again changed the lineup in the county commission. The new board voted on January 15 to stop work on the U.S. 27 site and build the new courthouse on the original square. Kirk's third suspension order raised the possibility that the site might change yet again, but the appointed board chose to wait and see what the Senate would do about the governor's suspensions. Once the Senate rejected the governor's latest order and the elected board returned for good, work proceeded on the new courthouse downtown. Big Chief, Inc. of Ocala began demolishing the 1908 courthouse on February 26, 1969. The new building was completed the following year and dedicated on May 24, 1970.[72]

Sentiments on the new courthouse were mixed from the beginning. Many locals found the new building bland and uninspiring compared with the ornate style of the one it replaced. Gwen Faulkner once referred to it as a "mausoleum"—no doubt the building's original stark white color did nothing to help that impression. The county later had the exterior painted, which warmed up the courthouse's appearance considerably.[73]

The current Taylor County courthouse when it was still painted white.

(Photo courtesy of the Taylor County Historical Society)

Seen from another perspective, however, the new courthouse also stood for the immense growth and progress Taylor County had experienced in just a few decades. A lot had been accomplished since World War II to make the area more prosperous. The lumber and pulpwood industries were thriving, as were other businesses that had moved into the area, like Sportscraft and Martin Electronics. Even with these developments, Perry had managed to remain essentially a rural community, retaining its small town charm and its trove of forests and beaches for locals to enjoy. As we have seen, that progress did not come without challenges, and plenty more stumbling blocks would present themselves as the 20th century drew to a close. In the next and final chapter of this history, we turn to one of the most destructive and disastrous of those moments—the Storm of the Century.

Sign dedicating the bridge over Crab Creek at Dekle Beach to the Archer family members who died during the Storm of the Century of 1993.

(Photo courtesy of Susan Moody)

CHAPTER 9

The Storm

It was dark, the wind was gusting, and Janie Hamilton could not ignore it any longer. The 90-year-old Dekle Beach resident had been through plenty of storms before, but this one sounded different—felt different. The rain was falling harder, the wind was blowing faster, and it was not even hurricane season. It was around 4:00 a.m. on March 13, 1993, and Janie and her husband Lewis "Ham" Hamilton had grandchildren and great-grandchildren living all over Dekle at that time. This storm was serious, and Janie was worried for her family.

When she got out of bed and looked out her window, she had even more cause for concern. Across the street at the Dekle Beach boat ramp, she could see the water from the canal beginning to spill over into the road and the yards of the nearby houses. This was not completely unprecedented—the canal had overflowed before. Still, this meant it was time to at least move the vehicles to higher ground. She went to the phone and called her granddaughter, Cindy Goodman, who was staying just across the street in one of the rental houses occupying that corner of the beach. Cindy's husband David answered, and after taking a look outside agreed that it was time to 'head for the hill.' There was no time to pack anything; the water was rising too quickly. David rushed over to pick up Janie and Ham in his truck; Cindy just barely got their 6-year-old son dressed and into her car before water began trickling into the floorboard. Both vehicles carefully made their way up the flooded street to try to leave the beach.

On the other side of Dekle, Cindy's twin sister, Susan Moody, was also awakened when her house began to shake from the intense gusts of wind coming off the Gulf. From the window, it was difficult to see much, but she could just barely make out Front Street (now Good Times Drive) through the driving rain. The house began to shake more violently, and the power went out, prompting Susan to decide it was time to leave. Looking out the window a second time, however, she saw that the road had disappeared beneath the incoming tide. To make matters worse, water began coming in under the doors. Susan began stacking belongings up on countertops and furniture, thinking the water could not possibly reach much higher. But the water did rise, and quickly. Driving out was no longer an option, but staying in the ground-floor portion of the house was looking dangerous as well. Grabbing only a book and a flashlight, Susan forced open the door and waded over to the wooden ladder leading to the unfinished upper floor of her home. She climbed up to the second story to wait out the storm there.[1]

A few miles south at Cedar Island, Don and Kathy Everett had settled in for the weekend with their daughter and the three- and five-year-old sons of their friends Lee and Becky Nelsen. Matthew, the youngest of the kids, woke the Everetts after the wind began to pick up after 3:00 a.m. or so. Stormy weather had been in the forecast, and at first glance nothing appeared to be too out of the ordinary—just some unusually strong wind and rain. Don and Kathy could see the tide coming in, however, and it already looked to be abnormally high. Seeing that it was not stopping, the Everetts decided to dress the kids and head for Perry. The lights went out just as they were getting everyone awake, so they finished their hurried preparations by candlelight.[2]

Around that same time, the power was beginning to flicker down the coast at Steinhatchee. Ed and Monica Elliott, who operated the Woods Gulf Breeze RV Campground, had gone to bed feeling prepared for what they thought was coming. The loose odds and ends around the place were picked up, and the doors to their storage buildings were nailed shut. The furious sounds of the wind and rain woke them up around 4:00 am, however, and they quickly saw that this was more of a storm than the weather reports had called for. The Elliotts could see water creeping into the campground, but they felt sure it was just puddles of rain. By the time they realized the water was actually coming from the Gulf, it was too late to drive out. Their vehicles were flooded and would not start. All they could do was stay put and watch.[3]

These Taylor Countians and their neighbors could not have known it at the time, but they were awakening to a meteorological freak of nature—a monstrous and destructive weather system that would quickly be named the "Storm of the Century," or the "No-Name Storm." Unlike a hurricane that forecasters might track for many days, this storm was relatively young—it had started out only two days before as a normal low pressure system off the coast of Texas. Over the next day, however, a combination of factors allowed it to rapidly transform into what weather experts sometimes call a "bomb cyclone." By the afternoon of March 12, ships and oil platforms off the coast of Louisiana were reporting sustained winds above 80 miles per hour, and the speeds were still climbing.[4]

Mike Rucker, who had been a meteorologist at WCTV in Tallahassee for nearly two decades, watched these reports roll in on March 12, along with barometric pressure readings from the Gulf that looked eerily similar to a hurricane. "The only other time I had seen isobar readings like that was for Hurricane Kate in 1985," he later said. The National Weather

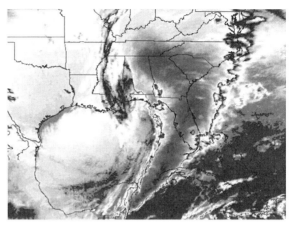

Satellite imagery showing the Storm of the Century just as it began lashing the Florida coast early on March 13, 1993.

(Image courtesy of the National Weather Service)

Service saw these same reports, but predicted the storm would produce conditions typical for a seasonal winter squall—thunderstorms, possibly some tornadoes, and winds topping out around 30 miles per hour. Forecast models correctly identified the storm and where it would go—what they had not counted on was the system's swift intensification. Most of the storm's sudden growth occurred in a "blind spot" in the Gulf where weather instruments were lacking at that time. At 3:45 pm local time on March 12, a flood watch was issued for the entire Gulf coast of Florida, followed by a gale warning at 4:30pm. State and local officials were aware of these warnings, but at no point did they issue an evacuation order.[5]

Rucker believed the situation was more serious. WCTV opened all three of its evening news broadcasts on March 12 with the latest on the weather, which gave him opportunities to describe the potential severity of the storm. He warned of likely coastal flooding, high winds, downed power lines, even the snow that eventually fell early the next morning. Station officials would not, however, allow him to publicly recommend evacuations or give warnings that deviated too far from the guidance given by the National Weather Service. "We tried to warn everyone as best we could," he later said. The national weather experts, for their part, did finally issue a coastal flood warning, but not until 5:08 a.m. on the morning of March 13.[6]

By that time, it was too late. The storm's powerful winds had already pushed a 12-foot wall of water onto the Taylor County coastline, carrying fishing docks, cars and trucks, boats, propane tanks, and entire houses with it. At Keaton Beach, Lynn Aibejeris, who owned the Old Pavilion Restaurant and Motel, watched with horror as her double-wide trailer began to split down the middle and the Gulf came pouring in. As the walls began peeling away, she, her son, and two others wrapped themselves around the exposed studs in one of the bedrooms and held on. Fearful for what might happen if they attempted to leave, they stayed that way for hours, suffering bruises and scrapes as furniture and appliances drifted around the flooded room and crashed into them. When the water finally receded, the current took Aibejeris and the others with it, forcing them to swim toward a neighbor's home for safety.[7]

At Cedar Island, Don and Kathy Everett had finished preparing to leave only to realize their vehicles were floating away in the surging flood outside. The water began pushing up the floors and breaking in through the windows of the house. Don tried at one point to go outside, but the waves were at his chest and nearly knocked him over. Even with the water several feet deep inside the house, he believed if they could hold out until the tide turned around 5:30 a.m., they would be alright. In the meantime, he and Kathy put the children on top of the kitchen counter and held on, staying put until the water receded.[8]

Over at Dekle Beach, many of the houses closest to the Gulf broke up entirely as the storm surge came ashore. Hud Lilliott and Laurie O'Quinn (later his wife) were staying at the Lilliotts' house on Front Street that night. They had already gotten up once to check on the tide, but they did not see anything too alarming at that point. Half an hour later, however, Laurie looked out and saw that the house next door had collapsed, and Hud's truck had floated away. The couple moved to the inland side of the house, but the floor boards were beginning to pop up from the pressure of the water beneath, and they knew they had to leave. Hud and Laurie had just gotten outside when the house began to give way. They jumped into the dark water below and made their way across the street to another home that was still standing. They looked around, hoping to find some life jackets they could use to stay afloat in the churning water if they had to swim again. Before they could find anything, this house too began to break apart. The pair climbed onto the roof, but were knocked off by a wave and ended up with only a floating board to hang onto as the current pushed them across the marsh toward the tree line.[9]

They ended up at the home of Carlton and Inez Hamilton, where they were confronted by some of the storm's most tragic costs. Melinda Sapp, whose family had rented a house on Front Street that weekend, had also made it to the Hamilton home. She had become separated from the others when their rental house collapsed, but she had managed to hold onto her 20-month-old daughter, Anissa. By the time she floated across the marsh and reached the Hamiltons, however, the baby had drowned. This was only the beginning of Melinda's nightmare; rescuers would later discover the bodies of her husband, son, brother, mother, and a family friend amid the debris.[10]

As the water began to recede, neighbors arrived at the Hamilton house and offered to take the occupants next door to the home of Ruth and Craig Harvey. Dozens of residents had ended up there, and there was a fire in the fire-place. Some, like Lewis Moody and Fred Morgan and their families, had been lucky enough to have boats near their homes when the storm surge hit, and they were able to make their way to the Harvey house that way. Others were forced to float their way inland at the mercy of the tide. Susan Moody, who had initially taken refuge in the unfinished upper floor of her house, ended up jumping into the water and swimming for her life after the house appeared to be on the verge of collapsing. "Swimming" is perhaps the wrong word; she later explained that the waves and current made it impossible to truly swim or even stay entirely above water. To make matters worse, debris was flying through the air and skidding across the surface of the churning water—propane tanks, pieces of houses, sheets of tin and plywood. Miraculously, one of Susan's own boat cushions came floating by and she was able to hold onto it and drift with the current across the marsh toward the tree line. Once she reached a place she could finally touch the ground, she waded over to the Harvey house and was reunited with the other survivors there. Not long afterward, her neighbors Charles and Diane Carlton arrived as well, having made the same perilous trip across the marsh.[11]

Janie and Ham Hamilton and David and Cindy Goodman also ended up at the Harvey house. After picking up the elderly Hamiltons in his truck, David took them to safety at the Harveys' while Cindy attempted to leave the beach in her car with their young son. Just past the

Storm surge gutted the home of Janie and Lewis "Ham" Hamilton not long after they left for higher ground.

(Photo courtesy of Susan Moody)

Harvey house, however, the car stalled and began to float, forcing the two to abandon it. David saw his wife's headlights dip below the water and hurried over to help. Cindy and their son climbed into the cab and the family tried once again to leave the beach. They made it only a few more yards, however, before the truck also stalled and began slowly drifting toward the ditch. Out of options for leaving, David and Cindy made their way to the top of the banked curve on the road leading into Dekle Beach, their son perched atop David's shoulders. The water was chest-high in places, and they were forced to stop periodically to let a refrigerator or a piece of a dock float by. In time, however, the Goodmans made it back to the Harvey house unscathed.

*　　*　　*

The true magnitude of the storm's destruction was only revealed when the sun began to rise on the morning of March 13. Up and down the Taylor County coast, many of the houses that had not been raised up on pilings were either gutted or blown away completely. The final count was 115 homes destroyed and 252 damaged. Sometimes even the houses on taller pilings, like many of the ones on Dekle Beach's Front Street, were obliterated. Only clusters of twisted wooden poles remained to show where houses had once been. Some homes remained intact but floated off their foundations. Lewis Moody's home at Dekle, for example, was carried more than a quarter of a mile across the Jug Island Road before settling down in the marsh at the tree line. When the family later located the house and looked inside, the floor was covered with a layer of mud but almost everything remained intact, even most of the dishes in the kitchen cabinets.[12]

As the storm surge receded that morning, it deposited the splintered remains of homes and their contents wherever they happened to stop floating. The roads and canals were piled with walls, roofs, shingles, refrigerators, cabinets, and household goods of every description. Broken glass was everywhere, and bits of insulation and torn fabric were twisted around practically every nail. Even today, if you look in sandy spots at the hardest hit beaches, you can still find bits of glass and the asbestos shingles that were commonly used for siding on pre-storm houses.

Cleanup was the last thing on the minds of law enforcement and EMS officials as they rushed to the beaches that morning, however. The first calls for help began coming in around 4:00 a.m., although only a few could get through before the storm surge wiped out the telephone equipment. Around 4:30 a.m., Deputy Sheriff Audie Towles and his brother John drove down the Beach Road as far as they could and then launched a boat just south of the water plant and rode the rest of the way into Keaton Beach to rescue survivors there. Firefighters Marty Tompkins, Pete Bishop, and Carl McAfee used the same strategy with Tompkins's boat at Spring Warrior and rescued at least nine people before moving on to the beaches farther south.[13]

Boats, appliances, lumber, and the contents of homes clog the canal between Palmetto and Mexico roads at Dekle Beach.

(Photo courtesy of Susan Moody)

Don Gutshall, administrator at the Taylor County Jail, was one of the first rescuers to venture into Dekle Beach. The road was strewn with debris and the storm surge had not yet fully drained away, so Gutshall and another man rode in the bucket of a front-end loader. Waves crashed in on the men as they headed down the road. At first, the only survivors they could find were at Susan Moody's house—about ten people had taken refuge there sometime after she decided to leave. The wooden ladder leading to the second story was gone, so rescuers evacuated the survivors by lifting up the bucket and carrying people out two at a time. Later, they began evacuating people from the Harvey house as well.[14]

In Perry, emergency management and disaster recovery crews snapped into action. Doctors Memorial Hospital activated its "Code D" disaster plan around 7:00 a.m., drawing in nearly all employees and associates, including doctors Nelson, Shugar, and Rawls. More than 40 patients were treated in the emergency room that morning, mostly for hypothermia, cuts, and other minor injuries. Nine patients were admitted to the hospital for further care.[15]

The American Red Cross established a shelter at the old Perry Primary School to house affected residents. By 10:00 a.m., most of the survivors had been rescued and either released to relatives and friends or transported to the shelter on school buses. Volunteers were everywhere—registering storm victims, entertaining children, offering sandwiches and hot coffee and dry clothing. Local churches brought in tables full of food, plus clothing and shoes.

Many survivors had not been able to salvage anything before they left; some people arrived with freezing cold wet shoes and socks or no shoes at all. Perry residents went to the local stores and bought hundreds of dollars' worth of underwear and towels and necessities to distribute.[16]

Once friends and relatives were accounted for and basic needs were met, beach residents quickly became anxious to get back to their shattered homes to see what was left and protect what property they could. There were still people missing, however, particularly at Dekle Beach, and law enforcement officials established a checkpoint at Deadman's Curve on the Beach Road to prevent anyone from entering the area. Officers from the Coast Guard, Customs Service, the State Fire Marshal, and agencies as far away as South Georgia descended on the beaches and combed through the tangled debris with search dogs, looking for survivors or bodies. Once the officials finished looking through a house, they scrawled a large red "X" on the front in red spray paint. Many of those X's disappeared in the ensuing months as homes were bulldozed or repaired. Other residents left theirs right where they were—a sobering reminder of their experiences.[17]

By Sunday afternoon (March 14), search and rescue teams had counted seven fatalities, six at Dekle Beach and one at Keaton Beach. The deaths at Dekle included Anissa Sapp, plus two other members of the Sapp party that had rented the house on Front Street. Three members of the Mike Archer family were also found—his mother Sibyl, his wife Charlene, and his step-son Derek Johnson. The one death at Keaton Beach was Edward A. Hunter, affectionately known by the locals as "Mr. Ed." On Monday, once residents were allowed back into Dekle Beach, three more bodies were found, all members of the Sapp family. That brought the total number of fatalities to ten.[18]

Rebuilding

Even in the midst of such tragedy and destruction, many of the people who lost their homes and property vowed almost immediately to rebuild. "This is a very tough community," Mimi Briglio, owner of the Paradise Motel, said of Steinhatchee. "We could sit on the curb and cry, but we don't have curbs." Instead, she told reporters she and her husband planned to build back their home and their business better than ever. For many residents, the beaches were a way of life, something not easily abandoned even with the sacrifices they would have to make to rebuild. "I was raised down here during the summers," Charles Carlton later said of Dekle Beach. "I loved it and I said when I was grown, I was going to live here. The cost of building after the storm was quite a bit more expensive, but I did it." A number of Taylor County families shared Mimi and Charles' strong desire to return to the beaches. Turning that dream into a reality often proved difficult, however, and for some it never came true at all.[19]

The first step was getting government officials to understand the extent of the storm's destruction. Governor Lawton Chiles flew over the Taylor County beaches as part of a tour of affected areas all along the Gulf coast. "It's devastated," he said of the wreckage he saw below. "We've never had a storm like this." Chiles declared disaster areas in 23 Florida counties, while President Bill Clinton made the same dec-

Looking south down Front Street (now Good Times Drive) at Dekle Beach after the storm had washed away most of the waterfront homes.

(Photo courtesy of Susan Moody)

laration at the federal level. This opened the way for the Federal Emergency Management Agency (FEMA) to come to Taylor County and offer crucial assistance to local families.[20]

By Wednesday of the week following the storm, FEMA had set up a disaster response center at the National Guard armory in Perry. The agency served as a funnel point for disaster recovery services from a number of agencies. FEMA itself gave out small grants to cover disaster-related unemployment and some home repairs that insurance didn't cover. The agency also provided travel trailers for displaced families to use while they rebuilt their homes or made other arrangements. The Small Business Administration (SBA) offered low-interest loans of up to $100,000 to help people repair or replace their homes, and up to $500,000 to help business owners get their businesses back up and running. These loans were especially valuable for storm victims, whose homeowner's insurance generally did not cover flood damage.[21]

These were helpful services, but in practice it took more than just signing on the dotted line to take advantage of them. Many of the homes at Taylor County's beaches had been built in the 1940s and 1950s, when building codes were practically non-existent and state and federal authorities only barely regulated dredging and filling activities along the coast. By 1993, however, much had changed, and while the old houses had been grandfathered in as long as they stood, any new construction would have to comply with the newest codes. And, thanks in part to Hurricane Andrew the previous year, those codes had become stricter than ever.

One of the biggest problems confronting landowners was that the "land" they owned had often ceased to be land, partly because of the storm and partly due to years of coastal erosion that had eaten away at the sand. This wasn't such a big deal as long as the houses stood—their pilings kept them out of harm's way even when water went all the way underneath them at high tide. When the time came after the storm to pull a building permit to replace a house, however, county building inspectors had to say no. Florida law prohibited building houses over water. Furthermore, the state claimed all land covered by the Gulf at high tide, even if that land had been high and dry when the owner bought it. These restrictions completely shut out most landowners along Front Street at Dekle Beach, plus several others at Ezell and Keaton beaches. Tyson and Janet Hicks, for example, lost a vacation home near the Old Pavilion at Keaton that had been standing for nearly 40 years. The house was originally built over dry land, but the ebb and flow of the Gulf tides had washed much of the sand away over the years. When they sought permission to rebuild, state officials assessed their lot and said it said it legally extended only ten feet out from the road.[22]

Septic tanks were another major sticking point. All new construction had to include an approved septic system with an adequate drain field to qualify for a building permit. Crucially, that meant being able to install a septic tank at least 50 feet from water or marshland and two feet above sea level. Even those residents who hadn't suffered as much erosion as the Hicks or the Front Street landowners often had trouble meeting this requirement. In some cases, landowners were allowed to bring in fill dirt to bring their lots up to par, but getting permission to do the filling required a whole separate permitting process that involved the Florida Department of Environmental Protection and the Army Corps of Engineers. These agencies did grant a number of fill permits, but not if the filling appeared likely to encroach on protected marshes or tidal waters.[23]

Local and state officials took steps to streamline the process and work with landowners, but anger and frustration set in fairly quickly when it became clear that many would be unable to rebuild their homes or even use the land they had enjoyed for decades. "We're not trying to fight the rules," Betty Ann Hatcher of Dekle Beach told a reporter. "We just want to put our house back." The Hatchers were lucky in some ways—they had to pay thousands of dollars to fill in their lot across Front Street from the Gulf, but eventually they were able to put in an acceptable septic system and rebuild.[24]

Others were not so lucky. Nearly 30 landowners were originally told they could not rebuild because too much of their land had eroded away. Within a year, ten of those landowners had received permission to rebuild, provided they installed self-contained "gray water" sewage systems. Others sued the state for the right to reclaim the land they had purchased, although that litigation sometimes lasted for more than a decade. Some gave up entirely. Representative Allen Boyd tried for a couple of years to pass a law that would waive the state's strict building requirements for victims of the storm, but federal authorities warned that such a measure could jeopardize Florida's eligibility for future disaster aid. The bill did not pass.[25]

Everyone who rebuilt, even those who faced little to no trouble getting their permits, encountered another major obstacle when they began designing their new homes. To qualify for a bank loan, landowners had to purchase flood insurance. To qualify for flood insurance, the home had to be built at a certain height above the mean high water level—meaning the average local water level at high tide. As a result, most coastal homes in Taylor County had to be built or raised to an average of 18 feet above the ground. This requirement greatly increased the cost of building at the beaches, to the point that some families made the difficult choice not to rebuild at all.[26]

* * *

The Storm of the Century proved to be a turning point for Taylor County, at least as far as the beaches were concerned. As the disaster unfolded, it brought out the best and bravest in ordinary citizens, who often put their own lives at risk to help friends and neighbors get to safety. "The response was unbelievable," Sheriff John Wesley Walker said. "The death toll would have been much greater if private citizens did not help neighbors." That same spirit of generosity continued in the days and weeks that followed, as the community rallied around families who had lost homes, possessions, and loved ones. In many ways, this was an illustration of what so many people had valued about the beaches—the sense of togetherness, tradition, and belonging.[27]

That way of life did not die with the storm, but it did change. A number of old regulars whose families had been around for decades were suddenly absent, their property vacant. The noise and bustle of hangouts like the Old Pavilion and the Dekle Beach store were silenced. Permits, building standards, and huge mortgages added a level of complexity to beach living that had previously been virtually unknown. Not least of all, residents were much more cautious about storms and their destructive power. "A burnt child is scared of fire," Ralph Carlton said, for example, when explaining his extensive preparations for Hurricane Allison two years after the storm.[28]

In a word, the beaches lost some of their innocence after that dark, frigid March night—some of the simplicity and familiarity that had made them such a source of joy to so many Taylor County families, and to countless people from other places. That is not to say, of course,

The Dekle Beach store and dock in 1969.

(Photo courtesy of the State Archives of Florida)

that plenty of good things have not happened along the Taylor County coast in the three decades since the storm. On the contrary, the future of the beach communities looks bright. For the people who can look across the shoreline at those bare wooden pilings and remember what was once there, however, it can never be the same.

Afterword

The View from 2020

Taylor County has experienced some exciting milestones in recent decades. The population increased by 12.5% between 1990 and 2000, and then by 17.2% between 2000 and 2010. New schools, new businesses, a new hospital, and extensive efforts to revitalize downtown Perry have all helped give the community a boost. The Florida Forest Festival is still a major focal point on the local calendar, and new events like the Fiddler Crab Festival in Steinhatchee and the Pickin' in the Pines Bluegrass Festival are gaining in popularity and drawing visitors from around the region. There's a lot to be proud of.

That being said, some changes have provoked more wariness than celebration. The pulpwood mill at Foley, still the county's largest employer, has been sold twice, once in 1993 and again in 2013 when it was acquired by its current owner, Georgia-Pacific. The land once owned by Buckeye Cellulose, which includes more than half the land in Taylor County, has also sold twice, and is now held by a company controlled by billionaire Thomas Peterffy. So far, even with these developments, the pulpwood industry has continued uninterrupted, and the timberland owners have declined to make any radical changes. Still, with the local economy so heavily dependent on pulpwood and related industries, and with control of so much land concentrated in the hands of so few, residents cannot help but wonder—sometimes apprehensively—what's in store for the future.

The issue of development remains especially prickly. Taylor County is not as remote as it once was, thanks to modern communication and transportation, and outsiders are beginning to see it as the hidden gem that it is. From one perspective, this is a very exciting trend. More visitors and residents will likely generate more demand for goods and services, which means more jobs and hopefully a more prosperous life for both the newcomers and the locals. Looking around at other parts of Florida, however, it's no secret that development can come with a cost, and not just the kind you can calculate in dollars and cents. One of the essential challenges of our time is to carefully decide how to strike a balance between the benefits of growth and the strong desire of many residents to preserve the rural character that makes Taylor County special. The solution to this puzzle, like so many things, is a work in progress.

Notes

Chapter 1: Before 1856

[1] Alan Yuhas, "Sinkhole Discovery Suggests Humans Were in Florida 14,500 Years Ago," *The Guardian*, 14 May 2016.

[2] Don Serbousek, "Explorations of a Paleo-Indian Site on the Aucilla River," *The Florida Archaeologist* 36, no. 1-2 (March-June 1983): 88-97; Robin C. Brown, *Florida's First People: 12,000 Years of Human History* (Sarasota, Fla.: Pineapple Press, 1994), 14.

[3] Gordon R. Willey, *Archaeology of the Florida Gulf Coast* (Gainesville, Fla.: University Press of Florida, 1998), 15; Clarence B. Moore, *Certain Aboriginal Remains of the Northwest Florida Coast*, 2 vol. (Philadelphia: P.C. Stockhausen, 1901-02).

[4] Florida Master Site File reports for Site 8TA127, Florida Division of Historical Resources.

[5] Jerald T. Milanich, *Florida's Indians from Ancient Times to the Present* (Gainesville, Fla.: University Press of Florida, 1998), 72-77.

[6] Ibid., 171-177; John E. Worth, *The Timucuan Chiefdoms of Spanish Florida,* vol. 1 (Gainesville, Fla.: University Press of Florida, 1998), 3-4.

[7] Allen C. Morris, *Florida Place Names* (Coral Gables, Fla.: University of Miami Press, 1974), 138; William A. Read, *Florida Place Names of Indian Origin and Seminole Personal Names* (Baton Rouge: Louisiana State University Press, 1934), 32-33.

[8] Read, *Place Names*, 10.

[9] John Lee Williams, *The Territory of Florida* (Gainesville, Fla.: University Press of Florida, 1962), 48

[10] Ibid., 7.

[11] J. Lee Williams, *Map of Florida* (New York: Greene and McGowan, 1837).

[12] John Mackay and J.E. Blake, *Map of the Seat of War in Florida* (Washington: W.J. Stone, 1839).

[13] Knight of Elvas and Luys Hernandez de Biedma, *Narratives of the Career of Hernando de Soto in the Conquest of Florida* (New York: Bradford Club, 1866), 231-234.

[14] Mark F. Boyd, "Mission Sites in Florida," *Florida Historical Quarterly* 17, no. 4 (Apr 1939): 255-280.

[15] Charlton W. Tebeau, *A History of Florida*, 3rd ed. (Coral Gables, Fla.: University of Miami Press, 1999), 17-20.

[16] Michael Gannon, "First European Contacts," in *The New History of Florida*, ed. Michael Gannon (Gainesville, Fla.: University Press of Florida, 1996), 22-23.

[17] Ibid., 23-24.

[18] Ibid., 24-30.

[19] Worth, *Timucuan Chiefdoms*, vol. 1, 3; Tebeau, *A History of Florida*, 27-34.

[20] Worth, *Timucuan Chiefdoms*, 63-72.

[21] Ibid., 35; W.T. Cash, "W.T. Cash Letter – Taylor County History," in *Cash Writings of Taylor County Florida* (Perry, Fla.: Taylor County Historical Society, 2007), 23-25; Ernest F. Dibble, "Captain Hugh Young and His 1818 Topographical Memoir to Andrew Jackson," *Florida Historical Quarterly* 55, no. 3 (Jan. 1977): 327-328. See also a reprinting of Captain Young's memoir, *Florida Historical Quarterly* 13, no. 3 (Jan. 1935): 145.

[22] Michael V. Gannon, *Florida: Short History* (Gainesville, Fla.: University Press of Florida, 1993), 17.

[23] Paul Johnson, *A History of the American People* (New York: HarperCollins, 1997), 163-167.

[24] John Hambly, a Panton, Leslie and Company employee who also served occasionally as an agent of the Spanish government in St. Augustine, chronicles two different trips through the vicinity of Taylor County in 1794 that mention local rivers and San Pedro Bay. See Daniel J.J. Ross and Bruce S. Chappell, eds., "Visit to the Indian Nations: The Diary of John Hambly," *Florida Historical Quarterly* 55, no. 1 (July 1976): 60-73; and Richard K. Murdoch, ed., "Mission to the Creek Nation in 1794," *Florida Historical Quarterly* 34, no. 3 (Jan. 1956): 266-284.

[25] John K. Mahon and Brent R. Weisman, "Florida's Seminole and Miccosukee Peoples," in *The New History of Florida*, ed. Michael Gannon (Gainesville, Fla.: University Press of Florida, 1996), 190-191.

[26] Ibid., 191-192.

[27] The 1848 plat is accessible from the General Land Office Records database of the U.S. Department of the Interior's Bureau of Land Management (glorecords.blm.gov). Jackson's description of the battle near the Econfina River is described in his April 20, 1818 letter to Secretary of War John C. Calhoun, *American State Papers*: Military Affairs 1:700-701.

[28] Jackson to Calhoun, April 20, 1818, *American State Papers*: Military Affairs 1:700-701.

[29] Mark F. Boyd and Gerald M. Ponton, eds., "[Captain Hugh Young's] Topographical Memoir on East and West Florida with Itineraries of General Jackson's Army, 1818," *Florida Historical Quarterly* 13, no. 1 (July 1934): 30-31.

[30] Tebeau, *A History of Florida*, 102-104.

[31] Eli B. Whitaker to the Secretary of the Navy, October 1, 1831 and November 23, 1831, *American State Papers: Naval Affairs* 4:99.

[32] Tebeau, *A History of Florida*, 137-139.

[33] Ibid., 139.

[34] Elizabeth H. Sims, *A History of Madison County* (Madison County Historical Society, 1986), 28. Regarding Hayward, see Edward E. Baptist, *Creating an Old South: Middle Florida's Plantation Frontier before the Civil War* (Chapel Hill: University of North Carolina Press, 2002), 127, 151-153.

[35] Ibid., 20, plus roster of Livingston's company in the Appendix; John K. Mahon, *History of the Second Seminole War, 1835-1842*, 2nd ed. (Gainesville, Fla.: University of Florida Press, 1985), 210-226.

[36] James F. Sunderman, ed., *Journey into Wilderness: An Army Surgeon's Account of Life in Camp and Field during the Creek and Seminole Wars, 1836-1838 by Jacob Rhett Motte* (Gainesville, Fla.: University of Florida Press, 1953), 83; *The Floridian*, 8 July 1837; *Tallahassee Watchman*, 25 July 1838.

[37] Mahon, *History of the Second Seminole* War, 161.

[38] Ibid., 249-251.

[39] Woodburne Potter, *The War in Florida* (Baltimore: Lewis and Coleman, 1836), 98.

[40] Fort Pleasant's location is given in an appendix of George Washington Cullum, *Biographical Register of the Officers and Graduates of the U.S. Military Academy from 1802 to 1867* (New York: D. Van Nostrand, 1868), 31. Its date of establishment is given on the initial post return from the fort. See *Returns from U.S. Military Posts, 1800-1916* (National Archives Microfilm Publication M617), roll 941.

[41] Florida Master Site File record for Fort Frank Brooke (site 8TA276), Florida Division of Historical Resources; Zachary Taylor to Richard Keith Call, 3 Jan 1839 in Document 278 of US Senate, *Public Documents*, vol. 5 (Washington, 1839), 165-166.

[42] Zachary Taylor's report to the Adjutant General, 4 Jan 1838 in John T. Sprague, *The Origin, Progress, and Conclusion of the Florida War* (New York: D. Appleton and Company, 1848), 210.

[43] *Army and Navy Chronicle,* 23 May 1839.

[44] James Belgen to John Green, 21 July 1839 and S. Woods to William Davenport, 20 Aug 1839 in Box 2, William Davenport Papers (MS 22), Special Collections, University of Florida.

[45] Samuel Woods to John Green, 19 Aug 1839 and Samuel Woods to William Davenport, 20 Aug 1839 in Box 2, Davenport Papers.

[46] *The Floridian,* 28 Dec 1839; *Army and Navy Chronicle*, 16 Jan 1840; *Niles' Register*, 20 Jun 1840.

[47] Captain John Mackay and Lieutenant J. Black, "A Map of the Seat of War in Florida" (1840), State Library of Florida. See also W.T. Cash, "Taylor County History and Civil War Deserters," *Florida Historical Quarterly* 27, no. 1 (July 1948), 34; and Sprague, *The Florida War*, 434.

[48] Sprague, *The Florida War*, 434; Donald D. Spencer, *Florida's Historic Forts, Camps, and Battlefields: A Pictorial Encyclopedia* (Ormond Beach, Fla.: Camelot Publishing, 2006), 155. See also post returns from Fort Pleasant dating as late as October 1842 in *Returns from U.S. Military Posts*, roll 941.

[49] "Table Showing the Number of Indians Remaining Out," 14 Feb 1842, *Territorial Papers of the United States* 26, 520-521; Worth to Adjutant General of the Army, 10 April 1842 in House Doc. 262, 27th Congress, 2nd Sess., v. 5, 20-21.

Chapter 2: Early Settlers

[1] These calculations are based on data from the 1860 census.

[2] Edward E. Baptist, *Creating an Old South: Middle Florida's Plantation Frontier Before the Civil War* (Chapel Hill: University of North Carolina Press, 2002), 37-44.

3 In addition to census records, see Fred T. Foster and Patricia O'Quinn Foster, *Descendants of Allen O'Quinn and Mary Ann Brown O'Quinn, Residents of Florida* (San Diego: n.p., 1990), passim. For more information on the English family, see *Pioneers of Wiregrass Georgia*, vol. 3, p. 87-88; and vol. 5, p. 141-142. For information on the Robert McFail Hendry family, see Rev. James A. Hendry, *By the Name of Hendry* (n.p., 1962).

4 For more on squatting and preemption, see Baptist, *Creating an Old South*, 45-51.

5 For records of federal land sales, visit the U.S. Department of the Interior, Bureau of Land Management's Official Federal Land Records Site at glorecords.blm.gov. For records of state land sales, visit the Florida Department of Environmental Protection – Bureau of State Lands' Land Document Search page at prodenv.dep.state.fl.us/DslBtlds/public/welcome.

6 Land patents from the US Department of the Interior, Bureau of Land Management's Official Federal Land Records site.

7 Henry Parker mortgage, 5 June 1860 in Taylor County Deed Book AB, 40. Deeds for William Bevan and William McMullen are available from the Department of the Interior – Bureau of Land Management.

8 "Important Legislation," *Floridian and Journal,* 15 Dec 1855; "Census Returns," *Floridian and Journal,* 8 Sept 1855.

9 Chapter 806, Laws of Florida (1856), 48-50; Tract Book for Township 4 South, Range 7 East, 169.

10 B.J. Nettles, "Taylor County," a report written for the Historical Records Survey of the Works Progress Administration, circa 1940. Manuscript copy held by the State Library of Florida.

11 See, for example, a deed between William McMullen and J.H. Sappington, 6 Aug 1859 in Taylor County Deedbook AB.

12 Application to open Rosehead post office, 11 Feb 1869, in Post Office Department, Reports of Site Locations, 1837-1950 (National Archives Microfilm Publication M1126), roll 99; minutes of the Taylor County Commissioners' Court for 12 Apr 1869 and 2 Apr 1870 (Series L 326), State Archives of Florida.

13 Minutes of the Taylor County Commissioners' Court for 22 Mar 1870 (Series L 326), State Archives of Florida.

14 See Asher and Adams' 1873 map of Florida, State Library of Florida. For Tillman's explanation of the Rosehead-Perry post office conundrum, see Tillman to John L. Routt, Second Assistant Postmaster General, ca. 4 Dec 1874 in Post Office Department, Reports of Site Locations, 1837-1950 (National Archives Microfilm Publication M1126), roll 99.

15 John Grantham's deed is in Taylor County Deed Book AB, 12.

16 "Moving Day for 109-Year-Old Whiddon Homestead," Tallahassee Democrat, 18 Aug 1972; Elizabeth H. Sims, A History of Madison County (Madison, Fla.: Madison County Historical Society, 1986), 35-36.

17 "Life of the Early Settlers" in Cash Writings of Taylor County Florida (Perry, Fla.: Taylor County Historical Society, 2007), 32-33.

18 Household inventory of Julia A. Willis, 1 July 1863 in Taylor County Deed Book AB, 47; and household inventory of Mamie Delilah Wilcox, 29 Dec 1871 in Taylor County Deed Book AB, 180.

[19] "Taylor County's Old Watermills Gone Now," in Cash Writings, 118-120.

[20] James H. Wentworth estimated that on Taylor County land where cows had been penned, sugar cane would produce as much as twelve barrels of syrup or eight barrels of granulated raw sugar. The yields went even higher for hammock land. See Wentworth's report in Florida Lands and Immigration Commission, Florida: Its Climate, Soil, and Productions (Jacksonville: E.M. Cheney, 1873), 113.

[21] Slave schedules from the 1860 federal census of Taylor County; and the 1857 tax rolls, Box 120, Series 28, State Archives of Florida.

[22] "Dancing Called Sin Long Ago," Cash Writings, 149-150.

[23] Tommie Stanaland, "Rocky Ford Primitive Baptist Church," manuscript in possession of the author; "Shiloh Primitive Baptist Church," manuscript held by the Taylor County Historical Society.

[24] Pat Rosier, "155 Candles Lighted for Springhill," manuscript in Ephemera Collection, Taylor County Historical Society; Marjorie R. Woodell, History of Education in Taylor County (Perry, Fla.: Taylor County Retired Educators Association, 1998), 3-4.

[25] "History of Taylor County," Cash Writings, 19.

[26] "Robert McFail Hendry," They Were Here, vol. 4, 1; "Thomas B. Hendry," They Were Here, vol. 1, 34; "John Wright Hendry," They Were Here, vol. 1, 7; 1860 federal census for Taylor County; private correspondence with Donna O'Steen Mixon.

[27] Contract between John W. Mixson and members of the Pisgah community, 1850, Vertical File, State Library of Florida.

[28] Florida State Department of Public Instruction – Research Division, Narrative Reports of County Superintendents, 1869-70 to 1879-80 (Tallahassee, Fla., 1962), 16-17.

[29] Ibid.

[30] Woodell, History of Education in Taylor County, 9-10.

[31] "Log Schools Common Here at Turn of Century," Cash Writings, 79-80.

[32] Wentworth's quote comes from his 1873 report to Florida's Secretary of Agriculture. See Florida: Its Climate, Soil, and Productions, 116.

Chapter 3: The Civil War

[1] Herbert J. Dougherty, Jr., Richard Keith Call, Southern Unionist (Gainesville, Fla.: University of Florida Press, 1961), 158.

[2] John F. Reiger, "Deprivation, Disaffection, and Desertion in Confederate Florida," Florida Historical Quarterly 48, no. 3 (January 1970): 279-283.

[3] Charlton W. Tebeau and William Marina, A History of Florida, 3rd ed. (Coral Gable, Fla.: University of Miami Press, 1999), 179-180.

[4] Ibid., 180; W.T. Cash, "Taylor County History and Civil War Deserters," The Florida Historical Quarterly 27, no. 1 (July 1948): 28-58.

[5] Cash, "Taylor County History," 45.

[6] Compiled Service Records of Confederate Soldiers Who Served in Organizations from the State of Florida (National Archives Microfilm Publication M251), roll 2; Confederate Pension Applications (Series S587), State Archives of Florida.

[7] Fred L. Robertson, ed., *Soldiers of Florida in the Seminole Indian, Civil, and Spanish-American Wars* (Live Oak, Fla.: Democrat Printing Company, 1903), 42-43; Letter from Dr. Wilson T. Hendry to the State Comptroller's Office, 11 Dec 1961, contained in the pension application file of John Wright Hendry (A02762), in Box 68, Confederate Pension Application Files; Florida Department of Military Affairs, *Special Archives Publication No. 92* (St. Augustine: State Arsenal, 1989), 78-89; 135-153.

[8] Confederate pension applications for James G. Green (A01928) and James B. Watts (A05467), Confederate Pension Application Files; James Hamilton Wentworth diary transcript, Alton Wentworth Collection, Taylor County Historical Society.

[9] Tebeau and Marina, *History of Florida*, 217-219.

[10] The *Sentinel* article is quoted in Robert A. Taylor: *Rebel Storehouse: Florida in the Confederate Economy* (Tuscaloosa: University of Alabama Press, 1995), 45-46. For Cash's description of saltmaking along the Taylor County coast, see Cash, "Taylor County History," 46.

[11] Taylor, *Rebel Storehouse*, 46.

[12] Ibid., 99-100

[13] Joe A. Akerman, Jr., *Florida Cowman: A History of Florida Cattle Raising* (Kissimmee: Florida Cattlemen's Association, 1976), 84-91.

[14] Ibid., 91-95; Confederate pension applications of Thomas L. Gunter (A01671), William H. Ezell (D22165), and Edward Benjamin Sanders (A02483) in Confederate Pension Application Files.

[15] Unpublished manuscript of S.M. Hankins' recollections (Series S1725), State Archives of Florida; Earl English to Gideon Welles, 10 June 1862, *Official Records of the Union and Confederate Navies in the War of the Rebellion* (hereinafter *ORN*), series I, vol. 17, 262.

[16] William C. Rogers to Gideon Welles, 6 Apr 1863, *ORN*, series I, vol. 17, 411; F. Burgess to C.H. Rockwell, 25 Jan 1865, *ORN*, series I, vol. 17, 804.

[17] Joseph P. Couthouy to William W. McKean, 7 Jun 1862, with enclosures, *ORN*, series I, vol. 17, 254-257.

[18] This estimate of the number of Taylor County men in the 2nd Florida Union Cavalry is based on a careful comparison between the 1860 federal census for Taylor County, the muster rolls for the Union's Florida cavalry units, and U.S. pension records. Where names could not be positively matched, they were left out of the estimate.

[19] Canter Brown, Jr., "The Civil War, 1861-1865," in *The New History of Florida*, ed. Michael Gannon (Gainesville: University Press of Florida, 1996), 234-236; E.Y. McCauley to Theodorus Bailey, 30 July 1863, *ORN*, series I, vol. 17, 519-520; petition by Taylor County officers to Governor John Milton, 11 Aug 1863, *The War of the Rebellion: A Compilation of the Official Records of the Union and Confederate Armies* (hereinafter *OR*), series IV, vol. 2, 839-840.

[20] Sworn affidavit of William Standley regarding the military service of Tullius Kinsey, 3 May 1913, and William B. Davis to W.A. McRae, 10 Feb 1913, in the Confederate pension application file of Tullius Kinsey (A08299), Confederate Pension Application Files; George E. Buker, *Blockaders, Refugees, and Contrabands: Civil War on Florida's Gulf Coast, 1861-1865* (Tuscaloosa: University of Alabama Press, 1993), 98-99; David W. Hartman and David Coles, eds., *Biographical Rosters of Florida's Confederate and Union Soldiers, 1861-1865*, vol. 5 (Wilmington, N.C.: Broadfoot Publishing Company, 1995), 1785.

[21] Tebeau and Marina, *History of Florida,* 212; Stanaland and Fulford appear on the muster roll of William W. Strickland's Union Rangers, as well as the muster rolls of the Second Florida Union Cavalry.

[22] Joseph Finegan to Thomas Jordan, 7 Oct 1863, with enclosed letters detailing Blackburn and Bird's mission to Taylor County, *OR,* series I, vol. 28, part ii, 401-403.

[23] Ibid.; Thomas Jordan to Joseph Finegan, 12 Oct 1863, *OR,* series I, vol. 28, part ii, 413; proclamation of Brigadier General William M. Gardner, 18 Mar 1864, *OR,* series I, vol. 53, 320-321.

[24] Henry D. Capers to J.L. Cross, 27 Mar 1864, including as an enclosure the muster roll of William W. Strickland's Independent Union Rangers, *OR,* series I, vol. 53, 316-318.

[25] William W. Strickland to Henry D. Capers, 27 Mar 1864, *OR,* series I, vol. 53, 319.

[26] Susan Bradford Eppes, *Through Some Eventful Years,* 2nd ed. (Tallahassee, Fla.: Board of State Institutions, 1968), 220-224; John Milton to Patton Anderson, 20 Jun 1864, and Milton to Anderson, 5 May 1864, *OR,* series I, vol. 53, 342-343; 351-352.

[27] The refugee women's letter to John Milton is quoted in full in Cash, "Taylor County History," 55.

[28] Buker, *Blockaders, Refugees, and Contrabands,* 100-101; David Harmony to Theodorus Bailey, 21 Feb 1864, *ORN,* series I, vol. 17, 649-650; Theodorus Bailey to Gideon Welles, 6 Mar 1864, *ORN,* series I, vol. 17, 648-649.

[29] David Harmony to Daniel P. Woodbury, 29 Feb 1864, *OR,* series I, vol. 35, part ii, 14; Buker, *Blockaders, Refugees, and Contrabands,* 115-131.

[30] "'My National Troubles': The Civil War Papers of William McCullough," *Sunland Tribune* 20 (1994): 66,68, 70; Buker, *Blockaders, Refugees, and Contrabands,* 163-164; Hartman and Coles, eds., *Biographical Rosters,* vol. 5, 1844-1848; and an affidavit of Dr. Samuel Wilcox attesting to Henry Poppell's cause of death, included in his wife's application for a widow's pension. See Civil War Widow's Pension Files on Fold3.com.

[31] S.M. Hankins's recollections; Buker, *Blockaders, Refugees, and Contrabands,* 166-167.

[32] S.M. Hankins's recollections; Confederate pension application of Green C. Denmark (A02406), Confederate Pension Application Files.

[33] Cash, "Taylor County History," 56-58.

[34] Florida Department of Public Instruction, *Report of the Superintendent of Public Instruction of the State of Florida* (Tallahassee: Charles H. Walton, 1870), 33-34.

[35] "An Excerpt from the Papers of Joseph A. Groom, Sr.," www.fl-genweb.org/jefferson/fgroom.html.

[36] Nancy Poppell to Pension Commissioner, 7 Feb 1908 and Colon Blue to Pension Commissioners, 7 Feb 1908, both in the case file for Henry D. Poppell's federal pension, in Case Files of Approved Pension Applications of Widows and other Veterans of the Army and Navy Who Served Mainly in the Civil War and the War with Spain, National Archives.

[37] Cash, "Taylor County History," 58.

Chapter 4: Frontier Cattle Country

[1] Jack Murray, "Florida's Flaming Six Guns," *Adventure* 112, no. 5 (March 1945), 80-85; Wesley Stout, "The Beachcomber," *Fort Lauderdale News,* 3 Feb 1964.

[2] Ibid.

[3] David Lang to William H. Towles, 18 Jan 1898 in vol. 50 of the Governors' Letterbooks (Series S32), State Archives of Florida.

[4] Population figures from the 1870 and 1900 federal censuses.

[5] Minutes of the County Commissioners' Court, 12 Apr 1869 (Series L326), State Archives of Florida.

[6] William Watson Davis, *The Civil War and Reconstruction in Florida* (New York: Columbia University, 1913), 332-334.

[7] *Journal of Proceedings of the Convention of Florida, 1865* (Tallahassee, Fla.: The Floridian, 1865), 4.

[8] *United States Statutes at Large*, XIV, 428-49; XV, 2-4, 14-16, 41; Charlton W. Tebeau and William Marina, *A History of Florida*, 3rd ed. (Coral Gables, Fla.: University of Miami Press, 1999), 227-230.

[9] Davis, *The Civil War and Reconstruction in Florida*, 466-467.

[10] Voter registration rolls for 1867-1868 (Series S98), State Archives of Florida.

[11] Ibid.

[12] Davis, *The Civil War and Reconstruction in Florida*, 496; House reports, 42nd Congress, 2nd session, no. 22, v. 13, 176-177.

[13] Tebeau, *A History of Florida*, 243-250.

[14] J.E. Quentin's monthly reports for March and May 1866, in Records of the Assistant Commissioner and Subordinate Field Offices for Florida, Freedmen's Bureau (National Archives Microfilm Publication M1869).

[15] A.A. Knight's December 1868 report of homesteads located, Records of the Assistant Commissioner and Subordinate Field Offices for Florida, Freedmen's Bureau.

[16] Samuel A. Wilcox to Ossian B. Hart, 23 Jan 1873, in Box 4, Folder 10, State Governors' Incoming Correspondence (Series S577), State Archives of Florida.

[17] J.E. Quentin to J.H. Lyman, 9 Oct 1866 in Records of the Assistant Commissioner and Subordinate Field Offices for Florida, Freedmen's Bureau. See also Judge William Bryson's testimony in *Testimony Taken by the Joint Select Committee to Inquire into the Condition of Affairs in the Late Insurrectionary States*, vol. 13 (Washington: Government Printing Office, 1872), 258.

[18] Jerrell Shofner, "Reconstruction and Renewal, 1865-1877" in *The New History of Florida*, ed. Michael Gannon (Gainesville: University Press of Florida, 1996), 257; Elizabeth H. Sims, *A History of Madison County* (Madison, Fla.: Madison County Historical Society, 1986), 80.

[19] See Jonathan Gibbs' testimony in *Testimony Taken by the Joint Select Committee to Inquire into the Condition of Affairs in the Late Insurrectionary States*, vol. 13, 220-223.

[20] James M. Denham and Canter Brown, Jr., eds., *Cracker Times and Pioneer Lives: The Florida Reminiscences of George Gillett Keen and Sarah Pamela Williams* (Columbia: University of South Carolina Press, 2003), 159.

[21] WPA History of Taylor County, Florida Historical Record Survey Files, State Library of Florida.

[22] Minutes of the Taylor County Commissioners' Court for 2 Apr 1870 and 8 Oct 1870, Taylor County Commission Records, 1864-1882 (Series L326), State Archives of Florida.

23 John S. Gallagher, *Florida Post Offices* (Lake Grove, Oreg.: The Depot, 1997), 177-178; Post Office Department Reports of Site Locations, 1837-1950 (National Archives Microfilm Publication M1126), roll 99; see especially the applications and correspondence relating to Rosehead and Perry.

24 See the 1870 federal census returns for Taylor County, as well as "Taylor County in 1886, *Cash Writings of Taylor County, Florida* (Perry, Fla.: Taylor County Historical Society, 2007), 28, "How Communities Received Names Used Now," *Cash Writings*, 115, and "Jeff L. Davis Was Taylor County's First Newspaperman," *Cash Writings*, 252; Publisher information in the *Taylor County Herald*, 30 Aug 1918.

25 U.S. Commission of Fish and Fisheries, *The Fisheries and Fishery Industries of the United States*, section II (Washington: Government Printing Office, 1887), 553-554.

26 Tina Bucuvalas, *Greeks in Tarpon Springs* (Charleston: Arcadia Publishing, 2016), passim.

27 Morrell and Associates, *Steinhatchee, Florida: A Brief Historical Overview* (n.p., 2009), 4.

28 Memorial to John Baptist Carrin by Shawn Riley, 9 Mar 2010, findagrave.com; Charles Carrin, "Peace on the Suwannee River," https://civilwar.illinoisgenweb.org/photos/carrin2.html; Post Office Department Reports of Site Locations, roll 99; see especially the applications for Deadman's Bay and Stephensville.

29 John B. Carrin, "Southeastern Taylor County," *The Florida Dispatch*, 22 Nov 1886; Carrin, "Homes for Soldiers," *National Tribune*, 24 Dec 1885; Carrin, "Florida A Delightful Home: A Defence of That State," *Boston Weekly Globe*, 13 Oct 1880.

30 U.S. Department of the Interior, Office of the Census, *Report on Cotton Production in the United States,* part II (Washington: Government Printing Office, 1884), 3, 47-48; Edward E. Baptist, *Creating an Old South: Middle Florida's Plantation Frontier Before the Civil War* (Chapel Hill: University of North Carolina Press, 2002), 20.

31 Taylor County Marks and Brands Record, vol. 1, Taylor County Courthouse.

32 Taylor County Tax Roll for 1873 and 1880 in Box 121, Tax Rolls (Series S28), State Archives of Florida.

33 Towles's letter to Lesley is reproduced in Joe A. Akerman, Jr., *Florida Cowman* (Kissimmee: Florida Cattlemen's Association, 1976), 106.

34 "Funeral Services Capt. W.H. Towles," *Tampa Tribune*, 27 Jun 1921; Karl H. Grismer, *The Story of Fort Myers: The History of the Land of the Caloosahatchee and Southwest Florida* (St. Petersburg Printing Company, 1949), 286-287; W.T. Cash, "James X. Towles, Pioneer Resident of County, Known for Sense of Humor," *Cash Writings*, 301-303.

35 Gregg M. Turner, *A Journey into Florida Railroad History* (Gainesville, Fla.: University Press of Florida, 2008), 106-107.

36 Ibid.; Alfred P. Tischendorf, "Florida and the British Investor: 1880-1914," *Florida Historical Quarterly* 33, no. 2 (October 1954): 120-129.

37 John F. White to William D. Bloxham, 15 Oct 1898 and L.E. Roberson to William D. Bloxham, 15 Oct 1898, both in Box 11, Folder 3, William D. Bloxham Correspondence (Series S578), State Archives of Florida.

38 David Lang to William H. Towles, 18 Jan 1898 in vol. 50, William D. Bloxham Letterbook (Series S32), State Archives of Florida; "Considering Pardons," *Marion Star*, 4 May 1887; "Pardoned after Escaping from Prison," *Troy Messenger*, 19 May 1887.

39 "Murder in Taylor County," *Pensacola News*, 6 Jan 1892; [untitled article], *Fayette County Leader*, 8 Jan 1892.

[40] "Shot to Death," *Altoona Tribune,* 13 May 1895; "Race War in Florida," *The North Carolinian,* 28 Jul 1895.

[41] John F. White to William D. Bloxham, 22 Oct 1898 in Box 11, Folder 3, Bloxham Correspondence; "Shot to Death," *Altoona Tribune,* 13 May 1895

[42] I use the spelling "Bump" Padgett rather than "Bunk" because that is how his brothers spelled the name in their correspondence. John C. Calhoun to David Lang, 16 Feb 1898, and John F. White to William D. Bloxham, 22 Oct 1898 in Box 11, Folder 3, Bloxham Correspondence.

[43] Ward Padgett to D.B. Padgett, 10 Dec 1897, and John C. Calhoun to David Lang, 16 Feb 1898 in Box 11, Folder 3, Bloxham Correspondence.

[44] John C. Calhoun to David Lang, 16 Feb 1898 in Box 11, Folder 3, Bloxham Correspondence.

[45] D.B. Padgett to William D. Bloxham, 27 Dec 1897 in Box 11, Folder 3, Bloxham Correspondence; and William H. Towles to William D. Bloxham, 15 Jan 1898 in vol. 50, William D. Bloxham letterbook (Series S32), State Archives of Florida.

[46] David Lang to William H. Towles, 18 Jan 1898 in vol. 50, William D. Bloxham letterbook.

[47] David Lang to John C. Calhoun, 14 Feb 1898; and John C. Calhoun to David Lang, 16 Feb 1898 in Box 11, Folder 3, Bloxham Correspondence; and Governor William D. Bloxham's proclamation announcing rewards for apprehending the murderer of Bunk Padgett and the assailants of Thomas Brannen and Henry Horace, 19 Feb 1898 in vol. 50, William D. Bloxham letterbook.

[48] William H. Towles to William D. Bloxham, 2 Apr 1898 in Box 11, Folder 3, Bloxham Correspondence.

[49] John F. White to William D. Bloxham, 22 Oct 1898; and James X. Towles to William D. Bloxham, 23 May 1898 in Box 11, Folder 3, Bloxham Correspondence; minutes of the April 1898 term of the Taylor County Circuit Court (Series L327), State Archives of Florida.

[50] John F. White to William D. Bloxham, 22 Oct 1898 in Box 11, Folder 3, Bloxham Correspondence; minutes of the October 1898 term of the Taylor County Circuit Court.

[51] L.E. Roberson to William D. Bloxham, 15 Oct 1898; and John F. White to William D. Bloxham, 22 Oct 1898 in Box 11, Folder 3, Bloxham Correspondence.

[52] A.J. Head to William D. Bloxham in Box 11, Folder 3, Bloxham Correspondence.

[53] John F. White to William D. Bloxham, 22 Oct 1898 and 23 Oct 1898, in Box 11, Folder 3, Bloxham Correspondence.

[54] S. Hiram Peacock to William D. Bloxham, 26 Oct 1898; and proclamation by Governor Bloxham suspending Sheriff A.J. Head, 28 Nov 1898 in Box 11, Folder 3, Bloxham Correspondence.

[55] Francis M. Lipscomb to John F. White, 25 July 1899 in Box 11, Folder 3, Bloxham Correspondence; Wesley Stout, "The Beachcomber," *Fort Lauderdale News,* 17 Feb 1964; Jack Murray, "Florida's Flaming Six Guns," 80-85; Gwen Faulkner, *The Story of a Taylor County Feud* (1969), a manuscript in the Vertical File, State Library of Florida.

[56] "Circuit Court," *Madison New Enterprise,* 24 Oct 1901.

57 "Horace and Anderson Held," *Ocala Evening Star*, 22 Apr 1911; "Robbery Case to Be Heard Again," *Tampa Times*, 5 Mar 1914; "Intended to Buy a Home Says Horace," *Tampa Tribune*, 24 Apr 1911.

58 Faulkner, *The Story of a Taylor County Feud*.

59 Chapter 4098 (1891), Laws of Florida; George W. Pettengill and B.F. Simmons, "The Story of the Florida Railroads, 1834-1903," *The Railway and Locomotive Historical Society Bulletin*, no. 86 (July 1952): 58.

60 Taylor County tax roll for 1900; Turner, *Florida Railroad History*, 172-174.

Chapter 5: Timber and Turpentine

1 Drew Harrington, "Burton-Swartz Cypress Company of Florida," *Florida Historical Quarterly* 63, no. 4 (April 1985): 424-425; *Ocala Evening Star*, 23 Oct 1908.

2 *Ocala Evening Star*, 13 Nov 1902; "Flourishing Montbrook," *Ocala Evening Star*, 15 Jan 1906.

3 Description of a bond offering for the Dowling Lumber Company in *The Commercial and Financial Chronicle*, 1 Aug 1908, 288-289.

4 Jeffrey A. Drobney, *Lumbermen and Log Sawyers: Life, Labor, and Culture in the North Florida Timber Industry, 1830-1930* (Macon, Ga.: Mercer University Press, 1997), 194-198.

5 Chapter 4098 (1891), Laws of Florida.

6 Chapter 4263 (1893), Laws of Florida; Russell Tedder, "Seaboard's Covington Subdivision: The Tallahassee, Perry & Southeastern," *Lines South* 21, no. 1 (2004): 14-25.

7 Ibid.; "The Work in Progress," *The Railway Age*, 7 April 1899, 260.

8 Frank Drew to the chairman and members of the committee on railroads and telegraphs, 15 Apr 1901 in Box 22, Folder 3, Drew Family Papers (Collection M82-8), State Archives of Florida; "Want an Extension," *Weekly Tallahasseean*, 25 Apr 1901.

9 Tedder, "Seaboard's Covington Subdivision," 17.

10 Ibid., 18-19; Don Hensley, "The Rise and Fall of the Florida Railway, part II: The Suwannee & San Pedro Railroad" (2001), www.taplines.net; Harry Gardner Cutler, *History of Florida: Past and Present, Historical and Biographical*, vol. 2 (Chicago: Lewis Publishing Company, 1923), 34; plat of the town of Fenholloway, Jan 1902, Taylor County Courthouse.

11 Taylor County tax rolls for 1900-1903, Taylor County Courthouse; *Moody's Manual of Railroads and Corporation Securities* (1914), 1220; John William Leonard, ed., *Who's Who in Finance, Banking and Industry* (New York: Joseph & Sefton, 1911), 94; Gregg M. Turner, *A Journey into Florida Railroad History* (Gainesville, Fla.: University Press of Florida, 2008), 172-173.

12 Hensley, "The Rise and Fall of the Florida Railway"; Eric Musgrove, *Lost Suwannee County* (Charleston: The History Press, 2017), 134-135.

13 Don Hensley, "The Rise and Fall of the Florida Railway, part III" (2001), www.taplines.net.

14 Ibid.; Turner, *A Journey into Florida Railroad History*, 174.

[15] Turner, *A Journey into Florida Railroad History*, 174; Annual Report of the Atlantic Coast Line for Fiscal Year Ending June 30, 1909 in *The Commercial and Financial Chronicle*, 20 Nov 1909, 1353; "Railroads into New Territory," *Tampa Daily Times*, 22 Sept 1913.

[16] Pete Gerrell, *The Illustrated History of the Naval Stores (Turpentine) Industry* (Crawfordville, Fla.: Southern Yellow Pine Publishing, 1998), 1; Louise Childers, "Remember the Old Turpentine Stills?," *TaCo Times*, 15 July 1976; Lenthall Wyman, *Florida Naval Stores* (Tallahassee: Florida Department of Agriculture, 1929), 5.

[17] Louise Childers, "Remember the Old Turpentine Stills?," *TaCo Times*, 22 July 1976; "New Industries in Busy Florida," *Tampa Tribune*, 3 Nov 1904; R.L. Polk & Company, *Florida State Gazetteer and Business Directory* (1918), 923.

[18] *Tallahassee Democrat*, 11 Aug 1905; *Manufacturers' Record*, 28 Dec 1905, 631; "New Industries in Busy Florida," *Tampa Tribune*, 3 Nov 1904; [C.C. Rawls], *Ocala Evening Star*, 10 Jan 1906; [C.C. Rawls], *Ocala Evening Star*, 3 Nov 1908; Florida Geological Survey, *Annual Report* (1912), 151.

[19] Wyman, *Florida Naval Stores*, 9-11.

[20] John S. Gallagher, *Florida Post Offices* (Lake Grove, OR: The Depot, 1997), 177-178.

[21] Louise Childers, "Remember the Old Turpentine Stills?," *TaCo Times*, 22 July 1976; Margaret N. Burkley, "Andrew Dias Poppell, 1894-1955: A Taylor County Entrepreneur," *Florida Historical Quarterly* 74, no. 3 (Winter 1996): 304-318.

[22] Ibid.

[23] Wyman, *Florida Naval Stores*, 18-19.

[24] Ibid., Robert N. Lauriault, "From Can't to Can't: The North Florida Turpentine Camp, 1900-1950," *Florida Historical Quarterly* 67, no. 3 (January, 1989), 314.

[25] Gerrell, *Naval Stores (Turpentine) Industry*, 40.

[26] Wyman, *Florida Naval Stores*, 22.

[27] Ibid., 26; Louise Childers, "Remember the Old Turpentine Stills?", *TaCo Times*, 5 Aug 1976.

[28] Ibid., 26-31.

[29] Lauriault, "From Can't to Can't," 315.

[30] Ibid., 318-319; "Curl Brought Prisoner," *Gainesville Sun*, 21 Aug 1905.

[31] John H. Powell to B.E. McLin, 1 Mar 1909 in Box 7, Folder 2, Convict Lease Program Files (Series S42), State Archives of Florida; "Blacks Bring the Most Cash," *Tampa Daily Times*, 30 Sept 1913.

[32] *Tenth Biennial Report of the Commissioner of Agriculture of the State of Florida*, 1907-1908, 445; J.B. Thomas to W.A. McRea, 5 Apr 1913 in Box 5, Folder 5, Convict Lease Program Files.

[33] Drobney, *Lumbermen and Log Sawyers*, 156-159.

[34] J.B. Thomas to W.A. McRea, 30 July 1906; report of R.A. Willis, circa 1913; and J.B. Thomas to W.A. McRea, 5 Apr 1913 in Box 5, Folder 5, Convict Leasing Program Files.

[35] Punishment records for the Blue Creek Company, 1914 in Box 2, Folder 1; and J.B. Thomas to W.A. McRea, Aug 1913 in Box 5, Folder 5, Convict Leasing Program Files; "Fears There Are Others," *Pensacola News Journal*, 29 Oct 1908.

36 R.L. Polk & Company, *Florida Gazetteer and Business Directory* (1911-12), 356-357; "Perry Banking Company," *Bankers Magazine* 74, no. 5 (May 1907), 840-841; and articles of incorporation for the Perry Electric Company, 3 Feb 1909 in Corporations Record, Taylor County Courthouse; *Thirteenth Biennial Report of the Department of Agriculture of the State of Florida* (1913-14), 650.

37 Louise Childers, "Remember the Old Turpentine Stills?", *TaCo Times*, 5 Aug 1976; W.T. Cash, *The Story of Florida*, vol. 3 (New York: American Historical Society, 1938), 168.

38 Ibid., *Huxford v. US* (US Court of Appeals, 5th Circuit), 5 May 1971; Burkley, "Andrew Dias Poppell," 311.

39 "Five Billion Feet in One Pine Belt," *Pensacola News Journal*, 6 Oct 1905; [W.F. Hughey]," *Ocala Evening Star,* 8 Sept 1900.

40 "Ocala Twenty Years Ago," *Ocala Evening Star*, 13 Nov 1922; "Tallahassee, Fla.," *New York Lumber Trade Journal*, 1 Jan 1904; "Big Realty Deal," *Miami News*, 17 Mar 1904.

41 *Biennial Report of the Department of Agriculture of the State of Florida* (1895), 140; "Echoes of Dead Past Reverberate in Silence of Town That Is No More," *Tallahassee Democrat*, 15 Aug 1968.

42 Plat for "Nelray," filed with Clerk of Court John C. Calhoun on 10 Aug 1904; post office application for Boyd, filed 27 Apr 1904 by Sonora M. Parker; Taylor County tax rolls, 1904-1910; Taylor County Historical Society, *They Were Here*, vol. 1, 11; Karl H. Grismer, *The Story of St. Petersburg* (St. Petersburg: P.K. Smith, 1948), 349-350; "Taylor a Great Lumber Region," *Tampa Times*, 10 Mar 1919.

43 *Live Oak Democrat*, 6 May 1907; letters patent for Standard Lumber Company, 31 Aug 1910 in Corporations Record, Taylor County Courthouse.

44 "A Mill Operator's Challenge," *American Lumberman*, 14 Nov 1914; "Three Killed by Falling Wall," *Tallahassee Democrat*, 14 Nov 1925.

45 "Thomas Hamilton is the General Manager of the Standard Lumber Company," *The Lumber Trade Journal*, 1 June 1920; "About Sawmills and Rheumatism," *American Lumberman*, 14 Nov 1914; Gallagher, *Florida Post Offices*, 177; Valuation Docket no. 811 for the Live Oak, Perry & Gulf Railroad Company, 22 April 1927 in *Interstate Commerce Commission Reports*, vol. 125 (March-July 1927), 213; "New and Rebuilt Saw Mill Plants," *St. Louis Lumberman* 53, no. 9 (1914), 53.

46 "Econfena Plant Burns," *The Lumber Trade Journal*, 1 July 1917; *Interstate Commerce Commission Reports*, vol. 70 (June-December 1921), 886; World War I Army Card Roster, 1924 (Series S1204), State Archives of Florida.

47 "Florida," *Southern Lumberman*, 1 Jan 1932; *Moody's Analyses of Investments,* part II (1916), 1238.

48 Harrington, "Burton-Swartz Cypress Company of Florida," 423-424; Drobney, *Lumbermen and Log Sawyers*, 51.

49 "Large Lumber Operation Planned in Florida," *St. Louis Lumberman*, 15 Dec 1913; Drobney, *Lumbermen and Log Sawyers*, 53; Perry Town Council Minutes, 28 Jan 1914.

50 "Rapid Construction of New Mill," *American Lumberman*, 17 Oct 1914; "The Burton-Swartz Florida Company – The Model Cypress Plant," *Lumber World Review*, 10 Jan 1916.

51 "Rapid Construction of New Mill," *American Lumberman*, 17 Oct 1914; Harrington, "Burton-Swartz Cypress Company of Florida," 425-426.

52 Harrington, "Burton-Swartz Cypress Company of Florida," 426.

53 "A Short History of the Catholic Community of Taylor County," Taylor County Historical Society Ephemera Collection; History of St. James Episcopal Church, www.stjamesperry. org.

54 "Rapid Construction of New Mill," *American Lumberman*, 17 Oct 1914.

55 Bolling Arthur Johnson, "In the Realm of the Lumber Manufacturer," *Lumber World Review*, 10 Feb 1922; "Strictly a Logging Town," *American Lumberman*, 17 Oct 1914.

56 Louise Childers, "Carbur—A Look Back," *Buckeye Fiberscope* 5, no. 1 (March 1975); Harrington, "Burton-Swartz Cypress Company of Florida," 426.

57 Childers, "Carbur."

58 Ibid.

59 Ibid.

60 Report from County School Superintendent W.T. Cash to State Superintendent of Public Instruction W.S. Cawthon, *Biennial Report of the Superintendent of Public Instruction of the State of Florida* (1920-1922), 607-610; Marjorie R. Woodell, *History of Education in Taylor County* (Perry, Fla.: Taylor County Retired Educators Association, 1998), 35.

61 "An Important Transfer of Lumber Properties," *The St. Louis Lumberman*, 15 Nov 1917; Drobney, *Lumbermen and Log Sawyers,* 55-57.

62 Drobney, *Lumbermen and Log Sawyers,* 205; "The Community That Does Not Exist Anymore," an unsigned, manuscript in the Ephemera Collection of the Taylor County Historical Society, written circa 1966.

63 Case no. 18364, *Georgia Public Service Commission v. Atlantic Coast Line Railroad Company* in *Interstate Commerce Commission Reports*, vol. 146 (1928), 717-720; Louise Childers, "Foley—Its Beginnings," *Buckeye Fiberscope* 4, no. 3 (June 1974).

64 "To Move Town of 3000 People," *Tallahassee Democrat*, 20 Feb 1929.

65 "Perry," *Tallahassee Democrat*, 12 Dec 1929; Childers, "Foley"; "Lumber Co. Sells Railroad Interests," *Tampa Times*, 18 Jan 1929.

66 Jeffrey A. Drobney, "Company Towns and Social Transformation in the North Florida Timber Industry, 1880-1930," *Florida Historical Quarterly* 75, no. 2 (Fall 1996): 126.

67 Ibid.

68 Childers, "Foley."

69 Ibid.

70 An uncredited historical sketch from the 1949 Foley School yearbook titled "The Foley School," Taylor County Historical Society Ephemera Collection; Taylor County Historical Society, *They Were Here*, vol. 1, 7; *Biennial Report of the Superintendent of Public Instruction for the State of Florida* (1928-1930), 100.

71 "The Foley School"; "Perry Topples Palmetto, 25-20," *Tampa Tribune*, 17 Mar 1940.

72 Michael E. Keller, *The Graham Legacy: Graham-Paige to 1932* (Paducah, KY: Turner Publishing Co., 1998), 136; "[Perry]," *Orlando Sentinel*, 1 Apr 1928; "Perry Getting a Big Factory," *Tallahassee Democrat*, 28 Aug 1928; "Perry Selected for Auto Plant," *Tampa Bay Times*, 30 Sept 1928; Samuel Gilbert Register, *Memoirs of an Octogenarian* (n.p., n.d.).

73 Russell Tedder, *Map of Railroads and Logging Mainlines in Taylor County, Florida* (1998); "600 Pounds of Dynamite Explodes in Logging Camp," *Tampa Tribune*, 24 Oct 1916; *American Bankruptcy Reports*, vol. 48 (1923), 143-144.

74 "In the Realm of the Lumber Manufacturer," *Lumber World Review*, 10 Feb 1922; Drobney, *Lumbermen and Log Sawyers,* 58.

75 N. Gordon Carper, "Martin Tabert, Martyr of an Era," *Florida Historical Quarterly* 52, no. 2 (Oct. 1973): 116-117.

76 Ibid., 117.

77 Ibid., 118-119.

78 Ibid., 119-131; commission records for B.F. Willis and J.R. Jones in vol. 14, p. 194, State and County Officer Directories (Series S1284), State Archives of Florida.

79 "The Community That Does Not Exist Anymore"; June Parker McLeod, "Boyd," in *The Second Annual Town of Boyd Reunion* (n.p., 1999).

Chapter 6: Perry: Gateway to Florida's West Coast

1 Chapter 5359, *Laws of Florida* (1903), 493-503.

2 B.J. Nettles, "Taylor County," a report written for the Historical Records Survey of the Works Progress Administration, circa 1940. Manuscript copy held by the State Library & Archives of Florida; *Municipal Journal and Engineer*, 16 Jan 1907.

3 National Register of Historic Places application for the Old Taylor County Jail, April 1989, U.S. Department of the Interior.

4 Taylor County tax rolls (1895-1908), Taylor County Courthouse; Marjorie R. Woodell, *History of Education in Taylor County* (Perry, Fla.: Taylor County Retired Educators Association, 1998), 30.

5 Woodell, *History of Education in Taylor County*, 30-34.

6 Ibid., 53-54; Pat Rosier, "History of Jerkins High School," in *Jerkins Community Center Listen-Up* (Perry, Fla.: Taylor County Leadership Council, 1997), 3-4.

7 *Biennial Report of the Superintendent of Public Instruction of the State of Florida* (1918-20), 69-90.

8 Rosier, "History of Jerkins High School," 4.

9 Perry Town Council Minutes, 19 Sept 1911 and 8 Oct 1912; Register, *Memoirs of an Octogenarian*, 32-33.

10 "Dixie Highway Grade in Taylor Completed," *Tampa Tribune*, 20 May 1917; "Perry to Be One of Most-Paved Towns," *Tampa Tribune*, 28 Jan 1922.

11 Minutes of Perry Town Council, 21 Mar 1911 and 5 Dec 1928; "Work Progresses on Dixie Highway," *Tampa Tribune*, 13 May 1917.

12 "When Did Perry First Receive Electric Service?," *Perry News-Herald*, 2 Mar 2012; Florida Geological Survey, *Annual Report* (1910-11), 152; articles of incorporation for the Perry Electric Company, 3 Feb 1909 in Taylor County Record of Incorporations, 32; Sanborn Fire Insurance Maps for Perry, Florida (1913), sheet 1.

13 "Telephone and Telegraph," *Electrical Review*, 4 Feb 1905; "New Direct Dial System Begins in Taylor Today," *Tallahassee Democrat*, 22 Aug 1971; Order No. 493 in *17th Annual Report of the Railroad Commission of the State of Florida* (1914), 86-89.

14 "Phone firm's Pioneer Had 'Peanut' Past," *Tallahassee Democrat*, 4 May 1977; "Taylor County's 'Mr. Telephone,'" *Tallahassee Democrat*, 14 Feb 1973.

15 George T. Belding, ed., *Florida Railroad Gazetteer and State Business Directory* (Atlanta: Cotton States Publishing & Advertising Company, 1895), 217; United States Census for 1910 and 1930; plats for the Hendry Addition (1905), Brobston-Fendig Addition (1905), Blair-Hinley Addition (ca. 1905), Hendry Realty and Abstract Company Addition (1906), and West Brooklyn Subdivision (1908) in the Taylor County Subdivision Plat Book, Taylor County Courthouse; biographies of William Thomas Hendry and Wesley A. Hendry in Harry Gardner Cutler, *History of Florida: Past and Present, Historical and Biographical* (Chicago: Lewis Publishing Company, 1923), 14, 29; and biography of Edwin Brobston in B.F. Johnson, ed., *Makers of America: Florida Edition*, vol. 2 (Atlanta: A.B. Caldwell, 1909), 197-201.

16 Sanborn Fire Insurance Maps for Perry, Florida (1913), sheet 3, University of Florida Special Collections; Perry binder, Taylor County Historical Society Ephemera Collection.

17 *Florida Gazetteer and Business Directory* (Jacksonville: R.L. Polk & Co., 1911), 356-358.

18 "P.F. Bloodworth," *They Were Here*, vol. 2, 10; "Barney O'Quinn," *They Were Here*, vol. 1, 36.

19 "S.H. Peacock," *They Were Here*, vol. 1, 3; Sanborn Fire Insurance Maps for Perry, Florida (1913), sheets 1-4.

20 Register, *Memoirs of an Octogenarian*, 18; "Every Day is Christmas at the Old Greystone," *TaCo Times*, 29 Nov 2006; *Florida Gazetteer and Business Directory* (Jacksonville: R.L. Polk & Co., 1918), 858.

21 "Perry Citizens Build Community Hotel," *Tampa Tribune*, 13 Mar 1927; "Hotel Gets New Face, Mission," *Tallahassee Democrat*, 8 Feb 1978.

22 "A Bank for Perry," *Madison New Enterprise*, 20 Mar 1902; "New State Banks," *The Financier*, 29 Dec 1902; "Drive Begun to 'Save Old Bank Building of Perry,'" *Tallahassee Democrat*, 20 Dec 1972.

23 "Senator Faulkner is Now a Banker," *Pensacola News Journal*, 11 Jun 1905; "Cash Tells of George R. Battle, One of Perry's First Bankers," *Cash Writings of Taylor County, Florida*, 223-224; *Manufacturer's Record*, 10 Aug 1905; "Open for Business," *Tampa Tribune*, 19 May 1907; "Notice of Voluntary Liquidation," *Tallahassee Democrat*, 13 Mar 1908.

24 "The Perry Banking Company," *The Bankers' Magazine* 74, no. 5 (May 1907), 840-841; articles of incorporation for the Gulf Coast Investment Company, 2 Feb 1909 in Taylor County Corporations Book, 25.

25 "Drive Begun to 'Save Old Bank Building of Perry,'" *Tallahassee Democrat*, 20 Dec 1972.

26 "38 Schools, 1200 Students," *Perry News-Herald*, 7 Mar 2014; "Judge J.O. Culpepper," *Cash Writings of Taylor County, Florida*, 248-249.

27 Ibid.

28 Mary Lou Whitfield, *815 West Bay: Views from the End of the Street* (Perry: Pretty Pond Press, 2007), 294-295.

29 *Ocala Evening Star*, 2 Mar 1906; "Fenholloway News," *Taylor County Herald*, 3 Jan 1919.

30 Booklet for the Perry Rotary Club's 75th Anniversary Jubilee Celebration (1998), Taylor County Historical Society Ephemera Collection.

31 Field Representative's Final Report for the Perry Kiwanis Club (August 1924), Taylor County Historical Society Ephemera Collection.

32 "100 Years and Counting," *Progress 2014: A Guide to Perry-Taylor County* (Perry Newspapers, 2014), 10; "Reports on Three Clubs Given on Reciprocity Day at Live Oak Club," *Miami News*, 5 Feb 1916; "Perry Woman's Club is Active," *Tampa Times*, 19 Jun 1920.

33 Ibid.; "Perry Woman's Club," *Orlando Evening Star*, 12 Aug 1916.

34 "Reports of Section Three," *Tampa Tribune,* 10 May 1925; Register, *Memoirs of an Octogenarian,* 20-21.

35 "Club Work of Boys and Girls," *Taylor County Herald*, 27 Feb 1920.

36 "Dixie Highway Grade in Taylor Completed," *Tampa Tribune*, 20 May 1917; "Perry Loses Out as Military Campsite," *Tampa Tribune*, 3 Jun 1917.

37 [A.C. Kirby], *Tampa Bay Times*, 10 Sept 1926; Register, *Memoirs of an Octogenarian*, 21-22.

38 Register, *Memoirs of an Octogenarian,* 12-13; "Carbur – A Look Back," *Fiberscope*, March 1975.

39 "Getting Ready for Baseball," *Taylor County Herald*, 2 Apr 1920; "Many Important Matters Before Chamber Commerce," *Tallahassee Democrat*, 21 Mar 1923; "North Florida League New Baseball Group," *Orlando Evening Star*, 3 May 1928.

40 Akerman, *Florida Cowman*, 234-235; "Taylor County Medical Association," *Taylor County Herald*, 10 Jan 1919.

41 "Popular Fred Warde Secretary of Taylor County Board of Trade, *Tampa Tribune*, 3 May 1917; "Work Progresses on the Dixie Highway," *Tampa Tribune,* 13 May 1917; Taylor County Board of Trade, *Taylor County, Florida: The Great Gulf Coast Country* (Perry: Taylor County Herald, 1924).

42 "Steel Rails for the New Route," *Atlanta Constitution,* 11 Feb 1901; *Madison New Enterprise*, 23 Jan 1902; editorial in *The Robesonian*, 13 Mar 1903.

43 "From Hampton Springs," *Madison New Enterprise*, 14 Jul 1904.

44 Louise Childers, "Taylor County's Famous Hampton Springs Area: Oglesby Builds Hotel," *TaCo Times*, n.d.; "Likes Hampton Springs," *Gainesville Daily Sun*, 23 Feb 1907.

45 "Florida's Good Road Statistics in Detail," *Tampa Tribune*, 6 Nov 1913.

46 "Perry is Interested in Tallahassee Route," *Tallahassee Democrat*, 1 May 1915; "Perry Folks Want to Get on Dixie Highway," *Tampa Tribune*, 25 Apr 1915; "Why Taylor and Lafayette Counties Want Dixie Highway Loop," *Tampa Times*, 24 Aug 1915; "Scales Logs 161 Miles of Dixie Highway," *Tampa Times*, 7 Sept 1915; "Nearly $10,000,000 Now Pledged for the Dixie Highway," *Tampa Times*, 24 Jul 1915.

47 "Taylor County to Do Its Part," *Tampa Times*, 19 Jun 1916; "Taylor Falls in Line," *Orlando Evening Star*, 27 Jul 1916; "Big Bond Issue is Passed," *Fort Myers Press,* 26 Jul 1916.

48 "Meeting to Urge A.C.L. to Build Link in Road to Be Held November 8," *Tampa Tribune*, 21 Sept 1917; "Interest High on West Coast Short Route," *St. Petersburg Times*, 29 May 1919; "Rail Outlet for Tampa on West Coast is Blocked for More Than Thirty Years," *Tampa Times*, 26 Jul 1923; "Long Desired Road to Southwest Seems Assured," *Tallahassee Democrat*, 16 Oct 1917; "Frame-Up Ended Work on Road to North West," *Tampa Times*, 8 May 1919.

49 "Taylor County to Send a Committee," *Tampa Times*, 18 Aug 1917; "Wrong Time to Build Railroad," *Tampa Times*, 27 Jul 1917; "Must Prove it a Necessity," *Tampa Times*, 3 Aug 1917; "Jacksonville Hoggish Again," *Tampa Times*, 28 Jun 1918.

50 "Northwest Outlet Sure," *Tampa Times*, 8 Mar 1919; "Seaboard Must Build Cut-Off Line to Perry," *St. Petersburg Times*, 7 Jun 1919.

51 "States Perry Cut-Off Suit of No Value," *St. Petersburg Times*, 28 Oct 1923; "Buford Declares That He Could Act as a Demagogue and Institute Proceeding," *Tampa Tribune*, 11 Nov 1923.

52 "Important Railroad Link is to Be Built," *Miami News*, 27 Apr 1921; "Organize West Coast Railway," *Palm Beach Post*, 12 Mar 1924; "Dr. Kelly Proclaiming a Big Slogan," *Tallahassee Democrat*, 11 Sept 1924.

53 "Railroad Developers Are Here Looking Over the West Coast Prospect," *Tallahassee Democrat*, 27 Sept 1924; "West Coast Road May Be Constructed," *Smith's Weekly*, 3 Jul 1925; "Financial Giants in Huge Development," *Sarasota Herald*, 17 Jan 1926.

54 "Atlantic Coast Line May Build Extension," *Palm Beach Post*, 20 Oct 1925; "A.C.L. Will Open New Gateway to Florida," *Palm Beach Post*, 1 Nov 1925; "Big Crowd Meets New Train Upon Initial Trip to City," *Tampa Bay Times*, 5 Dec 1928.

55 Plat of the town of Steinhatchee (1921), Taylor County Subdivision Plat Book, Taylor County Courthouse.

56 Articles of incorporation for the Perry and Gulf Coast Traction Company, 17 July 1919 in Taylor County Record of Incorporations; "I.C.C. Refuses Rail Extension," *Evening Independent*, 27 Apr 1926.

57 Plat of the Boneta Beach Club, Units 1 and 2 (1926), Taylor County Subdivision Plat Book, Taylor County Courthouse.

58 Plats for the Hampton Springs Improvement and Hampton Springs Villa, Taylor County Subdivision Plat Book.

59 "Hampton Springs Property Leased to Chicago Firm," *Atlanta Constitution*, 21 Aug 1927; "Acquire Hampton Springs Property," *Tallahassee Democrat*, 17 Aug 1927.

60 "Gulf Coast Highway the Greatest Project Undertaken," *Pensacola News Journal*, 1 Mar 1925.

61 "Gulf Coast Highway is on 2nd List," *Tallahassee Democrat*, 3 Aug 1926; "Taylor Route of Gulf Coast Road Changed," *Tampa Times*, 29 Aug 1928; "New Federal Highway Aids Florida Trips," *Chicago Tribune*, 30 Dec 1951.

62 Cutler, *History of Florida*, vol. 2, 3.

63 *People of Lawmaking in Florida* (Tallahassee, Fla.: Florida House of Representatives, 2017), 34.

64 "With Friends All Over the State This Worker Is Much in Demand," *Miami News*, 15 Nov 1918; "Woman May Be Member of Lower Florida House," *Tampa Tribune*, 7 May 1922; "Myrtice McCaskill Defeated Four to One," *Tallahassee Democrat*, 7 Jun 1922; *Tallahassee Democrat*, 16 Oct 1931.

65 "Taylor County Men Bound Over to United States Court," *Weekly Tallahasseean*, 28 Feb 1902.

66 "Taylor County in Peculiar Situation," *Pensacola Journal*, 2 Jul 1907; "[Perry]," *Ocala Evening Star*, 2 Sept 1907; "Tired of Blind Tigers," *Ocala Evening Star*, 12 Oct 1908; "Taylor County Went Wet," *Ocala Evening Star*, 5 Jul 1909; "[Whiskey Distillery]," *DeLand News*, 26 Nov 1909.

67 "Prohibition Amendment is Defeated," *Pensacola News Journal*, 9 Nov 1910; "Taylor County Dry," *Tampa Tribune*, 7 Oct 1911.

68 "Wonderful Record of Distillery Destruction," *Smith's Weekly*, 26 Dec 1924.

69 United States Congress, *Official Records of the National Commission on Law Observance and Enforcement* (Washington: Government Printing Office, 1931), 160-161.

70 John J. Guthrie, Jr., "Hard Times, Hard Liquor, and Hard Luck: Selective Enforcement of Prohibition in North Florida, 1928-1933," *Florida Historical Quarterly* 72, no. 4 (April 1994): 442.

71 "Alleged Slayer of Two Taken to Duval," *Pensacola News Journal*, 29 Dec 1926; "Taylor County Man Gets Death Charge," *Palm Beach Post*, 2 Jun 1929..

72 "Pepper's Novel Defense in Murder Case Launched Career," *Tampa Tribune*, 13 Mar 1983; "J.W. Buchanan Waits 14 Years for Doom; Natural Death Near," *Miami News*, 3 Sept 1944.

73 Florida Department of Military Affairs, *Summary Statistics – Florida – Army, Navy, Marine Corps, Coast Guard – World War I* (St. Augustine: State Arsenal, ca. 1980), 18; "Theo Faulkner Reported Missing in Action," *Taylor County Herald*, 30 Aug 1918.

74 "It Must Be Kept Up," *Ocala Evening Star*, 14 Nov 1917; *Taylor County Herald*, 22 Nov 1918.

75 *The Clyde Log* (July 1918), 143; "Must Keep Up W.S.S. Sales," *Tampa Times*, 8 Oct 1918; "Bonds Sold by the Women's Liberty Loan Committee Throughout State," *Tampa Times*, 29 Nov 1918.

76 "Close School, Churches, Shows," *Taylor County Herald*, 13 Feb 1920; "Local and Personal," *Taylor County Herald*, 20 Feb 1920; "[J.H. Scales]," *Taylor County Herald*, 2 Apr 1920; "[The Perry Schools]," *Taylor County Herald*, 21 May 1920.

77 "Body of Murdered Teacher Is Found by Crew of Train," *Tampa Tribune*, 3 Dec 1922; "Believe Murderer of Teacher Surrounded," *Tampa Tribune*, 6 Dec 1922; "Posse in All-Night Search for Alleged Murderer of Woman," *Miami News*, 7 Dec 1922.

78 Meghan Martinez, "Racial Violence and Competing Memory in Taylor County, Florida, 1922" (M.A., Florida State University, 2008), 5-6; "Tension Tightens in Taylor County," *St. Petersburg Times,* 7 Dec 1922.

79 "2 Accused Negroes Wanted in Perry Arrested in Georgia," *Tallahassee Democrat*, 8 Dec 1922; "Slayer of Perry Teacher Burned at Stake by Mob," *Tampa Tribune*, 9 Dec 1922.

80 "Slayer of Perry Teacher Burned at Stake by Mob," *Tampa Tribune*, 9 Dec 1922.

81 "Another Lynching at Perry, Florida," *Orlando Sentinel*, 14 Dec 1922; "Second Negro Is Lynched at Perry," *St. Petersburg Times*, 13 Dec 1922.

Chapter 7: Depression and War

1 T.H. Watkins, *The Great Depression: America in the 1930s* (Boston: Little, Brown & Company, 1993), 40-41.

2 Nick Wynne and Joe Knetsch, *Florida in the Great Depression: Desperation and Defiance* (Charleston: The History Press, 2012), 17-18.

3 Ibid., 21-25.

4 "Woman's Club Urges All to Help in Cause," *Taylor County Herald*, 5 Nov 1931.

5 "First National Bank in Perry Closes Doors," *St. Petersburg Times*, 19 Oct 1930.

[6] An Act for the Relief of James R. Jackson, Clerk of the Circuit Court of Taylor County, on Account of Moneys on Deposit in the First National Bank of Perry, Florida, belonging to the State of Florida and Taylor County for Tax Redemptions (Chapter 14867), *Laws of Florida* (1931).

[7] "Many Animals Dipped in June," *Tallahassee Democrat*, 7 Jul 1928.

[8] Joe A. Akerman, Jr., *Florida Cowman* (Kissimmee: Florida Cattlemen's Association, 1976), 235-237.

[9] Ibid., 240-241; "Death Knell for Range Cattle," *Tallahassee Democrat*, 5 Apr 1927; "Early Cattle Raisers Recall the 'New Era' Following Eradication of Deadly Ticks," *Perry News-Herald*, 14 Nov 1968; "Taylor County to Fence 12,000 Acres for Cattle," *Tampa Tribune*, 29 Nov 1936.

[10] "Hogs in Taylor County," *Palm Beach Post*, 21 Oct 1934; "Early Cattle Raisers Recall the 'New Era' Following Eradication of Deadly Ticks," *Perry News-Herald*, 14 Nov 1968.

[11] Undated, unsigned article titled "Scanlon: An Unforgettable Era in Taylor County," Taylor County Historical Society Ephemera Collection; "Boyd May Get 'New Lease on Life,'" *TaCo Times*, 5 Dec 1984.

[12] "Rowell's Store Moves to the Old Post Office Room," *Taylor County Herald*, 3 Oct 1935; Mary Lou Whitfield, "Storm of '35 Recalled," *Perry News-Herald*, 9 Apr 1999; "35 Storm Flattened Timber, Leveled Church," *Perry News-Herald*, 12 Jun 1998.

[13] "Red Cross Survey Shows Heavy Damage in Taylor County," *Palm Beach Post*, 9 Sept 1935; "Sholtz Finds Damage Heavy," *Tallahassee Democrat*, 10 Sept 1935; "Red Cross Seeks to Assist 2,726 Florida Families," *Fort Myers News-Press*, 15 Sept 1935.

[14] Letter from "unknown parties" to Governor Dave Sholtz, 2 Jun 1933 in Box 110, Folder 7, Dave Sholtz Subject Files (Series S278), State Archives of Florida.

[15] "$100,000 Dry Haul Made in Taylor County," *Fort Myers Press*, 12 Aug 1929.

[16] "15 Are Nabbed in Prohi Raid in This Area," *Pensacola Journal*, 18 Jan 1930.

[17] Letter to Governor Dave Sholtz, 18 Sept 1934 in Box 110, Folder 8, and letter to Dave Sholtz, 12 Mar 1935 in Box 110, Folder 9, Dave Sholtz Correspondence (Series S278), State Archives of Florida.

[18] Samuel Gilbert Register, *Memoirs of an Octogenarian* (n.p., n.d.), 14-15.

[19] Claude Pepper to Doyle Carlton, 7 Oct 1929; T.R. Hodges to Doyle Carlton, 12 Mar 1929; Doyle Carlton to Claude Pepper, 11 Oct 1929; and Claude Pepper to E.C. Strickland, 24 Jan 1930 in Box 81, Folders 5 and 6, Doyle Carlton Subject Files (Series S204), State Archives of Florida.

[20] Claude Pepper to Kosmas Gealourakis, Domionas Gealourakis, and Bill Gealourakis, 23 Jan 1930 in Box 81, Folder 6, Doyle Carlton Subject Files.

[21] "Standing Pat," *St. Petersburg Times*, 17 Oct 1930; *Tallahassee Democrat*, 11 Dec 1930; *Miami News*, 5 Jan 1931.

[22] "Sponge Divers Win Injunction in Hooker War," *Tampa Tribune*, 19 Sept 1931; "Taylor County Sheriff Makes More Arrests," *St. Petersburg Times*, 11 Nov 1933; "State Pledges Assistance to Sponge Divers," *St. Petersburg Times*, 24 Nov 1933; "Taylor County Holds Greek Sponge Divers," *St. Petersburg Times*, 21 Mar 1935; "Kaminis to Patrol Gulf Sponge Beds," *St. Petersburg Times*, 3 Nov 1935.

[23] Ray Evans, "Growing Up in Perry, 1925-1943," *Perry News-Herald*, 2003.

24 Minutes of the Perry Town Council, 14 Jan 1930, 29 Jan 1930 and 19 May 1931, Taylor County Historical Society.

25 Petition from Taylor County citizens to Dave Sholtz, 8 Dec 1933 in Box 110, Dave Sholtz Correspondence (Series S278), State Archives of Florida; "New Auto Tag Prices Go Into Effect July 1," *Tampa Times*, 5 Jun 1933; "Auto 'Rackets' Seen by Wilder," *Tallahassee Democrat*, 19 Apr 1933.

26 "Lights to Be Discontinued in Short Time," *Taylor County News*, 27 Aug 1931.

27 Minutes of the Perry Town Council, 9 May 1933 and 20 Jun 1933, Taylor County Historical Society.

28 "School Board Slashes Salaries of Teachers," *Taylor County News*, 4 Aug 1932; "Taylor County Schools Will Run the Full Eight Months," *Taylor County News*, 23 Feb 1933; "School Board Let Contract New Building," *Taylor County News*, 17 Sept 1931.

29 "Contributions for Christmas Tree Solicited," *Taylor County News*, 27 Nov 1930; "Help Yourself Woman's Club Local Talent," *Taylor County News*, 21 Jan 1932; "Foley School is to Have Soup Kitchen," *Taylor County News*, 17 Sept 1931; "Fine Success Soup Kitchen Perry School," *Taylor County News*, 19 Nov 1931; "Public Asked to Help with Soup Kitchen," *Taylor County News*, 16 Feb 1933; "Woman's Club Met Thursday in Regular Session," *Taylor County News*, 9 Mar 1933.

30 "Kiwanis Club Fall Garden Club Now On," *Taylor County News*, 17 Sept 1931; "Vacant Lots to Be Used for Gardens," *Taylor County News*, 4 Feb 1932; "Truck Farm Is Being Started by Welfare Board," *Taylor County News*, 16 Mar 1933.

31 "Farmers Association Will Erect Canning Plant Here," *Taylor County News*, 2 Mar 1933; "Cannery to Be Operated by Local FERA," *Taylor County News*, 16 May 1935.

32 "Summary of Home Demonstration Work," *Taylor County News*, 23 Jun 1932; "Statement of Red Cross in Taylor County," *Taylor County News*, 5 Nov 1931; "Red Cross Secures Carload of Flour for Taylor County," *Taylor County News*, 21 Apr 1932; Walton H.Y. Smith, "Perry School Tooth Brush Drill," *Journal of the Florida Medical Association* 29, no. 1 (July 1932): 37.

33 "Royal Theatre Giving Fine Program Daily," *Taylor County News*, 3 Mar 1932; advertisement for Good Will Sale, *Taylor County News*, 1 Sept 1932.

34 "Events Pass Quickly," *Taylor County News*, 9 March 1933.

35 See table 5 in Florida Emergency Relief Administration, *Unemployment Relief in Florida, July 1932 – March 1934* (Jacksonville, Fla.: The Administration, 1935), 150; "Surplus Projects Piling Up," *Orlando Sentinel*, 16 Dec 1933.

36 "Rotary Club Hears FERA Official Tell About New Work Relief Plan," *Taylor County News*, 24 Jan 1935; "County Planning Board is Organized Here to Study Projects for New Federal Work Plan," *Taylor County News*, 31 Jan 1935; "Planning Board Busy Setting the Plans for Work Relief Projects," *Taylor County News*, 7 Feb 1935.

37 "WPA Gives Okeh to 15 Projects in This Section," *Tallahassee Democrat*, 28 Aug 1935; "School Board Arranges for New Building," *Taylor County News*, 28 Oct 1937; "Schroder Gives Four Major WPA Projects Okeh," *Pensacola News Journal*, 5 Mar 1939.

38 "Taylor County Sewing Rooms To Be Continued," *Tampa Tribune*, 22 Dec 1938; "Many Women Leave Relief Sewing Work," *Palm Beach Post*, 13 Aug 1941.

39 "Florida Ghouls," *Miami News*, 17 Jun 1939.

40 "Perry Concert Band is Making Progress," *Taylor County News*, 1 Apr 1937; Ray Evans, "Growing Up in Perry, 1925-1943 (part 8), Taylor County Historical Society Ephemera Collection.

41 Watkins, *The Great Depression*, 130-131.

42 "Eighteen Taylor Young Men Leave for Camp Monday," *Taylor County News*, 25 May 1933.

43 "C.C.C. Boys Will Plant Pines on Vickrey Place," *Taylor County News*, 17 Jan 1935; "CCC Birthday is Celebrated at Camp Foley," *Tallahassee Democrat*, 4 Apr 1937; *Camp Hurricane Chronicle* 1, no. 30 (September 1936).

44 *Camp Hurricane Chronicle*, issues from 1936.

45 "Road to Mandalay Leads to Rustic, Cracker Retreat," *Tallahassee Democrat*, 2 Feb 1973.

46 "County Judge Named Chairman for Service Registration Day," *Taylor County News*, 3 Oct 1940; "Draft Board Here is Ready for Drawing," *Taylor County News*, 24 Oct 1940.

47 "Taylor County's First Drafted Men Go to Camp Blanding This Week," *Taylor County News*, 12 Dec 1940; "92 Taylor County Army Boys Are Serving in Foreign Lands," *Taylor County News*, 26 Jul 1943.

48 "Our Boys in the Service," *Taylor County News*, 5 Oct 1944.

49 "Our Boys in the Service," *Taylor County News,* 10 Aug 1944; "Our Boys in the Service," *Taylor County News*, 7 Sept 1944; "Our Boys in the Service," *Taylor County News*, 23 Aug 1945.

50 "Our Boys in the Service," *Taylor County News*, 28 Sept 1944.

51 "92 Taylor County Army Boys Are Serving in Foreign Lands," *Taylor County News*, 26 Jul 1943.

52 "Byron Butler Called to Army Service," *Taylor County News,* 26 Mar 1942; "Judge Butler," *St. Petersburg Times,* 24 Feb 1944.

53 List of officers of the Taylor County Defense Council, 19 Dec 1941 in Box 48, Folder 4, State Defense Council Subject Files (Series S419), State Archives of Florida.

54 U.S. Office of Price Administration, *Rationing in World War II* (Washington: The Administration, 1946), 2.

55 Report from Manilla Welles, 15 Apr 1942 in Box 48, Folder 4, State Defense Council Subject Files.

56 "Rubber Collection is Continued; 62,000 Pounds Brought in Now," *Taylor County News*, 2 Jul 1942; "save Metal Tubes to Help Win the War," *Taylor County News*, 19 Feb 1942; "Final Figures on Scrap Campaign," *Taylor County News*, 29 Oct 1942.

57 "Key Club Members Sell Defense Stamps," *Taylor County News*, 18 Dec 1941; "Taylor County Citizens Help to Pay for the 'Road to Victory,'" *Taylor County News*, 1 Oct 1942.

58 "'Enlist Your Books,'" *Taylor County News*, 29 Jan 1942; "Drive Being Made to Supply Cigarets," *Taylor County News*, 3 Jun 1943; "Local Red Cross Chapter Will Open Sewing Room," *Taylor County News*, 15 Jan 1942.

59 "Volunteers Wanted for Plane Spotting," *Taylor County News*, 23 Jul 1942; "More Volunteers Are Needed for Plane Reporting Station," *Taylor County News*, 30 Jul 1942; "Aircraft Reporting Starts Here Friday," *Taylor County News*, 6 Aug 1942; "Local Coast Guard Starts Its Patrol," *Taylor County News*, 22 Jul 1943.

60 "Great Crowd Was in Perry for Defense Rally Last Friday," *Taylor County News*, 4 Mar 1943.

61 John F. Woods, Jr., "History of the Perry Army Air Field – Month of February 1944," Taylor County Ephemera Collection, Taylor County Historical Society.

62 "3,000 Pilots Trained at Perry Army Air Base," *Perry News-Herald*, 31 Aug 2012.

63 Ibid.; "Local People Cooperate by Housing Soldiers' Families," *Taylor County News*, 17 June 1943.

64 "Army Flier Killed Saturday Afternoon," *Taylor County News*, 1 Jul 1943; "3,000 Pilots Trained at Perry Army Air Base," *Perry News-Herald*, 31 Aug 2012; "Two Planes Collide; One Pilot is Killed," *Taylor County News*, 15 Jul 1943.

65 "Service Men Use Womans Club House," *Taylor County News*, 1 Jul 1943; Mary Lou Whitfield, *815 West Bay: Views from the End of the Street* (Perry, Fla.: Pretty Pond Press, 2007), 295; "Dan Cupid Shooting and Marriages Are Many," *Taylor County News*, 16 Sept 1943.

66 "Our Boys in the Service," *Taylor County News*, 17 Aug 1944.

Chapter 8: Becoming the Forest Capital

1 "Biggest Sawmill to Close; Pulp Mill May Replace It," *Tampa Tribune*, 25 Feb 1948.

2 Ibid.

3 Federal census statistics for 1930-1950.

4 "Florida Leads in Turpentine," *St. Petersburg Times*, 21 Oct 1923; "Forestry Facts," *Taylor County News*, 27 Feb 1947.

5 World's Largest Cypress Mill Handles South Florida Timber," *Tallahassee Democrat*, 26 May 1946; "Biggest Sawmill to Close; Pulp Mill May Replace It," *Tampa Tribune*, 25 Feb 1948.

6 "Timbuctoo… Trees for Tomorrow!," *Brooks-Scanlon News*, November 1948.

7 "Forestry Facts," *Taylor County News*, 24 Apr 1947; "Forestry Facts," *Taylor County News*, 1 May 1947; "First County Forester," *Tallahassee Democrat*, 10 Dec 1946.

8 "Background Memorandum: Buckeye Cellulose Corporation, Taylor County and the Fenholloway River," February 1967, Taylor County Historical Society Ephemera Collection; "Taylor Welcomes Location of Mill," *Tallahassee Democrat*, 8 Aug 1946.

9 Chapter 24952, Laws of Florida (1947); "Passage of Local Legislation Made by Representative Dekle," *Taylor County News*, 8 May 1947.

10 "Background Memorandum: Buckeye Cellulose Corporation."

11 Ibid.

12 "Work Starts on $20 Million Plant," *Tallahassee Democrat*, 28 Feb 1952; "Foley Plant Contract Let," *Tallahassee Democrat*, 13 Apr 1952; *Miami News*, 16 Nov 1953.

13 "Taylor Group Backs Plans for Big Plant," *Tallahassee Democrat*, 21 Sept 1951; "Industry Planning 3 Housing Projects in Taylor County," *Tampa Tribune*, 26 Oct 1951; "Foley Lumber Mill is Closed," *Tallahassee Democrat*, 22 Feb 1953; "Homes on the Move in Florida," *Danville Bee*, 27 Apr 1955.

14 "$20,000,000 Plant at Perry to Boost Florida Industry," *Tampa Tribune*, 30 Nov 1952; "New Foley Cellulose Pulp Plant Will Make First Shipment Today," *Tallahassee Democrat*, 9 July 1954; "Foley Well Drilling Successful in Test," *Tallahassee Democrat*, 21 Sept 1952; William F. Diehl, Jr., "Buckeye Doubles Up in Florida," *Pulp & Paper* (October 1959): 78.

15 "Buckeye Firm Buys Big Tract," *Tallahassee Democrat*, 4 Mar 1956; "Buckeye Cellulose Buys More Land," *Tampa Tribune*, 29 Aug 1956; "Woodland Property is Sold," *Tallahassee Democrat*, 9 Feb 1967; "Buckeye Ups Holdings in Bend in Land Sale," *Tallahassee Democrat*, 9 Dec 1971; Diehl, "Buckeye Doubles Up in Florida"; "Timber, Motels in Taylor County Credited with Surge of Growth," *Tallahassee Democrat*, 11 Sept 1960.

16 "Lumber vs. Cattle Quarrel is Gradually Being Settled," *Tampa Tribune*, 1 Mar 1948.

17 Ibid.

18 Ibid.

19 Ibid.; "Successful Fire Control Promotes Forestry," *Southern Lumberman* 169 (15 Sept 1944), 40.

20 "Forest Fires Damage 5500 Acres in Area," *Tallahassee Democrat*, 20 Feb 1951; "Probers Say Forest Fire Purposely Set," *Tampa Tribune*, 31 Mar 1956.

21 "'The Woodsburners Are at It Again,'" *Tampa Tribune*, 26 Oct 1958; "Grand Jury Asks Stiffer Forest Fire Law Penalty," *Tallahassee Democrat*, 31 Mar 1955

22 "Taylor Puts on Pine Tree Fete in Fine Style!," *Tallahassee Democrat*, 14 Oct 1956.

23 Ibid.; "News from Perry," *Tallahassee Democrat*, 7 Oct 1956.

24 Donald Carroll Dies of Bite from Rattler," *Tallahassee Democrat*, 15 Oct 1956.

25 "Pine Tree Fete Launched with Burns' Branding Iron," *Tallahassee Democrat*, 20 Oct 1965; "Pine Tree Fete Gets State Name," *Tallahassee Democrat*, 31 Oct 1965.

26 "Pine Tree Fete Gets State Name," *Tallahassee Democrat*, 31 Oct 1965; "Forest Industry is Lauded at Perry Pine Tree Festival," *Tampa Tribune*, 31 Oct 1965.

27 "Taylor County and Perry Seek Army Air Base," *Tampa Tribune*, 8 Mar 1946; "Perry Granted Airport Permit," *Tallahassee Democrat*, 21 Jun 1946; "Perry Files Action to Bar Air Base Sale," *Pensacola Journal*, 17 Jan 1947.

28 "Scheduled Airline Service Starts for Perry April 7," *Tampa Tribune*, 1 Apr 1948; "Florida Airways at End of Line," *Tallahassee Democrat*, 27 Mar 1949.

29 "P.O. Lockhart New President of Chamber of Commerce," *Taylor County News*, 23 Oct 1947; "Many Trimmings for Santa Clause Being Made in Taylor County," *Tallahassee Democrat*, 28 Aug 1946.

30 "Ben Lindsey Heads Hospital Committee," *Taylor County News*, 27 Nov 1947; "Taylor County Clubs Meet on Hospital," *Tallahassee Democrat*, 21 Jul 1948.

31 "Citrus, Taylor Counties Get Federal Hospital Aid Funds," *Tampa Tribune*, 1 Apr 1955; *Report of the Secretary of State of the State of Florida* (1955-1956), 199-200; "Big Bend Briefs," *Tallahassee Democrat*, 16 Apr 1956; "Perry Hospital is Dedicated" *Tallahassee Democrat*, 2 Sept 1957.

32 "Perry Facility for Meetings Wins Approval," *Tallahassee Democrat*, 21 Dec 1965; "Doctors Memorial Gets Money for Expansions," *Tallahassee Democrat*, 28 Jun 1968.

33 "Hospital Fire," *Tallahassee Democrat*, 16 Aug 1972; "Perry Hospital Fire Damage is $400,000," *Tallahassee Democrat*, 17 Aug 1972.

34 "Passage of Local Legislation Made by Representative Dekle," *Taylor County News*, 8 May 1947; "Wakulla News," *Tallahassee Democrat*, 24 Jan 1954; "U.S. Highway 98 is Extended Southward to Palm Beach," *Panama City News-Herald*, 15 Nov 1951.

35 "Florida to Get Through Highway," *St. Petersburg Times*, 11 Aug 1948; "Major Highway from Roanoke, Va., Winds Up at Perry," *Tallahassee Democrat*, 29 Nov 1953.

36 "Bids Are Asked on Four-Laning," *Tallahassee Democrat*, 13 Jul 1961; "Low on Perry 4-Laning Job," *Tallahassee Democrat*, 20 Mar 1960; "Perry Road Project Over Half Complete," *Tallahassee Democrat*, 28 Mar 1961.

37 "Timber, Motels in Taylor County Credited with Surge of Growth," *Tallahassee Democrat*, 11 Sept 1960; "Perry Motel Owners Form Association," *Tallahassee Democrat*, 7 Sept 1960.

38 "Taylor Assured of REA Lines," *Tallahassee Democrat*, 3 Apr 1946; "New Highway Link is Open," *Tallahassee Democrat*, 30 Jun 1946; "Road Celebration is Being Held This Afternoon," *Taylor County News*, 30 Oct 1947.

39 "Keaton Beach is Developing," *Tallahassee Democrat*, 25 Oct 1959.

40 Ibid.; "'Miss Keaton Beach,'" *Tallahassee Democrat*, 8 Jun 1961; "Second Annual Sport Show," *Tallahassee Democrat*, 18 Jun 1961; "Fisherman Paradise is Found," *Tallahassee Democrat*, 16 Jun 1970

41 Subdivision plat for Dekle Beach Unit 2 (undated), a copy of which is in the author's possession.

42 "Steinhatchee Continues on Its Forward March of Progress," *Taylor County News*, 7 Aug 1947; "John R.T. Rives Will Build New Lodge on Steinhatchee," *Taylor County News*, 11 Sept 1947; "Roy George Karageorge," *Dixie County Advocate*, 31 Dec 2009.

43 Polly Waller, "Sun-n-Sandspurs," *Perry News-Herald*, 28 Jan 2011.

44 "Suit Against Perry Buckeye Firm Dismissed," *Tallahassee Democrat*, 30 Apr 1965; "Mill Denies Wells Harmed by Effluent," *Tallahassee Democrat*, 25 Jul 1963.

45 "Taylor Bills Ready Today," *Tallahassee Democrat*, 24 May 1965; "Taylor Okays 2 Industrial Site Streams," *Tallahassee Democrat*, 3 Nov 1965.

46 "Project Underway to Clean Up River," *Orlando Evening Star*, 23 Feb 1967; "Buckeye Aeration Lagoon is Pollution Control Step," *Tallahassee Democrat*, 12 Mar 1969; Notice of revision to Florida Department of Environmental Protection Permit FL0000876, 3 Aug 2015.

47 "Taylor Names New Teachers," *Tallahassee Democrat*, 10 Apr 1950.

48 "Taylor School Bonds Approved," *Tallahassee Democrat*, 15 Dec 1954; "Area Counties to Sell Bonds for School Use," *Tallahassee Democrat*, 11 Oct 1957; "Open House Set at Elementary School in Perry," *Tallahassee Democrat*, 15 Nov 1959.

49 "The Foley School," Taylor County Historical Society Ephemera Collection; "Survey Error Delays School Selling Move," *Tallahassee Democrat*, 27 Aug 1961; "Old Salem School Gutted by Fire," *Tallahassee Democrat*, 4 Apr 1980.

50 "Taylor Mixing Plan is Filed," *Tallahassee Democrat*, 2 Mar 1965; "'Willingness' Called Question," *Tallahassee Democrat*, 9 Nov 1967.

51 "Taylor to Lose Funds if Jerkins Not Integrated," *Tallahassee Democrat*, 12 Sept 1968.

52 "Florida County Wins School Aid Appeal," *Fort Lauderdale News*, 13 Aug 1969; "Taylor County's Mix Plan OKd by HEW Department," *Tallahassee Democrat*, 27 May 1970.

53 "Perry Policemen Resign Their Jobs," *Tallahassee Democrat*, 5 Apr 1958.

54 Ibid.; "Perry Police Quit; Charge Chief Allows Gambling," *Tampa Tribune*, 5 Apr 1958.

55 "Police Battle Leaves Perry with 3 Chiefs," *Tallahassee Democrat*, 19 Apr 1958.

56 "Both Perry Police Forces Still on Job," *Tampa Tribune*, 27 Apr 1958.

57 "Perry Chief Reinstated; New Investigation Slated," *Tallahassee Democrat*, 26 Apr 1958; "Both Perry Police Forces Still on Job," *Tampa Tribune*, 27 Apr 1958.

58 "Probe Opened in Perry Row," *Tallahassee Democrat*, 30 Apr 1958.

59 "Taylor Grand Jury Urges Perry Elect Police Chief; Says Town Not 'Wide Open,'" *Tampa Tribune*, 16 Jul 1958.

60 "Perry Mayor Quits in Hassle Over Police," *St. Petersburg Times*, 26 Sept 1959.

61 Presentment of the Taylor County Grand Jury at the Spring Term of the Circuit Court, 14 Jun 1967 in Box 119, Folder 2, Claude Kirk Correspondence (Series S923), State Archives of Florida.

62 Memorandum from Jack Ledden to Claude Kirk, with report by engineers Theodore Jenson and John Feira attached, 10 Aug 1967 in Box 119, Folder 2, Claude Kirk Correspondence (Series S923), State Archives of Florida.

63 "Taylor County Board Ousted," *Tallahassee Democrat*, 2 Apr 1968; "Five Men Appointed to Taylor County Board," *Tampa Tribune*, 4 Apr 1968; "Taylor Commissioners 'Discretion in Interest of Public,'" *Tallahassee Democrat*, 18 Jun 1968; "Old Taylor County Commission In Again," *Tallahassee Democrat*, 4 Jul 1968.

64 "Court Rules in Favor of Old Board," *Tallahassee Democrat*, 3 Jan 1969.

65 "Taylor County Politics Causes Statewide Concern," *Panama City News-Herald*, 30 Jan 1969.

66 Ibid.; "Senate Reinstates 10 Officials Removed from Posts by Kirk," *Miami News*, 18 Feb 1969.

67 Timeline of events regarding the Taylor County Courthouse, n.d., in Box 119, Folder 4, Claude Kirk Correspondence (S923), State Archives of Florida.

68 "Perry Courthouse Delay is Urged," *Tallahassee Democrat*, 5 Feb 1967; "Taylor To Build on Same Location," *Tallahassee Democrat*, 7 Feb 1967; "Citizens to Decide," *Tallahassee Democrat*, 21 Feb 1967.

69 "Taylor Straw Vote Backs Renovation of Courthouse," *Tallahassee Democrat*, 29 Mar 1967.

70 "3-Story Edifice Offered," *Tallahassee Democrat*, 28 May 1968; "Taylor Chooses Location," *Tallahassee Democrat*, 23 Jul 1968.

71 "Last Hurdle to Taylor Courthouse is Removed," *Tallahassee Democrat*, 6 Dec 1968.

72 "Taylor Courthouse Site Moved Again," *Tallahassee Democrat*, 16 Jan 1969; "Taylor Board Talks Tonight on Courthouse Site Issue," *Tallahassee Democrat*, 27 Jan 1969; "Taylor Project Started," *Tallahassee Democrat*, 26 Feb 1969.

73 Gwen Faulkner, *The Story of a Taylor County Feud* (n.p., 1969), 1.

Chapter 9: The Storm

1 Susan Moody's Recollections of the Storm of the Century, ca. 2002 in Box 1, Susan Moody Papers (Collection N2019-3), State Archives of Florida.

2 "Everetts Had 3 Kids Under Foot," *TaCo Times*, 17 Mar 1993.

3 "School's Doors Open Wide for Evacuees," *TaCo Times*, 17 Mar 1993.

4 National Weather Service, *National Disaster Survey Report: Superstorm of March 1993* (Washington: U.S. Department of Commerce, 1994), 2-1.

5 Ibid., 3-1—3-23; "Weather Expert Tells How & Why," *TaCo Times*, 17 Mar 1993; "Survivors Pick Up and Wonder Why," *Tallahassee Democrat*, 16 Mar 1993.

[6] National Weather Service, *Superstorm*, 3-21; "Weather Expert Tells How & Why," *TaCo Times*, 17 Mar 1993; "Trying for a Better View of Foul Weather," *Tallahassee Democrat*, 13 Mar 1994.

[7] "'We Were Never Told to Evacuate,'" *Tampa Tribune*, 16 Mar 1993;

[8] "Everetts Had 3 Kids Under Foot," *TaCo Times*, 17 Mar 1993.

[9] "Survivors Swam House to House," *TaCo Times*, 17 Mar 1993.

[10] Ibid., "Six Die at Gulf Coast Reunion," *Florida News*, 17 Mar 1993.

[11] Susan Moody's Recollections, Susan E. Moody Papers.

[12] "Winter Storm Destroys 115 Homes, Damages 242," *TaCo Times*, 16 Mar 1994.

[13] "Front End Loader Used in Early Rescue Mission," *TaCo Times*, 17 Mar 1993; "Residents, Rescue Workers Band Together for Survival," *TaCo Times*, 17 Mar 1993.

[14] "Front End Loader Used in Early Rescue Mission," *TaCo Times*, 17 Mar 1993.

[15] "Hospital Says Disaster Rehearsals Paid Off Big," *TaCo Times*, 31 Mar 1993.

[16] "Storm Rips Taylor Coast," *TaCo Times*, 17 Mar 1993.

[17] Ibid.; "Survivors Pick Up and Wonder Why," *Tallahassee Democrat*, 16 Mar 1993; "Help Comes from Nearby and Far Away," *TaCo Times*, 17 Mar 1993

[18] "Fatality Count Rises to Ten at Dekle and Keaton," *TaCo Times*, 17 Mar 1993.

[19] "Ravaged Town's Recovering Slowly from March Storm," *Tallahassee Democrat*, 2 May 1993; "Survivors Recall Horror of 'Storm of the Century,'" *Gainesville Sun*, 12 Mar 2013.

[20] "Swift Storm Takes Heavy Human Toll," *Tallahassee Democrat*, 15 Mar 1993; "State Asks Why No Evacuation," *South Florida Sun Sentinel*, 16 Mar 1993.

[21] "Help in Taylor County," *Tallahassee Democrat*, 18 Mar 1993.

[22] "Storm, Regulations Wash Away Dreams," *Tallahassee Democrat*, 20 Jun 1993; "After the Storm," *Tallahassee Democrat*, 13 Mar 1994.

[23] Ibid.

[24] Ibid.

[25] Ibid.

[26] Ibid.

[27] "Storm Rips Taylor Coast," *TaCo Times*, 17 Mar 1993.

[28] "Allison Lets Floridians Off Easy," *Atlanta Journal-Constitution*, 6 Jun 1995.

Index

4-H programs, 122-123

Abdoo, Tom, 158

Adams Beach, 160; destruction of salt works near, 47; saltmaking near, 38

Adams, Hal, 176

Adams, Tom, 177

African Americans: early educational opportunities for, 30; inequalities in the courts toward, 57-58; local population after the Civil War, 56; registered to vote during Reconstruction, 55; schools in Perry for, 111, 112; in the turpentine industry, 88; violence against, 140

Aibejeris, Lynn, 198

Airline, Josephine, 99

airport, 157, 177-178

Albritton family, 21

Allen, Richard C., 34

Allison, Abraham K., 54

American Legion, 166

American Red Cross, 139, 149, 155, 164, 201-202

Applewhite, George W., 60, 61

archaeological investigation, 1, 2

Archer, Charlene, 202

Archer, Sibyl, 202

Archer family, 194

Arnold, James, 179

Arrowheads, 2

Athena (community): early settlers near, 21; evidence of Weeden Island culture near, 3; turpentine operations near, 84, 91

Atlantic Coast Line Railroad, 78, 95, 104, 105, 124; construction of, 82-83; dispute with Brooks-Scanlon, 101-102; and the Perry Cut-off, 83, 128-131

Aucilla River, 1, 80, 134, 160, 180; attempt to destroy bridge over, 48-49; blockade running near, 40; evidence of Deptford culture near, 2; Hernando De Soto crosses, 6; mullet fishing near, 62; origin of the name, 4